Writ on Water

THE SUNY SERIES

HORIZONS OF CINEMA

MURRAY POMERANCE | EDITOR

Writ on Water

The Sources and Reach of Film Imagination

Charles Warren

Edited by
William Rothman and Joshua Schulze

Cover: Lea Massari in L'Avventura (Michelangelo Antonioni, Cino del Duca, 1960).

Published by State University of New York Press, Albany

© 2022 State University of New York

All rights reserved

Printed in the United States of America

No part of this book may be used or reproduced in any manner whatsoever without written permission. No part of this book may be stored in a retrieval system or transmitted in any form or by any means including electronic, electrostatic, magnetic tape, mechanical, photocopying, recording, or otherwise without the prior permission in writing of the publisher.

For information, contact State University of New York Press, Albany, NY
www.sunypress.edu

Library of Congress Cataloging-in-Publication Data

Names: Warren, Charles, 1948–2021, author. | Rothman, William, editor. | Schulze, Joshua, editor.
Title: Writ on water : the sources and reach of film imagination / Charles Warren ; edited by William Rothman, Joshua Schulze
Description: Albany, NY : State University of New York Press, [2022] | Series: SUNY series, horizons of cinema | Includes bibliographical references and index.
Identifiers: LCCN 2021054815 (print) | LCCN 2021054816 (ebook) | ISBN 9781438488097 (hardcover : alk. paper) | ISBN 9781438488110 (ebook) | ISBN 9781438488103 (pbk. : alk. paper)
Subjects: LCSH: Motion pictures—Philosophy. | Motion pictures—History. | Film criticism.
Classification: LCC PN1995 .W3567 2022 (print) | LCC PN1995 (ebook) | DDC 791.4301—dc23/eng/20220118
LC record available at https://lccn.loc.gov/2021054815
LC ebook record available at https://lccn.loc.gov/2021054816

10 9 8 7 6 5 4 3 2 1

Katherine
Sine Qua Non

What mad pursuit? What struggle to escape?
—John Keats, "Ode on a Grecian Urn"

Author's Note

I dedicate this book to Katherine Kimball, my beloved wife, who really made the book possible, helping and supporting me in a great variety of ways—inspiring me, critiquing what I had written, getting us both through the minefield of word processing techniques, always there with her sunny temperament.

The late Stanley Cavell must have been the most *encouraging* person since his own beloved Ralph Waldo Emerson. Cavell took an early interest in my project, helping me see what I had in me to say, to see, and fully to become who I am. And he gave me useful instructive criticism all along the way, as did at an earlier phase my late friend Gilberto Perez, whose own writing on film has been an inspiration to me. I would say the same of my alive and well friends George Toles in Winnipeg and William Rothman in Miami, for whom special gratitude is owed for his canny selection and arrangement of images.

To my collaborators at SUNY Press, including James Peltz, Ryan Morris, Brian Kuhl, Sue Morreale, and Amane Kaneko, a sincere thank you for caring so much about this book. And to Murray Pomerance, editor of the Press's "Horizons of Cinema" series, I am grateful for the inspiration of his conversation and writing going way back, and for taking an early interest in my book project and guiding me all along the way.

(Dictated before the author's death in March 2021)

Contents

Introduction   1

Long Takes

1 *Nashville*, West of the West   9

2 Whim, God, and the Screen: Jean-Luc Godard's *Hail Mary*   33

3 Earth and Beyond: On *WR: Mysteries of the Organism*   55

4 *Blonde Venus:* Experiment Successful beyond All Dreams   91

Short Takes

5 The Path of Art in *Chronicle of a Summer* and *Le joli mai*   167

6 Fiction and Nonfiction in Chantal Akerman's Films   177

7 Surprise and Pain, Writing and Film: On Ross McElwee's *Time Indefinite*   193

8 Two Women in *L'Avventura*   205

9 The Unknown Piano Teacher   215

10 Three Immersions: Jean-Pierre and Luc Dardenne's *Rosetta*   227

Postscript: The Integrity of Film	241
Notes	247
Works Cited	253
Index	259

Introduction

LIKE MANY PEOPLE, I GREW UP watching films and talking about them with friends. I was also reading books and studying music and occasionally seeing a play production—this was North Carolina off the beaten path, the small city of Fayetteville in the 1950s and early 1960s. As I began to see what the great traditional arts were, it dawned on me that I, and seemingly everybody, was involved in one such art with movies.

Foreign films and nonfiction films seemed to belong with the more popular variety. A neighborhood theater where I went as a child on Saturday afternoons to see double-feature westerns and science fiction serials, became a few years later the venue for a local literary club's Sunday film series, showing us *Last Year at Marienbad* (1961), *Night and Fog* (1956), *Les parents terribles* (1948) . . . A walk downtown to the two or three grander theaters might bring one to John Ford's *The Man Who Shot Liberty Valance* (1962) or Alfred Hitchcock's *The Birds* (1963). From the downtown, a descent came to the old Cape Fear River port of Campbellton, in whose eighteenth-century tavern building Carson McCullers lived for a time around 1940 and completed *The Heart Is a Lonely Hunter*, while gathering impressions from nearby Fort Bragg for *Reflections in a Golden Eye*. At the great oak tree on this spot Flora MacDonald, who had helped Bonnie Prince Charlie escape to the Isle of Skye, rallied Royalist troops against the American Revolution. Somewhere on the fringes of the old town had lived the remarkable turn-of-the-century black writer Charles Chesnutt, then and still unknown to most of Fayetteville's inhabitants.

As I was growing up there, traveling to play piano in competitions, getting involved in the horse world, coping with the books assigned in school and the many more books each of these led to, even then the power of film and the uncanny rightness of organization of whole films reached me and stuck in my mind. Film seemed to ask for the responsiveness and thought that books and plays and music had received.

I went off to New Hampshire for the last years of secondary school, where the educational atmosphere was tense with the ethics and aesthetic taste of, let us say, Thoreau—a spartan idealism. Yet there were crosscurrents. The Art Gallery presented a series of films, including Ingmar Bergman's *The Seventh Seal* (*Det sjunde inseglet*, 1957), which astonished me at what the medium of film could address and could do. A maverick English teacher summoned a group of the interested to a basement classroom for a secret screening of Kenneth Anger's *Scorpio Rising* (1963). Saturday nights at the gymnasium gave everybody *Bad Day at Black Rock* (1955), *Hud* (1963), *Zulu* (1964). Some of us who wrote stories and poems and put out a literary magazine found all of this film eminently discussible.

I studied literature at Harvard and Princeton in the late 1960s and early 1970s, where courses in film were not yet given. But outside the formal curriculum films were much screened and discussed, and I knew many people seriously interested in fiction and drama and the other arts who were ready to attend to film and give it its due, listening to what new it had to say. Friends and I at Princeton returned from our seminars on Spenser and Dickens and Calderón, and stayed up all night watching films on the New York television stations. We made trips into the city for retrospectives of D. W. Griffith and Buster Keaton. The intellectual stimulation was constant.

A well-developed criticism seemed to be called for. And it seemed about to happen; the way seemed to be opened. Some of Sergei Eisenstein's and André Bazin's daring, exploratory writings on film were current in English translation. Jean-Luc Godard's and François Truffaut's pronouncements on film were making an impression, as their own films continued to appear and give excitement. Andrew Sarris was making the case in articles and books for the artistic worth of American popular film (a high point of my graduate school years was walking into a Princeton newsdealer's and opening the *Village Voice* to discover they had printed an article-length letter of mine defending Sarris against a reviewer of one of his collections, who claimed that popular art could not have depth or be worth serious attention). Robin Wood, with an impressive background in literary study under F. R. Leavis, had turned to film and made the case in a fine small book for the artist who seemed popular film's most powerful voice, Hitchcock. Stanley Cavell published *The World Viewed*, reflecting on his lifelong attachment to movies and showing how much a distinguished philosopher of aesthetics found to think about in film. It reaches out to a reality we fear we do not possess; it reflects on itself, like the other modern arts. Good books on directors, free-thinking books on the medium, continued to appear.

Yet when I began to teach literature and film in the 1980s, it seemed that possibilities had shrunk. Film studies had caught on as an academic discipline, but the ways of thinking about film seemed to have narrowed. I was discouraged, as were others, by repeated talk of film as a component of bourgeois, capitalist culture, or as a distortion of women, in order to bolster the patriarchy. Discussions of film along these lines gave one second thoughts about our culture and general attitudes. But the rich and diverse art of film seemed not really to be listened to. Images and words and sounds, the variety of deep feelings a film could stir, the range of thoughts it could provoke, seemed mostly turned away from. Women's many anarchic appearances in film, their following out of their own destinies there, seemed overlooked. (Molly Haskell's critically astute 1974 book, *From Reverence to Rape: The Treatment of Women in the Movies*, was unfortunately not a factor in shaping academic film studies, though the book is still read and admired.)

Academic film studies also gave the call—and still gives it—for a strictly historical account of the production of films and their reception by audiences. A film, seen historically, is what its makers intended it to be, as well as what audiences have taken it to be. But the evidence for intention and reception is never good enough. The intention of a *work* is something broader than the consciously held intention of a maker. Reception is a matter of individuals.

My disposition as a critic is akin to that of the American New Critics, writers I love and admire—John Crowe Ransom, Allen Tate, Robert Penn Warren, and others. The New Criticism finds, and avers, that the work of art, looked at with openness, will always surprise one. An understanding of history, of psychology, of the ways of working of cultural assumptions, may help one to understand art. But understanding brought from the outside will never go far enough, and may distort what is there. The work needs to be followed out, paid attention to in detail, submitted to, sometimes talked back to. If the work is remarkable, it asks that the critic give testimony to it, wanting to save the valued experience and offer it up to others, using the various powers of language to evoke the experience and direct others into the life that is there. R. P. Blackmur is for me a supremely inspiring critic for riding out the waves of a work, getting thoroughly involved in it, and yet pushing for insight into what the gesture of art is, after all, what the giving of intelligent attention is, what indeed intelligence and aliveness are.

Crucial to me is the note of importance, of urgency, in criticism—as in Blackmur, the critical writings of D. H. Lawrence, F. R. Leavis, or Q. D. Leavis, Wilson Knight, Yvor Winters, Charles Olson, Susan Howe. How the art works, what it does, is taken to have immediate bearing on how we might live—how we might perceive the world, and use our imaginations, and act. The sense of art's urgency, and a liberating directness in writing about the work, often go with willingness to acknowledge the critic's self, to test by reflection the quite personal reaction and push it toward some general usefulness. Ezra Pound writes in *ABC of Reading*, "The critic who does not make a personal statement is not to be trusted" (30). In any case, I say something about myself here and in the chapters that follow—paint in my sensibility and my relation to the films I take up—hoping this will help to make clearer what I am saying about the films.

A film, like any work of art, becomes fully itself only in interaction with a thinking, responding reader, only in having its way of being, its meaning, its connections to other works of art and to life, acknowledged. Films ask for thought, and answer back to it. They were meant for thought, for being read. Is there a danger of critical subjectivity? One supposes so—yet there is a danger in fear of subjectivity, for there is a wild element to art that speaks to the open sensibility of a *person*, who may testify to a response, may reason or point or insist, looking to others for, as Leavis put it, a "yes" or "yes, but. . . ." (*English Literature* 47). Responding to art is, finally, a question of sensibility, of the nerves and heart and brain all at once. I see this. Do you see it?

I offer here extended essays in critical engagement—I call them "long takes"—with four films, taken up one by one and sequentially, from the film's opening to its close: Robert Altman's *Nashville* (1975), Jean-Luc Godard's *Hail Mary* (*Je vous salue, Marie*, 1984), Dušan Makavejev's *WR: Mysteries of the Organism* (1971), and (in the book's longest essay and the only one devoted to a so-called classical Hollywood film) Josef von Sternberg's *Blonde Venus*, with Marlene Dietrich (1932). The second part of the book consists of "short takes," more varied in format but addressing similar issues, on *Chronicle of a Summer* (Jean Rouch and Edgar Morin, 1960) and *Le joli mai* (Chris Marker, 1963); *Jeanne Dielman, 23 quai du commerce, 1080 Bruxelles* (1975), and other films by Chantal Akerman; Ross McElwee's *Time Indefinite* (1993); *L'Avventura* (Michelangelo Antonioni, 1960); the cinema of Michael Haneke; and *Rosetta* (Jean-Pierre and

Luc Dardenne, 1999). The volume concludes with a brief postscript, occasioned by the death (in 2016) of Victor Perkins, a film critic whose work I greatly admire, that serves to sum up my aspirations in writing the essays in this book.

All these films themselves reflect on the nature of film, its ontology, its sources in the creative imagination, film's ways of working and speaking, what film offers an audience or challenges an audience to undergo. A close look at the films draws these reflections out.

Further, all the films find and use the image of a reflective water surface as a pointer to film and its nature—thus my title. And all the films focus on a woman character who seems to be the creative source of the film, to generate its images and flow and thus the stream of thoughts it provokes, including reflection on the place of the woman or the feminine in film imagination and creative imagination more generally.

I pursue these themes throughout the book. Yet I have adhered to the idea of essays, tryings out, on individual films in order to let the films themselves be the source of instruction, sensing that the films have more to say than any set of ideas that might be used to frame them. The films have a way of going on talking, as from an endless depth, and ought to be allowed to talk themselves out, with their twists and rebuttals and qualifications. The work belongs "uniquely within the realm that is opened up by itself," says Martin Heidegger in his great essay "The Origin of the Work of Art," to which I often refer (41).

I offer this book believing that more is going on in film than has even yet been acknowledged—that there is more possibility in the contact of film and viewer than has been supposed.

I make strong claims about films, episodes in films, shots, words, sounds . . . and about the very medium of film, what it is, where it comes from. I claim connections from film to books and the other arts and philosophical ideas over a wide range. I write hoping that what I say will be acknowledged, will be accepted as true, whatever else may be true as well.

Long Takes

1

Nashville, West of the West

WHEN I WAS GROWING UP in eastern North Carolina, Tennessee was very decidedly the West. It was far away and difficult of access, over high mountains. There seemed to be more space there than in the East, and people seemed to live a simpler, purer, more honest life than ours. Tennessee was farming, but there was room for cultivation of the self. One could make oneself comfortable as one saw fit. People raised fine show horses. One could be religious, or drink. One could pursue learning—this was the country of John Crowe Ransom and Allen Tate, who with other poets and critics fostered a significant literary and intellectual culture at the University of the South in Sewanee, Tennessee, and at Vanderbilt University in Nashville. A young Robert Lowell left Harvard to move south and study with these people.

Nashville was a big and raucous city (bigger than any in North Carolina). But it was still a part of the Tennessee life. The city was dominated by sights like the Andrew Jackson plantation house—the Hermitage—and the imitation Parthenon, situated in a grassy flat area with trees looming about—tacky perhaps, but known for what it was, lived with and just enjoyed, not too much staked on it.

At the beginning of F. Scott Fitzgerald's novel *The Last Tycoon*, easterners traveling west to Hollywood stop in Nashville and visit the Jackson house:

> We drove for a long time over a bright level countryside, just a road and a tree and a shack and a tree, and then suddenly along a winding twist of woodland . . . somewhere we passed

a negro driving three cows ahead of him, and they mooed as he scatted them to the side of the road . . . presently the taxi turned down a long lane fragrant with honeysuckle and narcissus, and stopped beside the great grey hulk of the Andrew Jackson house . . . The Hermitage looked like a nice big white box, but a little lonely and vacated still after a hundred years. We walked back to the car. Only after we had gotten in and Mr. Schwartz had surprisingly shut the door on us did we realize he didn't intend to come along . . . I kept thinking of him all the way back to the airport—trying to fit him into that early hour and into that landscape . . . Manny Schwartz and Andrew Jackson—it was hard to say them in the same sentence. (11–16)

The stop in Nashville and visit to the Hermitage seem steps in a ritual for those who are movie-bound. The crossing of Nashville and Hollywood will come back here.

The city of Nashville seemed to us those years ago to give scope to Tennesseans' desires to shop; to hobnob, those who had money, with lots of others who had money; to dine out well; to see shows—all of this without making people into city folk like those of any other city. They were still Tennesseans, with the accent and smile and honest look in the eye.

My family was involved in a minor way in the showing of Tennessee Walking Horses, an activity which had spread from Tennessee to other southern states (these horses figure in Altman's film: the Haven Hamilton character [Henry Gibson] is said to raise them, and he makes a joke about the maverick, roving political candidate's name, Walker, being the same as that of the horse). My friends and I, once we were fairly independent teenagers, sought to spend as much time as we could in Tennessee, to stable and show our horses there and to live the life. Tennesseans understood these horses, and trained and showed them with effectiveness and grace. The one-night horse show in every country town brought out an audience of connoisseurs. I am happy to adopt the terms of D. H. Lawrence in *Studies in Classic American Literature* and say we went West to "get away" (15)—away from a world, back in North Carolina, that seemed a little degenerate, a little as if having given up, not alive to life's purposes as they might be. And we went to submit ourselves to, to be taken over by, "It"—to live a life answering to our sense of discovering our deepest selves, what mattered most.

And the music. My friends and I were not devotees of country music. In Tennessee we were aware that most people knew and more or less liked this music—had listened to the Grand Ole Opry on the radio growing up, if they did not listen still. Yet we could see that the music was not pervasive. It was all right to be a Tennessean and like other music, or not particularly any music. At times I listened to Roy Acuff or Hank Williams or one of the more modern stars like Tammy Wynette, and I admitted that this was a real art, fed by the soul and beautifully crafted, unlike anything else. One knew that it was commercial—that one reason Nashville existed was to process and sell the music, and to allow the stars a place for their mansions. Plenty of dull and trivial music was sold. One heard of the stars' divorces, wild living, and breakdowns. The music was a genuine creation, but sullied in its commerce and in the way some people lived its life.

Tennessee was a West for us. It admitted of human imperfection (and I have not mentioned the sins of the horse world). But it held the possibility of a plain life that was aristocratic—self-cultivating—for anyone who would embrace it, something like the Nebraska of Willa Cather, where every experience, dramatic or workaday or small-scale—walking down a ditch between fields, for example—had about it a sense of magic, of ritual—being an enactment of the transformative. And Tennessee had its own art—that special music and the show horses.

I came to Robert Altman's *Nashville* (1975) in the course of time, and here was the romance world of my adolescent years, portrayed—it seemed at first—as a chaos of idiocy and viciousness. The music is made fun of. The people are variously gullible, self-deluding, hypocritical, demented with lust. The city looks silly with its strutting drum majorettes, bouffant hairdos, Opryland, and the wretched Parthenon. And yet the film is exhilarating—and it was so to me on my first viewing of it—with its wide-screen exploration of the life of a city (forget that it is a city one knows); with its inventiveness as spectacle; with its grand—critical—conception of America in the microcosm of the music business here. The people may be pathetic or condemnable, but what performances! And how interesting the people become, after all, as one thinks about them and explores them on re-viewings of the film. One comes to feel a good deal for them. And the music, if made fun of, is fascinating to hear and see performed, always in the eye of Altman's wondering and very much alive camera.

I believe anyone looking at the film has to deal with the double experience of a shock at the critical portrayal of life and an exhilaration at the rendering of it all as a film. One may be prepared to be a snob about country music, Nashville, or the South (like the Michael Murphy or Geraldine Chaplin characters in the film). But this film makes it clear that it has to do with human beings in general, with America, with life itself (consider its great concern with death). One has to face a take on these bigger things. I wonder whether my own experience of romantic memories being affronted by this film may not stand for the experience of any viewer, who will bring a grasp of life to this film, or any other, and have it met by the unexpected.

I am outraged at this film and yet I enjoy something like an enormous vitality in it. I am delighted at the sheer event of it. In trying to account for this work that can do one thing seemingly in spite of doing another, I would like to call on D. H. Lawrence's idea of creativity, as developed in *Psychoanalysis and the Unconscious* and *Fantasia of the Unconscious* and in the essays of the *Phoenix* volumes. Creativity is the entirely new and absolutely unaccountable that always, on and on, wells up in life, the going ahead that is in no way repetition or recurrence, except in a Kierkegaardian or Nietzschean sense of repetition that goes beyond repetition or transforms what is repeated or recurs. In art the creative burns us free from any predispositions we may have had about the subject matter or the form. Altman's film in its creativity, I want to say, turns its elements of the recognizable world, along with problems we may have about the attitude Altman takes to this world, into a wholly new area, a world of film. This film world presents its own new challenge as to the attitude to be taken to it. Perhaps *Nashville* in working this change gives its own direction to a power of film that operates always, in any film. Stanley Cavell suggests in *The World Viewed* that the individual film, if pondered, will reveal something of the medium of film as it always is.

But what is a world of film? T. S. Eliot wrote, in a moment of pique over the concept of art as a "criticism of life," that "no phrase can sound more frigid to anyone who has felt the full surprise and elevation of a new experience of poetry" (*Sacred Wood* ix). It has been a besetting difficulty to reconcile our sense that we ought to acknowledge art as a criticism of life—as being about life, and having a position toward life to promote—with our sense that art rushes us beyond the area where we have to think in such terms—life in the world, interpretation of the world, and so on. F. R. Leavis faces this problem in his essay on Swift. Swift can look juvenile (not Leavis's word) in unremitting negativity about the world. But by his writing's resourcefulness, its effect of surprise that goes on and on, a new energy is put into play. There is an energy, as we read, that we can only direct back disruptively toward ourselves in our situation in the world. Finally we are forced to question ourselves and our world most deeply. With Swift's *writing*—as opposed to his imputable views—we are brought to face a mind, with its regard of the world, unlike anything we could have supposed a mind to be. This happens with *Nashville*, and with much other film.

The substantial beginning of *Nashville* is an episode in a recording studio. This is just after a parody television commercial for a record anthology of country hits, and a brief scene showing the emergence of the Walker political van, driving off down a Nashville street. The parody television commercial might precede various sorts of film. It is a thing of so odd a tone. It dazzles us for a few minutes, announcing the film as "Robert Altman's *Nashville*" and running through the cast with a lot of fast promotional talk and shifting still images and bits of songs. We know that what is to follow will have a measure of irony and comedy. Chiefly, we wonder where we are.

We might think the film has begun with the shot of the street, with the traveling van spouting its message. Here is a real street, and things are beginning to happen as they will in a film. But this is interrupted after so little. Strains of the beginning of a song intrude on the soundtrack, and there is a cut to the studio.

With this recording studio we feel we are being allowed to enter a privileged world—the place where artists work, an underworld or world of those who are more than human, a place curiosity would love to have a look. Altman calls on the power the camera has held since Lumière and Méliès, Griffith and Murnau, to show us something marvelous, perhaps real, that we are exhilarated to see.

The studio is a dark cave, or womb. (The cave/womb will come back in my discussion of *Blonde Venus* [1932].) Here the camera moves slowly, ritualistically, past spectators and musicians, with interesting objects continually emerging, the lighting carefully set for the effects of color and bright areas and shadow on film. We see dials, control boards, musical instruments, a projector creating a rectangle of bright red light, and more. The accompaniment of music—Haven Hamilton's "Two Hundred Years"—superficially silly ("We must be doin' somethin' right to last two hundred years"), but at a deeper level truly eerie, with drum rolls and a chorus singing nonsense syllables and particles of words and sentences—everything works to make us feel we are being taken into a mystery. Haven's song means to comment on the upcoming American bicentennial (1976), as does, in a different way, Altman's film as a whole.

Now credit titles begin to appear, "Associate Producers . . ." and so on, and these titles come and go at intervals well into this long scene.

One deep interest of the studio scene, something that helps to give it its weightedness like the images of a dream, is the suggestion that all this may be a film studio. It may be a "stand-in" for one, to use a term Haven uses later in the film. The singing artists here are conspicuously brightly lit in their glass booths, and they are the objects of a train of vision on the part of others in the room, seated in rows and watching. The glass screens before the artists suggest the projection screens it is the destiny of film artists to come to live in.

The cumbersome equipment and the effort at coordination are like what our impression is of the working of a film studio. Shortly into the scene Geraldine Chaplin drifts across the room, Opal from the BBC, as she repeatedly introduces herself, here wanting to join the spectators in the room, watching Haven record his song. Chaplin's face and presence eerily suggest her father, as if that Hollywood giant, Charlie Chaplin, gives his blessing to this film as a continuation of Hollywood's serious critical comedy—Capra, Lubitsch, Chaplin himself. In a way, *Nashville* is a successor to *The Gold Rush* (1925, about American ambition); *Modern Times* (1936, about the maddening pressures of work, taking in political tensions); and *Monsieur Verdoux* (1947, about the violence at the heart of things).

We may begin to reflect that this film is all about a city of productions and "stars" (the word is stressed in the film) and people wanting to break in, and so on. Nashville is a "stand-in" for Hollywood, perhaps. What we may be seeing in this studio episode is the place that generates the films, or this film—the source of creation. A cave or womb suggests a

woman at the origin of all this. The fact that credit titles begin to appear, and not cast credits but production credits, might seem to underscore the idea that we are getting a suggestion of this film's scene of production.

The recording studio episode announces the film, literally in the titles, and more richly if we see the scene as a film studio. In this announcing, the episode links with the opening parody television commercial, which announces the film literally in the voiceover and in written names for the cast, and figuratively in the still images of people that are turned clockwise on a wheel—the spool of film, a wheel of fortune of a sort. The television commercial and studio sequences declare that what we are seeing is a film: life deadened in order to come into new life, like the still images rotated in the commercial, and something born mysteriously in the dark—whether we think of the film studio or the cinema hall with its spectators.

With the shot of the street and the political van, here is a real street, I have said. One of the major impressions of *Nashville* as a whole is that we are getting something like a documentary of the city, or at least of the music world here. There are those frames so full of activity, and so much on the soundtrack, and the seemingly random movement among so many lives and stories. There are many natural settings. And here in the van sequence at the start is our first taste of all this. Further, the political theme is begun. The candidate is offering himself and telling us we are all involved in politics. But suddenly it is interrupted. We are removed to the studio scene that proclaims that we are watching a film. Is politics, is reality, film? The van the camera follows first emerges from a dark indoors, like the studio, and the overhead lettering NASHVILLE on the garage has been dissolved from the graphics of the television commercial. The music that wells up with the van, which might be radio music or conventional film scoring, is shown to be the product of the studio scene that follows. The little look at a Nashville street looks more and more to be the product of the two self-admittedly filmic sequences that surround it. What is the world? What is film? The quality of randomness of movement from scene to scene is very important to our sense of the documentation of a world we can believe in, in Altman as in Renoir. But even randomness is subverted, so to speak, in these first three sequences of *Nashville*. The television commercial sequence [1] and the political van sequence [2] feel uncertain in significance as they go by. But sequence [3], the recording studio, reveals their meaning, and makes it clear that [1] and [2] were put there to serve the interest of [3]. [1] and [2] are seen to have their full existence only as they stand in relation to [3], which underscores the power of film. These three sequences are each very different from the others—in material, in look—and there remains absolutely a randomness in moving from one to the next. But now we have to think of randomness differently. It can accord with things standing in relation to one another. This is a lesson of this film and of Altman in general, and perhaps a lesson Altman offers about all film, if we will look at it properly—and indeed a lesson about life.

The van sequence seems at first a documentation of reality. But of course the studio scene, giving us the sense of seeing something privileged, is also a documentation. We credit what we see. Now we are made to rethink "documentation." What, after all, must it be "of"?[1]

It is beginning to look as if the relation of film to reality is a true subject of this film. The film tells us that what might seem like reality in film, is film. And the film can hardly indicate this much without going further. It tells us, as well, that reality itself, what we live in our lives and always call "reality" (including politics), has something of the nature of film in it.

Altman in his own way provokes us to the question film has always provoked us to. The impression of Griffith is of grand visions of history, and melodrama, and yet also of abundant real settings and natural activities and believable, if intense, people. A recognizable, we might say reflected, real world and filmmaking imagination are inextricably mixed up with each other, so that we begin to ask—I begin to ask—if the world itself might not have such imagination in it or behind it. Murnau in *Nosferatu* (1922) and elsewhere, and others like him, take us into an immediately marvelous world, which we come more and more to credit as real, either expanding our sense of what the real is or recognizing that the world of these films exists at some deep level in our own lives as they are. We may all be monsters of desire.[2]

After our first good look at the recording studio, a second studio comes into the picture, where Linnea (Lily Tomlin) is singing gospel music with a black choir (the Fisk Jubilee Singers from Nashville's historically black Fisk University). "Do you believe in Jesus? Yes, I do," they sing with pulsing accentuation. More of Jesus later.

Eventually the credit "Produced and Directed by Robert Altman" appears over Tomlin and the choir going full tilt, clapping and swaying to the music. Altman would seem to identify the source of this film's creation with the black people and a woman—instinctual? suffering? eloquent?—as the clichés would have it—as opposed to Haven Hamilton and the thin, contrived white music being spun out in the first studio. But things are more complicated than this. The gleam and energy of movement in Haven's eyes as we first catch sight of him is arresting and not to be got over. Such aliveness is surely to be taken as a part of creation, of film direction. When Haven wants to do another take of his tune, and says to the technicians, "I want to hear a little more Haven in this one," there is an immediate cut to the needles on dials jumping up—but this is revealed to be occurring in the second studio, with Tomlin and the black choir. They "are" Haven in a sense. One thing is an aspect of the other. Altman lets us know that he is attuned to both the aggressive/contriving and the passive/intuitive/receptive sides of direction, or film imagination itself. And we look forward to more this film will have to say about film imagination, or the filmic nature of the imagination we always live with.

After the recording studio we go to the airport. Here the pure story of the film—events and characters and a look around the city—begins in earnest. It is here at first, and takes focus in a great piece of theater, the outdoor welcome for the singing star Barbara Jean (Ronee Blakley). And this theater is engulfed in a larger, self-declaring film event, giving us encounters among more and more of the film's characters, indoors and outdoors, all of it ending in a great car wreck and stall on the freeway into the city. Much of this film amounts to pieces of theater—in clubs, at the Opry, in church, even in homes—where characters of the film appear performing, or are momentarily parts of audiences or of backstage groups. The subject of the theatricality of life is raised, the pervasion of theater into life, as in Renoir. But always in *Nashville*, as at the airport, the theater event is enmeshed in a larger film event. The great show at the Parthenon at the end might seem to bring the whole film, in all its strands, into one final event of theater. But this show is itself outdone by the filmic exercise of Altman's coda, a long, thought-provoking flirtation with the crowd, as it listens, in a succession of many shots with much use of the zoom lens, to aspiring singer Albuquerque (Barbara Harris) sing, very soulfully, "It Don't Worry Me." The whole film up to the last can seem essentially a preparation for this protracted documentary-like episode, one of the most remarkable sequences in film.

Almost at the beginning of the airport episode comes the appearance of a television reporter seen through the viewfinder of a camera. And the television coverage continues throughout the episode, with cables and equipment in view. It is like the opening scene of Renoir's *Rules of the Game* (*La règle du jeu*, 1939), with radio people at the airport to greet the returning pilot. In these scenes from both films we are being reminded that a crew and camera are at work all the time in film, that what we get is the observation and work of filmmakers. But in both films the news media are overwhelmed by the onrush of events. We have the feeling that we are being thrown from the media onto nature itself. Of course, what is really happening is that we are being thrown on the full resources of film, this film, which knows that its medium is finer than others. (*Nashville* is reminiscent of *Rules of the Game* generally, with the subject of theater-in-life, the motive of eros, the pervasiveness of death, and the offer to make a breakthrough in film's ability to deal with reality, to keep up with reality.)

At the airport the film narrative takes us on a remarkable route. We go from the television reporter's announcement that security police are keeping the people inside, to a view of a record-selling booth indoors with a large black-and-white poster of actress Karen Black as the character Connie White, a singer in a cowboy hat. A sticker for Hal Phillip Walker, the political candidate, has been placed across the poster of White. Later someone walks by and remarks, "Wait a minute, wait a minute, Hal Phillip Walker looks exactly like Connie White." Onto this scene comes a young soldier in uniform, Vietnam veteran, as we hear later, and devoted fan of Barbara Jean, with questions about her arrival, getting the answer that he will not be allowed outside. Whom does regulation or law or things as they are keep in check? We are asked to ponder, in this respect, the repressed, mysterious Connie White; the maverick political candidate; the young man in uniform who, in a way, will be doubled in the story with another, more bedraggled young man who will come to fire a gun at people in this society; the musicians who are boxed and stacked and sold over this counter we face; the young woman behind the counter who works here and gives the soldier his answer, and whom we hardly notice, until we think. We are immersed further in this film's blurring and transforming of identities—Connie White and Karen Black here, like the earlier contrast and blurring of white and black music. Now, even female/male.

Again, upon the shot of Barbara Jean's plane touching down, with the television man's announcement of it, there is a cut to a man we will come to know as Mr. Green (Keenan Wynn), inside the airport café, standing, beautifully ruminative in profile, and then turning to walk toward us and descend onto a counter stool. A parallel/contrast is drawn between stars and ordinary people, which is to be explored so much in this film. Mr. Green's talk with a neighbor about domestic life—"I live here. My wife is sick"—gives way to a cut to a waitress whom we will know as Sueleen Gaye (Gwen Welles), singing her little song, "Let Me

Be the One"—"Oh I never get enough, of the love I'm hungry for"—addressed to a fantastically clothed silent man, played by Jeff Goldblum, who gives Sueleen back a magic trick with a handful of salt, performed at the counter. Asking for love seems to bring one a trick or illusion: although the waitress appears to enjoy and admire the performance, Sueleen's song might be commenting on Mr. Green as well as herself. Mr. Green's life is suggested to be frustrated. Then there is a cut to Del Reese (Ned Beatty), whom we will get to know as the husband of Linnea. Here he seems to have been listening to the waitress's song. He looks uneasy, interested, licking his lips nervously and then glancing down toward his lap, with the overtone of looking for an erection, or a semen stain. Finally he gets up and leaves. Mr. Green's frustrated home seems to make contact here with that of the Reese family.

When Barbara Jean at last appears outdoors, she mentions that she and "the boys" will be at the Opry this week and she invites everyone to come, with her invocation of baptism in her "granddaddy's" old quip, "If you're down to the river, I hope you'll drop in." Altman cuts to a view, like Barbara Jean's, but closer, of the fans pressing against the inside of the airport's glass doors and windows, looking out. The distance suggests the cinema hall with its screen at the end.

The fans, the audience, are willing (eager) presumably to respond to the artist's offer of contact as baptism—immersion, giving oneself over, death, new life. And these fans are seen now as transfigured and inhabiting the screen, in a state of identification with art, we may say. For a moment in this odd image the film touches its central subject, as I see it, the subject of the way we are caught up in creativity, as in death and new life.

The film narrative in the airport episode gives reality to people's words, follows hints from one image to the next, as with the cabinet's doors and the glass doors of the building, all in all opening significance we could not have anticipated. For a time this film narrative, which has called attention to itself by means of the television reporter, is where we live. We may reflect on film's value for exploring or knowing life. Or we may fix our attention on the film world itself, and reflect on the value of everyday reality as it is susceptible to being taken up into such a work. I am not suggesting that art is better than life, but that life is the better, as life, for its susceptibility to being taken up in the understanding of art. Heidegger argues in "The Origin of the Work of Art" that in Van Gogh's "A Pair of Shoes" we come to know actual peasant shoes. But which ones? The work has a reality that no particular shoes have.

Still, we are not worshipping a painting. What we come to know in the painting is actual peasant shoes.

Nashville seems to wander in a complex real world; after a while we feel that we are living in this world. At night after the Opry show,

Haven/Gibson meets Julie Christie as herself in a music club and urges her, "Remember what film facilities we have here in Nashville." Well into things, at the height of the second big day of the story, we have Haven Hamilton's party outdoors at his fine log-cabin-style house in its wooded setting. Very early Linnea comments, as someone arrives on a motorcycle, that life is beginning to imitate "that old *Easy Rider* movie." Opal "from the BBC" arrives and comments that the setting here looks like Bergman. "Of course the people are all wrong for Bergman," she says—are they indeed? Soon a real movie star arrives, Elliott Gould playing himself, remarking, "They've got a lot of photographers here," and "I'm promoting a movie." The party episode concludes with Opal getting out of hand, making a reporter's advances on Gould. Haven tells her she is behaving badly in front of "a star—no, two stars," and when she has been taken away, he remarks, "That's the price of success." Gould responds (a little archly), "It certainly is." Haven closes ranks with a movie star, in their common state of being laid open to hounding by the press. But Opal is not just a reporter. She is making a film. "I'm making a documentary about Nashville," she says repeatedly. This is Altman's film in a way. So the vulnerability of Haven and Gould—think of them as just men—is susceptibility to the attentions of a filmmaker, susceptibility to being filmed. We are being told throughout this party that we are attending to a film, that the life we may feel we are beginning to live, or get to know, is a film. Perhaps our own life is a film, outside this film, full of connections, as if created to embody them. After seeing *Nashville*, we leave the movie theater dazzled and exhausted. We have stepped up to enjoy this, or be shocked by it, and now we step down, walk out. But life is not the same as before this film. It starts to echo the film. It has the film in it now, radiating light and noise. Life begins to show the interplays, and the energies, of *Nashville*.

This film is full of what we might call *blendings* of people's words with images, of lives with one another. On the first evening in the film, the Deemen's Den episode, where people sell themselves onstage, intrudes itself on the home life of Linnea and Del Reese. A couple of phone calls are made between these settings. But no mere circumstance of the plot could account for what we learn by watching these intercut scenes through. A less than happy, but stable, home, restrained, brightly lit, is invaded by the dark, raucous world. The man and wife begin to give way, spiritually, to the darker world. The man will preside at a "smoker," with the look and feel of Deemen's Den, and force the waitress Sueleen to strip herself bare before an audience of men. Linnea will give way to the seductive offers of Tom (Keith Carradine), which begin with his phone call here.

We have a look at the Green home, where the young man who will become an assassin is settling in, then there is a cut to a hospital, where Barbara Jean is awakened (she has collapsed at the airport and has been hospitalized). She is saying she has been dreaming. Perhaps she dreamed of the young man at the Green home, who will eventually shoot her. When she sings later in the hospital chapel about her contact with Jesus ("He walks with me and he talks with me"), she leads to the scene of Opal walking among wrecked cars, calling the place a "graveyard," and eventually coming upon the young man, the assassin. Barbara Jean is in the graveyard. She summons up the man who will shoot her in her destiny's bid to have her imitate Christ—more of this later—whom she has been singing about. Barbara Jean's second number later at Opryland invokes a shot of the assassin in the audience on the words, "You've got your own private world . . ." At the earlier Opry show Connie White, Barbara Jean's "stand-in," has sung about being lost in life, and her words about its being "dark in here" invoke the assassin in the audience. Her second song, about domestic trials, leads to a hospital scene where Barbara Jean and her husband Barnett (Allen Garfield) quarrel bitterly. These singing women seem to create or project the film that will be their life.

On the night before what will be the great show at the Parthenon, the momentous scene of Sueleen's degradation—stripping at the political fund-raising "smoker"—is intercut with Tom's performance of "I'm Easy," charming the women in his life, who are now in the audience, each thinking the song is for her—as we look at them one by one, Opal, Mary (Cristina Raines) from Tom's folk-rock trio, L.A. Joan (Shelley Duvall), and at last Linnea, whom Tom has been after all along. Tom has the advantage over the women, as the men at the "smoker" have it over Sueleen. But Tom is like Sueleen in a way, thrown on his resources onstage before an audience that would like to have pieces of him. This film continually makes revelations of significance or connection. If the film impresses us mainly as a great show, we may start to consider whether a show is not capable of giving us meanings such as we know to be in life. Meanings especially, perhaps, about what a show is, what putting oneself up for show is (—like a horse? Vicki Hearne argues in *Adam's Task* that the training and showing of horses and dogs amounts to a self-realization for the animals, that the animals want and need to put themselves up for this).

Nashville is full of *contrasts*—like my contrast of North Carolina and Tennessee—turnings around, turning of things upside down. And with this we come to what has settled in with me as the central experience of the film, an experience of difference, let us call it, that represents the turning around anyone must undergo to come into understanding, or into the experience of art, or into art's of life, or into new life. A passage through fire, we might say, as Barbara Jean has gone through when we meet her at the beginning of the film.

Of course, contrast is an element of putting things together. Contrast might be pointed out in the blending of lives, of words and images, of sequences, that I have been sketching. But the film has more surprises still. This is the world of Tommy Brown, "the whitest nigger in town," as a sympathetic black character (Sueleen's true friend Wayne) calls him. Karen Black is Connie White. At a height of noncommunication, the young soldier hurries forward to Mr. Green in the hospital to tell about his own family's involvement with Barbara Jean at the time of her burn accident, while Mr. Green is totally abstracted, having just learned of his wife's death. An empty elevator opens in the background behind Mr. Green's head—an image of nothingness.

It is a moment from *Macbeth*, registering the surprise that one stands over the abyss. When the soldier leaves him alone, Green gives way to heaves of weeping. And now there is a cut to Opal and the Walker political agent Triplette (Michael Murphy) cackling with laughter in another setting. I think of Wilson Knight's noting a characteristic move of *King Lear*: "a shifting flash of comedy across the pain of the purely tragic" (159). Here grotesquerie more than comedy. Just after the political van, a bus of sorts, discourses through its loudspeaker on the scandal of tax-exempt churches, Opal appears walking in a storage lot for school buses, saying, "The buses are empty. . . ." She talks on into her recorder, "I must be more positive, no, negative." And she meditates on the color yellow, "the

color of caution . . . cowardice . . . sunshine." We live stuttering between opposites, or entities that jar one against another.

This film is striking in that it is bursting with life and energy. But it is full of death, beginning with the parody television commercial with its frozen images being turned as if on a mechanical wheel. The performances reach a new plane of the natural (I would single out Ned Beatty and Allen Garfield, and Michael Murphy's stuttering outburst at Garfield—"YOU'RE puttin' the knife in her back, B-B-Buster"—at the Parthenon). But the film proclaims itself to be theater, and film. The natural is formalized, becomes art, is seen for what it is through the work of art—perhaps as in all film, as in Van Gogh's painting. The film offers to be comedy, but it turns serious, and deals death. Destinies are obstructed or diverted. The politician about whom so much fuss is made, is not allowed to come before us as a person. The great star, Barbara Jean, has her Opryland performance by a breakdown, and her Parthenon performance by a shooting. Even as this film satisfies us in more than good measure, it frustrates us. Plots do not work out. People's love is frustrated, even Tom's, who gets so much of it.

Everybody wants to make it as a singer. The very atmosphere of the film is one of striving for, and frustration about, this prospect. Albuquerque is actually held by the arm from entering the Opry backstage, through a long sequence. She does finally make it, transcendently, on the Parthenon stage. But it is only by means of death first purging the stage. Shades of Aeschylus's *Eumenides*, where a Greek stage has given much play to death, and at last the transcendent going-forward can occur, with the goddess Athena's saving appearance.

In regard to turnings around, Tom Hopkins suggests, in a breakthrough essay on Altman, that any Altman film will have a midpoint after which the action goes in an opposite direction. In *Nashville*, I propose, the midpoint is the montage of church scenes, beginning with the camera's descent across a huge stained-glass representation of Christ as shepherd, conspicuously swaddled in clothes, after a cut from Tom and Mary naked in bed—sharp contrast there. The Christ image is so strange, so strikingly unlike anything seen in the film thus far, it must herald something. We go on to moments from several churches, including the enactment of a full immersion baptism. And finally Barbara Jean sings, "He walks with me, and he talks with me . . ." in the hospital chapel. It is her first song in the film. After this she moves into action as a singing star. We have already seen the last of Connie White. Tom and Sueleen now come to their destinies onstage, as does Albuquerque, first right away on Sunday, entertaining at the auto races, and eventually at the Parthenon. The next time we see Linnea after she sings with her black choir in a scene from the church series, she is giving way and agreeing to a rendezvous with Tom, just what she had resisted, or pretended to resist, in the first half of the film. Things have turned, though they are in a way the same, which is just the point.

There are certain reversals in technique after the midpoint of *Nashville* such as those Hopkins points out in detail in Altman's *Come Back to the Five and Dime, Jimmy Dean, Jimmy Dean* (1982), the main focus of his essay. The early recording studio scene is an exploration by the moving camera from left to right. And the important domestic interiors we come to know in the first part of the film are explored in the same way, by a camera moving left to right: the Green home, the Reese home, and Tom's motel room, first when Opal has spent the night with him and later when Mary has done so, just before the church scenes. The domestic scenes are linked to that first studio scene. They come from it and repeat it in a way. There is the same sense of our entering on mysterious ground. And it begins to dawn on us that the domestic scenes are scenes of creation too, scenes of the genesis of the film, like the studio scene. The world of the film is genesis, on and on.

Let us look at homes for a moment, and what they generate. We see the Green home when the assassin comes to rent a room there. It is the beginning of the large action that will lead the boy hurrying with Mr. Green out of a graveyard (for Mrs. Green's funeral) to do the shooting at the Parthenon, the thing the whole film heads toward. The assassin, too, is identified with the director (and us who watch the film) in an odd moment, so that this boy's coming to settle in the Green home, thereby in Nashville, is all the more a beginning for the film. Just before the assassin shoots, he contemplates a huge rippling American flag, as a cut to this image reveals it, and then he looks below it to the show onstage. It is exactly what the film itself—and we—have done just a bit earlier in this same scene. We realize that the boy's action when he shoots, carries out a potential in us, in the camera, in filmmaking—a potential to kill. The director, the film, and the audience, being identified with the assassin, suggests that film, this film, may kill us in some sense. There is a way to life-in-art, or life itself that matters, only through death of a kind.

As for *Nashville's* other generative home scenes, the one at the Reese is the first occasion for the intrusion of one life and setting upon another (Deemen's Den upon this home), which is a basic way of proceeding for the whole film. And in the scenes in Tom's room the lustful and uncaring, or highly unrealistic, find each other out. The state of mind here is basic to the film—raw desire, which has to be channeled, frustrated, perverted, creating the world of the film, as the naked in bed are supposed to create.

After the film's midpoint church scenes, the only new interior is Bill and Mary's room (Bill and Mary of Tom's folk-rock trio. And this scene is explored in a series of camera movements right to left, the opposite motion to what we have had formerly. We feel that we can know a thing in a new way, opposite to our former way of knowing. And yet what we come to know is much the same as before, another version of the unhappy home. This new scene is not mysterious like the earlier ones, with their sense of something being created and of our being on the special ground where such occurs—except here when Mary's pensive face summons a cut to Tom's room—another gesture of authorship on the part of a woman—and there is again movement from left to right, as if the film recollects itself. The Bill and Mary scene is realistic; it is bitter marriage comedy. We are asked to recognize realism, in its subject and in its manner, as a development out of mysteriousness, as being the same thing but different. Creation goes on and on.

The late scene with Linnea and Tom in bed is given at first with cuts between fixed-camera images (more matter-of-fact) rather than camera movement, but the action moves from right to left in the setting, in the new way. It is the same old scene with novelties. Linnea manages to have her shift on in bed after the sex. She retrieves her panties from under the covers, evoking the reality of the sexual encounter, which we do not see directly. And she proceeds to dress, reversing the action of the Sueleen strip in the scene just preceding this, the "smoker" (shades of the Devil at work). There Sueleen had tossed away her panties, evoking her full nudity, which we also do not see directly. Film is always doing this, offering the seen to evoke the unseen—meaning, depth, action.... Tomlin's scene here as Linnea is one of disillusionment—Tom shows himself to be a cad—a scene of de-creation that is yet a new creation. Linnea is not to meet a dead end in lust and the loss of a grasp on life. We sense she is great, a great person and a great talent. We are left asking just what she is, or where she is. We are asked to contemplate her, to wonder at her. The film is interrogative.

The central event of the church sequence, where things begin to turn around, is baptism. "If you're down to the river, I hope you'll drop in."

> Are you willing to be sponged out, erased, cancelled, made nothing?
> Are you willing to be made nothing?
> dipped into oblivion?
> If not, you will never really change. (Lawrence, *Last Poems* 80)

> I don't see how man will ever quite be able to get rid of purification, contemplation, and rebirth. Our orthodox sciences—sociology, social reform, psychiatry—and our orthodox prophets—Freud and Marx—still leave this loophole; alas, they must. (Lowell 50–51)

Barbara Jean's early invitation to her audience to drop in is taken up at the midpoint of the film, as we see a black youth being immersed in a Baptist Church tank. *Nashville* finds its way to the ultimate willingness that D. H. Lawrence wants to promote, the real action and experience that Robert Lowell says we shall never get rid of, never be able to do without. The result is that we can now have Barbara Jean sing. She will sing more and more in the film. Perhaps she will survive the shooting at the end (this is unclear) to come back and sing again—just as Ronee Blakley survives Altman's film shooting, and cutting, to become, to reach us as, Barbara Jean.

This woman artist is what the death and rebirth of baptism into art, into film, is meant to bring us into contact with. Reading back from Sunday, the day of her first song, in the hospital chapel: Barbara Jean collapses on a Friday afternoon, traditionally the time of the Crucifixion. Saturday night, when she fights with Barnett, is a descent into Hell. And the film's final gesture in this scene shows intense pity, rendering a close-up of her in profile, on her knees, an all but indescribable look on her face, complex and deep—a look of suffering, consciousness of where she is in life, despair, self-control. She rises on Sunday morning and sings of her contact with God. When she is carried off the Parthenon stage and out of the film, Barnett shouts, "I can't stop that blood, man!" It is the blood that will always flow for those baptized into it. The suggestion of the film, I think, is that the blood of art, this art—film, figured in country music and essentially Barbara Jean—flows to nourish those who will die and be born into it.

In *Contesting Tears*, Stanley Cavell discusses *Stella Dallas* (1937), *Now, Voyager* (1942), *Gaslight* (1944), and *Letter from an Unknown Woman* (1948) as exemplifying a body of film melodramas—the earliest he cites is *Blonde*

Venus (1932)—he calls "the melodrama of the Unknown Woman," which come into play as the agonized, dark alternative to the "comedies of remarriage" he studied in *Pursuits of Happiness*. *Nashville* is equally agonized, equally dark. Altman's film emphasizes the trauma and ecstasy of starting to face a work of film, taking the first step toward acknowledging the life of a person who may be the subject of film. The life we are invited into is figured in this film's vital images of the women singing, the heart of the work. They sing about wanting to go somewhere but not knowing the way, about never getting enough of what they hunger for, about the secrets of their love they will never tell (why? because life will not tolerate love?).

Karen Black's Connie White is very intriguing, and could well be the subject of a whole film. But here she is an aspect, a version, of the central singer of the film. She has to die out of the film before Ronee Blakley can begin to sing. Perhaps Connie has to give way because she is against nature, black-and-white, Black made White, too constrained, a walking dead woman, not a woman to whom an audience can be reborn. The deathly imagination about her is something Altman makes a central subject in *Come Back to the Five and Dime, Jimmy Dean, Jimmy Dean*, where her deathly imagination has much to teach (as Tom Hopkins explains). Hitchcock makes the deathly quality of Black a subject in *Family Plot* (1976).

Black is linked to Blakley and to the central utterance of the film in the early sequence of Connie singing at the Opry as a stand-in for Barbara Jean. This whole episode builds in excitement as Altman's camera moves about the hall, among points of view of audience, performers, backstage admirers. It is a magnificent exploration of theater, an exploration presented by film and thus made larger than theater. When Connie sings her parody songs—"Will you still love me in the mornin', when the baby makes you git up one more time"—it is fascinating, done by this woman and regarded by Altman's camera. He looks at her close up from a low angle as she holds the bulbous microphone just before her lips and sings intently. Altman—the viewer—is worshipful and questioning. And there are cuts to poetically invoked images during the song, such as that of the assassin in the audience. The singer has a power over images, or film has a power to appreciate the singer and follow her leads—perhaps a power we exercise in our own living of life—or a power we *might* exercise. When Barbara Jean appears at last outdoors at Opryland, the scene is shot with all the panache of the earlier one with Connie. The low-angle close shot of the singer is repeated.

But now it is daylight; there is more energy at hand—things seem more unpredictable. The cutting to orchestra musicians doing their work is more alive and spontaneous than before, giving a sense of the musicians' great enjoyment (contrast the brutal pan across the ensemble later at the "smoker" when Sueleen is forced to strip). But the chief new thing with Barbara Jean now is that the songs are real country songs done by a real singer. The parody songs—Haven's "200 Years" and so on—serve the satiric purposes of Altman's film whereas the real songs have much broader intentions and reach, and yet the film is able to face these songs. The parody songs are just art, in a sense, or artifice. The real songs are life. Here the film tells us that its concern with art is meant to point back into, or forward into, life.

With the rapid, propulsive Cowboy Song ("There's nothin' like the lovin' of a hard-ridin' cowboy man . . ." [the *a* drawn out, ma-a-an]) Barbara Jean/Blakley comes on revealing her inner life with something like the impact of Dietrich's first number in *Blonde Venus* (which we will come to: the quiet housewife and mother peeling herself out of a gorilla suit to sing about the "hot voodoo" in her blood). These songs point to our own recollections, or fantasies. With Barbara Jean's cowboy song—a stay against madness, it transpires—we know that *Nashville* has delivered itself fully. Out of the shocking contrasts and all the rest of it, we and Barbara Jean are born to each other.

Barbara Jean follows this number with "Dues," eloquent wailing, with some wordless singing and expressive hand gestures, painting in air, about the miseries of domestic life. Then she is unable to start a new number. Instead, Blakley gives a magnificent rendition of a nervous breakdown onstage, the character recounting her girlhood and difficult working life, finally descending into imitation chicken sounds. Barnet comes on to escort her off, and she repeats, "I ain't done, I ain't done." Done performing or done breaking down? The rest of the film might be regarded as a continuation of her breakdown.

Audiences are volatile in this film. They boo Barbara Jean when she breaks down at Opryland after her first two songs. They boo and torment Sueleen at the "smoker," pressuring her to strip; above all, there is the assassin rising up from the crowd at the Parthenon, figuring a potential both in the filmmaker and in us who watch the film. Film itself is an audience, to the singing performers and to all the others in the film, appreciating them, bearing down on them, holding dangers for them. Clearly audiences are a worry to Altman—the audiences to art, and art itself in its capacity as audience.

The long coda to *Nashville*, after the shooting, can be seen as an offer to come to terms with audiences. The camera both questions and celebrates people here as they mill around—the camera moves to follow people, the film cuts to close-ups. Altman seems to want to claim people, to claim *us*, as his own, fit to be the audience to his film. Or perhaps he just probes these people, and probes and shocks us. The sequence concludes with the camera rising into the sky, countering the many grand descending camera movements of the film—at the start of the first political van sequence, down the stained-glass Christ, at the start of all the big theatrical events. The final upward gesture may be one of resurrection, with the spirit of the crowd. Or is it may be a sorrowful turning away from the pit of this world.

My romantic memories of Tennessee are met with the critical, shocking images of *Nashville*. And I am rushed into a world of film imagination. My memories submit to shocks just so that I can enter and dwell in this world of film. If I do not close it off, the film will stand to do who knows what with my life, my picture of life, my sense of the play that imagination may have in life.

My romantic memories amount to an understanding of life. They are, I think, much like what anyone brings to a film. My West is like anyone's. A West is what we hope to find and do find and live in. *Nashville* asks, speaking strongly what art always speaks, that we break through our West into a further West. Perish and be changed.

John Donne exclaims in an early poem, in love, excited, "O my America! my new-found-land!" (87).

But we may go from West into West, which is East, the source again of the spirit, the land of creation. At any point in life we may be apt for re-creation. Donne speaks in "Goodfriday, 1613. Riding Westward" of being

> carryed towards the West
> This day, when my Soules forme bends toward the East. (259)

He summons up a cinema of the mind, the Passion scenes encountered one by one, and says of them,

> Though these things, as I ride, be from mine eye,
> They'are present yet . . . (259)

He is even delicate about the power of the gaze:

> durst I
> Upon his miserable mother cast mine eye? (259)

Finally, he will submit to being changed, to coming into identity with, as he takes it, the author of the images he has half looked at, so that he may look at them—at something—full:

> Burne off my rusts . . .
> Restore thine Image, so much, by thy grace,
> That thou may'st know me, and I'll turne my face. (259)

Henry Gibson, in his flagrantly western clothes, sings about America, "We must be doin' somethin' right, to last 200 years." But he also sings, urges, "Keep a Goin'," and ushers in Connie White, who sings, "I'd like to go to Memphis [which is west] . . . I'd love to go to heaven . . I'd like to tell you how I feel, but I don't know what to say." If we will look with the eyes of Altman—of this film—then we may come into a life of meeting those who would express themselves, including oneself, and responding. This is America beyond America.

2

Whim, God, and the Screen

Jean-Luc Godard's *Hail Mary*

CAN A FILM BE RELIGIOUS? Can it open doors into religious knowledge or experience?
Everyone comes to film either without religion—in a purely secular state of mind—or with some background in religious education and profession of faith still alive within one.

The background in my case was southern Presbyterian, very conscious and proud of its Scottish heritage. I was sent to Sunday School, and taken to church, where everyone recited together the Apostles' Creed. The Bible, both its story and its moral teaching, was presented as truth.

Among Presbyterians there was an emphasis on fatedness, the sense that life is lived out in the hands of a higher power, or (we may say) according to a previously ordained mythic pattern—a sense not incompatible with the experience of film.

In my early teens I took an interest in Roman Catholicism—the rituals, the images, the doctrine. My mother said to me at one point that her father, my grandfather, a McMillan and a staunch Presbyterian, who died when I was three (I do remember him, vaguely), would turn over in his grave if he knew I was interested in Catholicism. There has been much anti-Catholic prejudice in the South, as Haven's wife, Lady Pearl, protests in *Nashville* (1975). She is a fan of "the Kennedy boys."

I hasten to add that my grandfather worked for a large business owned and run by Catholics, with whom he was very friendly and got along well. My mother harbored really no prejudice. Nor did my father, of rural Baptist background, but never an enthusiast.

I matured, like many, I think, from a religious background into a fairly secular state of mind, in my case going north to secondary school, reading Freud, and conversing with atheists.

Could Jean-Luc Godard, the most inventive and self-reflective of contemporary filmmakers, bring religion and film into contact, and reach viewers with the quality of their interaction?

Hail Mary (*Je vous salue, Marie*, 1985) is a modern story whose characters do not speak of the Bible or the resemblance of their lives to biblical events. Yet the film is about a virgin named Marie (Mary; Myriem Roussel) who becomes pregnant while remaining a virgin, gives birth to a child, and feels that God is involved in all this. She has problems with her fiancé, Joseph (Thierry Rode), who eventually marries her. And a character named Gabriel (Philippe Lacoste) intervenes in their lives, rather bullyingly, to give advice and explanations. We seem to have here a presentation in a modern setting of the early phase of the life of Christ. Or is the film a presentation of something else—just a modern story? modern ideas?—using the life of Christ and Mary as a means to Godard's own end?

But we do not really know the difference between these two propositions. We do not know—do we?—exactly what the life of Christ was, or is, whether it is a mysterious fact to be faced; something we have made up, even if inspired by God, that serves as a metaphor for our life, a way of interpreting human life; or a way for us to make ourselves change. Godard's film asks us to ponder what the life of Christ is, and what our life is in relation to that.

The film does its work in part by getting us to ponder what is at stake in the act of telling the tale. *Hail Mary* quotes versions of the life of Christ (the Gospels, Bach's *St. Matthew Passion*) and suggests comparisons to still others (the many paintings and philosophers' accounts, such as Augustine's or Schopenhauer's or Simone Weil's). Godard seems to want to join the rank of tellers of the old tale, or to supersede them. At any rate he gets us to think: What has the very telling of this old, obsessing tale, the occasion and the form or manner that is found to tell it, got to reveal of what Christ's life, and ours, is?

Whim is a force commonly felt by tellers of this tale, and a force Godard feels and does something with in his own way. Our attitude to these events must be such, it seems, that we feel we half create them. There is the sense that anything might happen, and all will be well. We feel that to yield to the play of these things, coming from within us or from outside as it may be, is to realize a deep necessity, a veritable principle of life—rather in the way specified in Vedic and Buddhist teaching, or in Emerson. The speaker in T. S. Eliot's "Journey of the Magi" is at first down to earth, complaining of the camels, the cold, the unfriendly people and high prices on the journey. But he is open to strange moods:

> . . . a water-mill beating the darkness,
> And three trees on the low sky,
> And an old white horse galloped away in the meadow. (Eliot,
>   *Collected Poems* 99)

The man comes at last to witness a birth [Christ's] that is "like Death," and he is left uneasy and glad.

Hail Mary is a notably whimsical film, first in a way that is like other Godard films: there is a seeming arbitrariness about the flow of images and sounds. In Godard, and notably here, we constantly experience shocks, as our attention to the unfolding narrative—to *some* unfolding narrative, so it seems—is interrupted to have us look at a new, at first sight incongruous, image, or to have us take in someone's words from outside the present scene, or a strange sound or bit of music. Each of these items seems to offer a comment on what has been going on in the film, as if from a heightened, not to say nervous, consciousness on the part of the filmmaker—and from no clearly fixed or summarizable point of view. Is the new item a comment, or an extension of narrative in some sense? The more we attend, or re-view, the more right seems each of the surprising gestures. We think about meaning, and we adjust in ways that are beyond, or below, such thinking, reconciling ourselves to all the facts of the film. Whim seems to prove "better than whim at last" (Emerson 262).

Now Godard was first a critic and appreciator of film and then a maker of films, as if making the kind of film he already admired, or allowing something half hidden that he had seen in earlier film, to come to the fore and be plain in his own work. After we watch Godard, a great deal of film—Hollywood films such as *Blonde Venus* (1932), Renoir, and other work—looks more like Godard than it did before. There is much of the surprising and thought-provoking and difficult to contend with in the earlier work if only we will see it. Perhaps film of its nature is whim that is more than whim. Perhaps film is suited in general, of its nature, to deal with the coming of God into life. This is a theme Godard pursues explicitly in *Hélas pour moi* (*Oh, Woe Is Me*, 1993), a version of the Amphitryon story. *Blonde Venus*, I will argue, posits a goddess and brings her into ordinary life.

Hail Mary is particularly whimsical in eliciting something like the Annunciation and Christmas story from the lives of *these* people, driving their cars around a clean, electrified city, working in a gas station, playing basketball in a spiffy gymnasium. The people seem very much a part of the film's modern surfaces and ambiance. The lead couple are the familiar Godard sulking adolescents—self-absorbed, fighting over sex and commitment. The film seems just to *declare* that its characters are Mary, Joseph, and Gabriel. And the later part of the film, when the child is born, with shots of blossoming branches, and beasts ogling the camera, seems a joke in a way, a ritualized going through the steps of the Christmas scenario.[1] There is a willful turn to lightheartedness. The film's early use of Bach on the sound track, which has given way to an obsession through the middle portion with the Dvořák Cello Concerto—a whimsical turn in itself—now comes home with "Jesu, Joy of Man's Desiring" in a simple piano version.

But Christmas is like this. The most important Christian feast, inspired by the most astonishing of mysteries, Incarnation, has a way of going unaccountable and lighthearted. Romance, rather deliberate allegorization, humor, a certain excessiveness—such are the qualities of the Gospels' treatments, the late medieval *Second Shepherds' Play*, the things that people desire to do in ordinary life in the face of this inspiration.

Look at the *Second Shepherds' Play* for a moment. Mak and Gill, man and wife, are alive strictly speaking at the time of the birth of Christ. But they also exist, clearly, in present-day (medieval) England, suffering its conditions and swearing by Christ and Mary. Like Godard's Mary and Joseph, Mak and Gill are a modern couple who do not compare themselves to the Bible but still reflect the coming of God into their ordinary/extraordinary everyday lives. Mak and Gill live a life of poverty and go through the tensions and antics of sheep stealing, getting a sheep as if getting a child, and expecting to be saved by it.[2]

In the play there is constantly music in the air, as in *Hail Mary*, as in so many films. Mak comes on stage expressing lostness and freedom, a readiness for whim, we might say, and he is taken to be singing:

MAK: . . . thy will, Lord, of me tharns [is lacking]:
I am all uneven, that moves oft my harns [brains] . . .

SHEPHERD: Who is that pipes so poor?

MAK: Lo, a man that walks on the moor,
And has not all his will! (78–79)

Rhyme and a musical mode, and humor where we can see it, seem to express a transcendence of what things would be without these qualities. The discovery in the cradle of the sheep stolen by Mak is a joke, despite the deadly seriousness of the crime:

SHEPHERD: Give me leave him to kiss, and lift up the clout.
What the devil is this? He has a long snout. (72)

Soon an angel is heard singing "Gloria in excelsis!" and the shepherds go to see the actual baby Jesus, mysteriously presenting him with a bunch of cherries, a bird, and a tennis ball. They finally depart the stage calling for song, and singing.

The parallel of Mak and Gill and their sheep to Joseph and Mary and Jesus, and the parallel of Godard's characters, are suggestions in the imitation-of-Christ way of thinking about life—our life is like that of Christ and those close to him. The parallel offers a solution, a way of comprehending what happens in our life, and at the same time a problem, a challenge. How *can* a human life be taken to parallel Christ's? What is at issue here? What ought one to do?[3] The characters in a story may not think much about all this, but the audience can go further. *The Second Shepherds' Play* (and much of Christian art, much of Christian philosophy) seeks to reassess the life of Christ, to ask again what it is and what our life is in relation to that. Any such work means to supersede Christian art and thinking as it stands, perhaps as much as Godard's film may be thought to do.

Hail Mary suggests right off, and continually throughout, that the lives of its characters are in the hands of something like God, a sublime power comprehending and ordering all of life. The parallel with the life of Christ suggests even more: fatedness, even constriction to a certain pattern of life—including salvation, of course. But the film suggests too that the whole divine dimension to these lives is a matter of the way the characters live imaginatively toward one another. The film suggests this by identifying the characters, notably Joseph and Marie, over and over with the imaginative power that generates the film, these people's lives. Call this power the director, the power of film as it comes to be this film, life itself as it comes to be film.

⌇

The film begins with the title "*EN CE TEMPS LÀ*" (at that time), white letters on a black ground. It is biblical, historical, romance-like, suggesting that we shall see a fable with resonating significance. Then there is a long-held shot—with the sound of thunder—of a luminously green field on a hillside in the rain, with trees and a margin of sky in the background, dense marsh grass or some such stuff (it is blurry) in the foreground, moved by wind.

It is a very vivid shot, reminiscent of Tarkovsky and his hero Dovzhenko. The colors and motion really come to life. We are brought close into the natural world. Maybe it is the moment of Creation, as "*EN CE TEMPS LÀ*" might suggest. Or it could be read simply as nature standing opposed to the literariness, the art making, the idea, of the white words in the title frame. Of course, the new shot is not nature itself but a film shot, a wonder of the cameraman's art, and rather prettily composed, it might occur to us, for all its immediacy. Here the world and film art are inextricably mixed up in each other.

The title of the film and the credits follow (white letters on black), with shots interspersed looking down on a water surface reflecting a fixed point of light—maybe the sun, an element of nature; maybe an artificial light, a filmmaker's or cinematographer's equipment. And this surface is broken continually by objects—perhaps rocks—splashing into the water and making the reflected light ripple all over the surface. Perhaps this is, or points to, the primal action, getting the world into motion. With the first title, a Bach sonata for cello and harpsichord begins, which plays throughout the sequence—we will come back to this. At the same time, we constantly hear the sound of the splashing of objects into the water, and the cries of birds. The water and bird cries continue the creation theme from "*EN CE TEMPS LÀ*" and the shot of the field. We are taken further into the natural world. Perhaps *Hail Mary* will make a point about the primacy of nature, albeit a *created* nature, for any consideration of the events that happen in the film.

But the sight of water reflecting light suggests still more: film itself as a subject for this film. The surface is like a screen, the reflected light source suggesting a filmmaker's lamp.

Perhaps it is a director who throws the objects into the water, making the light move on the surface, bringing the surface to life. (And here the idea of water as an imaginative medium or power reflects back

to rain seen watering the earth in the film's first shot.) The opening of *Hail Mary* is strangely like the opening of *Blonde Venus*—just the sort of rich and conscious-of-itself Hollywood film that inspired Godard to begin analyzing film and eventually to make films. *Blonde Venus* gives us at its opening a shot down onto a water surface rippling with light; the main title and credits come, superimposed on the water surface; and then a woman emerges as if from behind the camera, swimming out and churning this surface. She will be the chief actor in the film. As we will see in the chapter on the film, *Blonde Venus* suggests throughout that the woman we see living her life is a woman giving us her story, creating it, as if she is the filmmaker making the film. *Hail Mary* in the opening sequence is just before getting to the woman, but the film reveals already that the created world—of nature, or of the film—and the story that will unfold are to be seen with an unusual consciousness as tied to the art of a film director—to the art of a person, or to the art of God, who, in this filmed view, is like a film director.

The Bach in this sequence might be taken as residing on the side of art. Godard in using it may be declaring that he is shaping the natural world and the story that is to come. He freely chooses—imposes—the music and determines the mood of the sequence. But the music of Bach has such character that it cannot merely serve Godard in this way. It takes us beyond Godard—to God, I would suggest. Bach's music evokes the harmony of the spheres: it is unremittingly contrapuntal—it never seems to need to stop. The music makes us think of mathematics: a grasp of the things of the universe in their essentials and essential relations, and as they may, on principle, be recombined. But the Bach is unpredictable, even shocking, in its moves. And this music is a great dance, animated by very material rhythms emanating from who knows where. Bach is thus in accord not so much with law as with an unaccountable, person-like spirit at the heart of things. The quantity of Bach's music, the speed with which it must have been written, suggests God working through the hand of a man. And the work is quintessentially sacred, even when it is secular (and Godard uses plenty of both kinds of Bach's music in *Hail Mary*). Sacred music before Bach is *of* the church; while impressive sacred music after Bach seems to be music addressing its own subjects with the forms of the church taken to give guidance, a taking off point (Mozart, Berlioz, Verdi, Fauré . . .). Bach points our minds to the sacred as happens not quite with any other music, because of his historical moment (which is apparent in his music). He represents music coming to consciousness of itself, with a destiny to be followed out, while still proceeding from a function defined by something other than music. (Consider, in regard to later sacred music, R. P. Blackmur's discussion of the place of Christianity in T. S. Eliot's poetry—the Christianity is distinct from the emotional subject matter of the poems and the very pressure to speak, though the Christianity is inextricable from the poems as they finally take shape; the poetry is thus Christian but not "devotional.")

All of this is not to say that Godard can simply play a passage of Bach and thereby give his story a dimension as if coming from God. Think of the human and highly expressionistic character Bach's music takes on in Pasolini or Bergman. Godard's gesture with Bach can actually throw the film to God because of the open, intellectually free way in which this film proceeds, its light/serious touch with its range of contents. Anything might happen and might come to any significance.

In the final shot of the water surface in the credits sequence, the water is reddish. Probably the light source is now red; perhaps the sun is setting. In any case, something happens. We are made aware that film registers events in the passage of time. The story of Christ comes to blood, and the meaning of the story, its redemptive force, is subsumed in our being offered blood to drink symbolically—we are to take something within us. Does such redemption amount, now, to our being offered Godard's red water surface, the screen, the film? (The very next scene will focus on eating and drinking.) Mary tells us in the film, when she "knows," as she says, that she is pregnant, that nevertheless her period "came very intense" on Friday (the day Christ bled and died). We come to Mary and her motherhood, and strangely at the same time to her menstrual blood. The latter, because brought up unexpectedly, seems suddenly the most important thing about her. Mary's story, epitomized in her blood, is offered us to contemplate, to taste, as is Christ's, and as the screen is offered us to do whatever it is we do with the screen.

Just after the credits there is a café scene, virtually a parody of 1960s Godard. A woman's voice says, "Out of my mouth is shit." We are bound to wonder if this is Mary. We know Mary is our subject, and we shall wonder about her until we locate her. Because the camera is trained on the man here (Joseph, as we learn later) eating and listening, and the woman's voice is from someone outside the frame, except for her hands—imaging her executive power—we might wonder if the woman is to be identified with the film director. "Out of my mouth" means what is said, what we have, this work. The film will end with the image of a woman's open mouth—red lips, black depths within—and the final, "reconciliation" chorus of Bach's *St. Matthew Passion* pouring from the sound track, the image and the music seeming to subsume all of the film, Mary delivering God. "Shit" sounds disappointing. The woman in the present scene cannot get the man to be involved with her, to respond. But shit is also fructifying. Excrement nourishes the earth. Menstrual blood is excrement. Any blood, once it is bled, or as it is being bled, is excrement. Speech, writing, art, are all in a sense excrement.

With a cut to a view of the woman (Juliette Binoche), the rattling of crockery and Godard's other café sounds give way to the opening flourish of Bach's dramatic organ Toccata in D Minor. It is the dimension of God again, if we like, but the music fits the temperament of the scorned woman angrily trying to assert herself. And this music, of all the Bach, seems to foreshadow and justify, to give birth to, the Dvořák Cello Concerto, romantic and stormy, used so much in later scenes. The gripping solo cello entry of that piece comes with a close look into Mary's face when Gabriel and a child angel discover her in a gas station, her home (where "excrement" is purveyed to keep the world running).

In sum, the woman in the café scene is identified with the director by her position outside the frame as she speaks, with God by the music, and with Mary by our wondering and a sort of in-advance musical symbolism (stormy organ toccata/stormy Dvořák). Indeed, a number of women in the film are identified with Mary in various ways, as we shall see, until a woman thanks Mary "on behalf of all women" in a scene after the birth of the child. The question of the film-author and God merges into the question of Mary and woman in general.

In the café scene, the unsatisfactory conversation ("All women want something unique." "Can't you see I'm not listening?" etc.) brings Joseph to comment, "Men think they enter a woman," and there is a cut to the next scene, women's basketball. Joseph's comment implies that perhaps men don't enter a woman but are rather imposed on, or entered by, a woman, perhaps woman as God or author. On the other hand, perhaps men enter something, but it is not a woman; rather, a realm of men's imagination—here the man is author. The man as author or imaginer is confirmed by the cut to the next scene, invoked by Joseph's words. We "enter" this basketball scene, a deep rectangle full of life, something eminently worthy to be entered. But already we have been caught up in the film as the woman's, as the director's, as God's. God, Godard, woman, and man are all confounded. We are involved, the film seems to say, as we live with others and with God, in something like film imagination, with no fixable point of origination for events. I think back to *Nashville* and its melding of identities. Film is very suited to suggest, or convey, a melding of identities.

The women's basketball game is in a way the real beginning of the film after the rather abstract credits sequence and Godard self-parody café scene. A character, Mary, is now given us and named for the first time (named by the woman of the café scene in a little continuation of the scene's dialogue bled over into the basketball scene). And this scene has a curiosity and a developing life that is more than any author could impose on it. We know now that *Hail Mary* will be a good film. The basketball is a staged scene. But it has the look of something that once set going, has its own interest to offer. The activity of the game at a distance down the court, something to be looked at, something one wants to get closer to; then a closer shot of the extra players watching on the side; then Mary's lovely preparation exercises, then her participation in the game—all of this offers a liberation, so to speak, from the filmmaker's art as artificial or arbitrary. What we have here is entirely part of the film, yet it is more than the film, more than film itself. This scene justifies the treatment of life as answering to film imagination, just because life here is given so much ground.

We look hard at Mary, cued as we are (by the film's title) that she is the Madonna, or some sort of Madonna. But her individuality as a young woman, the modern character playing basketball and the actress Myriem Roussel, is utter.

Godard here challenges comparison with Renaissance painting. The realism of this religious painting is famous—the settings and perspective, the modeling, the faces seemingly taken from everyday life—altogether, bringing religion home or finding it at home. But still, this painting is transporting. A film frame is not a painting: it may be very interesting, but however long we contemplate it, stopped on a machine or looked at in a book or in the mind's eye, the point must be finally to come back to the frame in context, its place in what is happening. Godard asks us to wonder how like or unlike painting of the Madonna is the filming of Myriem Roussel, alive and moving, playing this role, where the strange and the familiar are here, what is the basis in the real, what starts, or what inhibits, our being transported.

Mary moves to the fore now. She does her warm-up exercises skipping along the sidelines, and the sounds of the ball game give way to a rippling Bach piano prelude—the dimension of God in lightness of spirit.[4] Mary enters the game and shoots, and suddenly there are brief images of the full moon, echoing the shape of the basketball and suggesting the divine and the generalized feminine at once, and per-

haps the outdoors of this gymnasium scene, where we may be going, where Mary may be sending us in a sense. Her shooting at the basket, which I take as a metaphor for shooting film, making a film, gives us the moon image. Mary seems to have the power to determine where the film goes. Mary now begins a voiceover, "I wondered if some event would happen in my life" (picking up the theme of the woman in the café—"all women want something unique"). And Mary's voiceover runs over into what is in fact the next scene, a classroom with a foreign professor and Eva, as we will come to know them—suggesting that Mary creates or projects this scene, with these characters who will run a sort of parallel course to her story in the rest of the film, not knowing or interacting with Mary and those close to her (the exception proves the rule: Joseph gives the professor and Eva a brief ride in his taxi, a sort of movie-generating machine, as we shall see). Mary's voiceover becomes very important later in the film, making the action and images of the film seem generated by her intense concern about what is happening to her, her questions about the relation of the spirit and the body. In the basketball scene, we discover Mary as the film's principal subject, and we see her begin to act, more strongly than anyone, as if she is the author of the film.

The classroom scene, possibly Mary's projection, introduces the idea of the creation of life on Earth from the outside. "It was willed, desired, anticipated, organized, programmed," says the professor. God, in short, if he is the creator, has acted like a human being in his forethought and imagination and taking of action—the only way we can conceive of God, Thomas Aquinas says, even while we recognize that our terms are not suitable. God, more specifically, has acted like a human being as artist, as filmmaker. The professor does not speak of God, just of the transplanting of life from a distant point in the universe to Earth. Still, his argument about the unlikelihood of natural evolution on Earth is that the time required, with its chance actions, is just too long—"one hundred times the life of the universe." Then how did the life at a distant point arise? Where did it come from, before? It seems that with the question of our lives we are thrown to the outside, whether to God or to beings from a distant point, who must themselves originate from another distant point, and so on and on. But still, this is to be thrown to ourselves in a way—to God as like ourselves, or to alien beings who are in fact us, strange as it may sound. "We wonder what an extraterrestrial looks like. Go to a mirror and look at yourself," says the professor as Godard's camera contemplates a fascinating-looking, ordinary young man with a walrus mustache, a listener in the classroom.

We must go to the outside—and it is ourselves—but still it is outside ourselves. It is all something of an intellectual bind, a bumping of the head against wall after wall, yet it is full of promise. T. S. Eliot gives the experience of the situation in *Ash Wednesday*:

> Because I do not hope to turn again
> Because I do not hope
> Because I do not hope to turn (Eliot, *Collected Poems* 85)

Mary perhaps projects it, the scene of it succeeds to her, because she looks forward to an "event" in her life, what might be caused from the outside. This question of the outside becomes a chief preoccupation of hers, and ours, in the film. Is what happens from the outside? Is the spirit other than body and from the outside?

Mary implicates herself in the present scene in a number of ways. The scene begins with a shot of another woman in the classroom, looking contemplative, as Mary's voiceover from the previous scene trails away. This woman seems another aspect of the generalized woman the film seems to be about, all individuals to be related to Mary. The woman sits before a large plate-glass window, as if projected on a screen, as if having power, herself, to project her own life as if on a screen. The whole classroom episode ends with a shot of this woman again sitting before the window, now with darkness outside and a vivid reflection of herself issuing back from the window. Perhaps the whole episode has been her meditation. This woman, the scene reveals, is Eva, her name suggesting she may be pure and art-inspiring like the heroine of Wagner's opera *Die Meistersinger von Nürnberg*. The professor calls her Eve, whom theology identifies as the first of sinners, historically redeemed by Mary, the two being in a sense alter egos of each other. Eve is always alive in us to be redeemed in Mary, the teaching tells us, just as the "old Adam" is always alive in us to be redeemed in Christ. It is a matter of contemplating them and becoming imbued with their spirit.

After the first shot of Eva/Eve and the shot of the mustached young man, during all of which we hear some of the professor's theory about origins, we get a lengthy shot of the professor before a white board on which there is a red graph, an amorphous elongated figure representing an analysis of light received from a cloud distant in the universe. The professor points to a "dip in the curve," likely indicating the presence of bacteria—life—out there. "We are from there," he says. The film asks us to contemplate for a moment, as the sign of its science, its knowledge, a red mass spread over two dimensions, reminiscent of the reddened water surface earlier and the idea of the issuing of blood—the screen, Mary's product, Mary's film. The color red is threaded through the film. Later Eva will appear in a small red car to give the professor an angry send-off after the end of their affair, exulting in her independence.

The sense of who Eva is, is deepened as the classroom scene goes on. After the professor's remarks about the red graph, Eva is asked to help a young man solve a puzzle cube. The young man is seen first from the back of the head for a time, his crazy and beautiful white hair making us think again of the extraterrestrial and the strangeness of the human. There is an exciting cut to a straight-on view of the young man's face—this gesture of suspense and cut to the face will be repeated toward the end of the film for the boy "Jesus" at his mother's table. To solve the puzzle, the young man will have his eyes covered, and Eva will say "yes" and "no" as he makes moves with the cube. It will prove how "direction" gets us to the place chance will hardly ever bring us. There is a wonderful close-up shot of Eva and the young man (Pascal—perhaps like Blaise Pascal a mystic and a scientific thinker at once) working along. The shot of the two suggests sex—or the movies, where people make out—with softened light and physical intimacy, Eva saying, "yes . . . no" as the activity (out of frame) proceeds. Finally she cries ecstatically, "Yes . . . yes . . . yes," as the solution is reached. Eva is the woman who makes love in this film.

Making love is inextricably tied up with the scientific pursuit of the film, in the present scene and throughout. And making love, living sexually at all, is an aspect of Mary that Mary is curious about, wants and shies off from, projects and creates. "God counts on ass," Mary says much later in the film, somewhat bitterly, though she is reconciled to giving her own. Eva, while more than ass, is distinctly that from the start. How different she looks walking around naked in a later scene, carnal, at her lover's house, with what a different world in her mind, from how Mary looks in the many shots of her nude—Mary, this unearthly being Godard's film has created, not carnal despite all, until perhaps the final moments of the film.

During the close-up shot of Eva and Pascal working together, the Bach D-Minor Toccata begins again. I have suggested that this music, free-form, moody, dramatic, gives birth to the Dvořák. And this is exactly what happens in the present scene. After the Bach, the next music we hear is the Dvořák welling up during the scene's final shot, Eva against the plate-glass window. The Dvořák is Czech, like the professor. Bach's Toccata, the Dvořák, God, the professor, woman in general, and Mary—all are to be identified with one another in a sense. Such is the play of something like film imagination in the going forward of our lives, in our identifying of God—call it that—in ourselves, in others, or at all. The Dvořák continues and is entirely the music for the succeeding scene, the angels' arrival by airplane. So the early start for the music, while we are still with Eva, makes the airplane scene seem projected by Eva and the classroom events. But it is all very soon brought home to Mary, who started everything anyway. Just a moment into the airplane scene a shot of Mary looking into a mirror is inserted—as if she is seeing a movie, or running one.

With the arrival of the Gabriel figure and the child angel, the film starts in some new directions. The story parallel to the Annunciation and the birth of Christ now begins. Also, from here on until the highly whimsical "Christmas" section at the end, the film can be regarded as a familiar Godard story, the extended emotional debate between two young people over the question of their intimacy, what is it to be, exactly, a question that seems to subsume the questions of virginity-with-pregnancy and intervention in our lives from the outside. These questions

can seem just wrinkles, figures, things as they sometimes appear, to be taken against the solid base of the emotional set-to between Joseph and Mary. Now we can be caught up in a story, biblical or Godardian. We can take things more crudely.

And yet, from the airplane arrival scene on, the succession of images and ideas carefully develops the interests of creativity and imagination already begun in the opening sequences. First now we get, with the Dvořák, a shot of a plane with lights approaching in a dark sky, seen through a mass of tangled black trees in the foreground, like the tangles of a woman's hair—Mallarmé's *cheveux impurs*. Cut to the shot of Mary looking in a mirror, surely hearing, perhaps summoning, the sound of the airplane. She looks at herself in the glass, looks at an extraterrestrial, if you like, as the professor has said to do. Perhaps she is doing the bidding of a man or of God, rather than her own. Perhaps she is bringing an event to her life, such as she reflected on earlier. Cut to a beautiful red sun on the horizon, one of those artistic, somewhat arbitrary images that suggest a metacontext for the film—perhaps the divine realm, perhaps nature—and similar to the image of the great round moon that occurred in Mary's beginning voiceover at the basketball game. Mary might seem to command the divine, or nature. Cut to the plane flying into a reddish sky. Mary seems to send it into her "work," her red production. Seemingly, this is the plane that lands to produce Gabriel and the child angel in the airport—what we come to next.

We see the little girl looking at us close up through a pane of glass. Perhaps she is what Mary screens, having the power herself to screen something. She, who is never named and who is not part of the original Annunciation story, in a sense represents Mary herself. She is assistant to and instructor of Gabriel—a projector, projected, Mary's intervention to make sure the outside coming to her does what it is supposed to do. We see Gabriel and the child together awkwardly tie Gabriel's shoelace, and the camera makes us concentrate on the silly two-tone shoe, the lace, and the hands—concentrate as if on work, somebody's achievement, the white string against red leather, a reverse of the professor's graph, his red string upon white. The shoe and lace epitomize the whole scene as someone's work. Mary's. Gabriel and the child go out into a night of cars and fast-moving lights, a world like a darkened cinema hall with its flickering light—an image much repeated in the film. A car (Joseph's—but where does he come from?) will take them now to Mary and the moment when she looks at them and at the camera, and we hear the stirring solo cello entry of Dvořák's Concerto. Mary's film brings about what happens to her.

⤺

Here, thinking about the film, I want to ask, Does *Hail Mary* have to be read inch by inch, so to speak, with a very active consciousness? What about the film's larger storytelling, after all, its larger action? Our involvement with the film is a being torn between the potential to think about the moment, and on the other hand our interest in the succession of events, always going forward.

Film would seem to ally itself, as many have noted, with stage drama and prose fiction, where the interest, what makes drama and fiction what they are, is events that happen, what goes forward. Still—and here a connection to the Bible and other sacred history becomes apparent—the drama and fiction that interest us most ask for, or allow, analysis, taking thought, letting ourselves register more and more deeply what is there, with the moment or back and forth over the interconnections of the work. Perhaps with an interesting work we never do stop and think; we may just go forward, the work having a supercharged quality for us, like a dream. But with what interests us as action, in life or in storytelling (or story-presenting), we always know the *potential* to stop and reflect, maybe forever. F. R. Leavis said that the nineteenth-century novelists are the heirs of Shakespeare. The novels, like the plays, are "dramatic poems." I have come to regard film directors as the heirs of Shakespeare and the novelists. Perhaps all of these are the heirs of the writers, or writer, of sacred books. In any case, I have come to regard good, rich films as dramatic poems.

Whether *Hail Mary* does in fact move forward can never be answered to the point of proof. For me, *Hail Mary* does move forward, and I am interested first and last by its large things that happen, even though, I can testify, the film on a first viewing can be confusing about characters and their relationships and what exactly is occurring. One's interest on a first viewing, as with other Godard films of the time (*Every Man for Himself*, *Passion*) may be only in how people look and how they relate to the objects in their world, and what moods in the film, taken rather abstractly, supervene upon what other moods. *Hail Mary*'s action is, as films (dramas, stories) go, highly *particular*: the direction changes often and drastically; the film seems continually to be beginning anew, not only in episodes but on the smallest scale (as with the musical movement of Schönberg's opera *Erwartung*[5]—a melodrama about a woman facing her apartness and making something of it, beginning anew, reconceiving). And Godard's moments, more than those of most films, "tend toward" being ideas, as T. S. Eliot said of the moments and patterns of some poetry, such as Valéry's, considered relatively to other work. Moments with Mary invite thought about imagination, when we have not developed for Mary the full emotional sense of a human being, such as we develop for characters in other films. When we stop and think with *Hail Mary*, the thinking will be relatively "intellectual." With *Blonde Venus* or *Now, Voyager*, we stop and think (about the causes of this story we are watching, about the nature of film), and our reflecting, without being any the less thinking, is, more than with Godard, a flowering of our emotions, a deepening of our sympathies. To look at this Godard is more like reading Melville than, say, Jane Austen or Tolstoy.

Overall, the parallel of Godard's modern story with that of Mary and Joseph in the Bible is more than arbitrary because of the genuine element of whim about it, the sparks that leap to connect the two stories and that appear, all the more on consideration, to come of necessity. Consider a crucial scene and its aftermath. In her gynecologist's office, there is the question of Mary's being in pain, the question of her being pregnant (although her period came on Friday), and also the question of her being a virgin (although she avers she is pregnant). These issues are not taken up and answered one by one, to say the least. The doctor appears to examine Mary vaginally (the film image is indirect here, the camera a bit high and to the side of the action) and then says, "It's true." And it is not at all clear what he means to be saying. He is modest about his knowledge, perhaps with a false modesty, as he washes his hands and prepares to have a look at Mary: "I always wondered what we know about a woman, and found that all you can know is what a man already knew." Then he really learns his lesson about this, finding out the unclear and mysterious state of affairs that Mary knows and speaks of. Yet there is a suggestion of God about the doctor, as if he knows all and has power over all. "I was there when you were born." At the end of the scene, Mary asks him to "tell Joseph," and in subsequent scenes we see Joseph being instructed by the "angels," suggesting that the doctor is in league with divine forces.

But then there is plenty of evidence that the angels are projected by Mary or by Joseph, a part of the way each communicates with the other—and the priority of either Mary's or Joseph's authorship is impossible to establish, just as in the early sequences of the film. What the film's editing presents as an exchange of glances between Joseph beside his taxi and Mary in her bathroom, just after the doctor's office scene, gives rise to an appearance of the angels to Joseph. Whose glance started this—Joseph's or Mary's? And a little later, Mary at the gas pumps at night, after reading in a book on the spirit and the flesh, is suddenly, by a cut, made to appear as if she is the image on a screen projected by Joseph and his luminous machine, the taxi and its lighted sign, now in the foreground with Mary at a distance. Whether Joseph is the projector, or whether Mary projects Joseph projecting her, this projection carries forward in time, if we like, to the subsequent scene in a clothes shop, with the angels' crucial instruction of Joseph, and on to the scene a few moments later with Mary in Joseph's room, much of it played on or about Joseph's bed, a sort of parody of the bedroom scene in *Breathless*. (*Breathless* has given rise to this. Or perhaps the essence of this is the essence of what gave rise to *Breathless*.) Joseph concludes in this scene, "I'll only be your shadow [as it were, cinema image]." Cut to a close-up of Mary, possibly in a new space—divine space?—as her voiceover begins, "God's shadow . . . Isn't that what all men are . . . for a woman who loves her man?" "Your [Mary's] shadow"/"God's shadow." Is Mary God? Is she so by virtue of loving a man?

My point about all this is that in the interview with the gynecologist and the events this seems to generate, there is an openness of terms—pregnancy, virginity, telling, and knowing—that eludes what we might expect a modern, recognizable sort of story to be. These people's story has its impossibles-to-know, its confusions. Godard makes us wonder whether any story, any film, hasn't its impossibles-to-know, its confusions, if we do not close them out.[6] This story's gestures toward God's story do not so much explain, or alternatively confound, this modern story as develop it, allow it to flourish. The film, in Eliot's phrase, "tends toward" being a recognizable modern story and also toward being the divine story, without allowing us to have it either way definitely.

Mary proclaims her virginity first to last. It is the great issue between her and Joseph, creating much tension, and at the end of their long reconciliation scene on this issue in Mary's room, Joseph says, "I'll never touch you . . . I will stay." The Roman Catholic Bible tells us in the footnotes that Mary and Joseph never had carnal relations, even after the birth of Christ. Surely we cannot deny that Mary is a virgin *in some sense*—if she and the film tell us anything, it is that. But *in some sense* is just the point. Mary is not visibly pregnant until late in the film, and Joseph has said, in his taxi just after the doctor's office scene, "It must be mine!" Perhaps he proceeds, induced by Mary, to make it his. Perhaps he in fact fathers the child, though neither physically nor by formal adoption, so far as we see. In the bedroom scene, Mary says "No!" repeatedly as Joseph offers to touch her, but later "Yes" as he places his hand merely *close* to her belly. Or perhaps he in fact touches her. One cannot tell for sure. Then he draws his hand out, as if swelling out the belly. This is a strange interchange for sure between the two of them. Does it represent the engendering of the child, in whatever way, which we do not see? Does it stand for a carnal relationship in the future for these two, living together, where this relationship is to have a different tone or nature from what we are used to thinking of as a carnal relationship? When Joseph says, "I'll never touch you," he is actually stroking Mary's hair. I take it that Mary's "virginity" obtains between them. Perhaps virginity signifies integrity, psychological intactness, even power, as with Queen Elizabeth I or with the heroines of the epic poem she inspired, Spenser's *Faerie Queene*. In any case, we cannot simply deny that Godard's Mary and Joseph have carnal relations.

The Bible's Mary and Joseph minister to the spirit's becoming flesh. More and more in the film Mary ponders, in voiceover, the spirit and the flesh and their relation, and more and more Mary's nude body becomes the subject of the camera (as was Eva's at one point). Much of the film suggests the camera is Mary's. If so, these sequences might represent the effort of the spirit, figured by filming, and fashioning a film, to come into interaction with the body, figured in Mary's body specifically, as film's subject taken generally. Of course, film's subject, and notably in these sequences, is the body *and* the spirit, so that the spirit of film in a sense just repeats the spirit that is already there before it. If we all live by something like the act of film imagination, then we imitate Mary in bringing the spirit into a dance with spirit-and-body—a way of acting that is never of a settled sort and certainly never answers to a view of spirit and body as more than provisionally separate identities (while the body still lives).

Mary and Joseph are not fully conscious of who they are, though they do much thinking and talking and though their situation is so suggestive. Their significance is for *us* once we get involved in the work, as is the case with other figures in imitation-of-Christ stories and art—and indeed much other art. This film asks us to think of the screen as like a water surface, which might reflect us. But we may break the surface, scattering light—as it were, fashioning a film as we relish the film. We may be said even to swim in it, like Mary in her bath or the infant Christ put dangerously beneath a surface of water near the end of the film—baptized as it were by Mary, his mother acting as John the Baptist.[7] The first appeal of the screen is that it reflects life, or something lifelike. But as with other poetic media, what we become involved with on the screen may mean a shocking reforming and redirecting of ourselves. We may touch divinity. The possibility is to live out in the work and to foster in ourselves, what we then to an extent *are*. The screen life may be not just our reflection, or just a beyond for us, but our life's blood, our child.

Hail Mary brings about a confrontation with a woman who seems the source of her world and life. And this originality and creativity that are met and are comprehended through film, and seem only comprehensible through film, through its specific way of being and of working. Indeed, the woman, her originality, and her creativity seem simply to *be* film, and to show us what film is. For us to yield to the intensity of this film, to the specifics of its intensities, is in a sense to be this woman and to live her originality and creativity. I say "in a sense" because what is at issue is not delusion or simple emotional identification, but a deepening of consciousness. I am film. This woman, her originality and creativity, are, I see, my own. To summarize it thus is to make a huge abstraction. What is to be known here is in the particulars, the film work and the work of our engagement.

Nashville suggests the transformative power of film, identifying itself with the eloquent, mad woman artist who bleeds to nourish us into new life. And I have suggested that in *Nashville* we meet a mind something like what we encounter in the writing of Swift (beyond Swift the man), unnerving us at every point, setting loose an energy that will go in unpredictable directions. What the strange mind of the film has to do with Robert Altman remains unclear. Godard, of all figures in film, impresses one as being a mind, comprehensive, informed, reflective on all it takes in, conscious of what it does at every turn. And yet Godard can seem lost in his films, overcome by what is going on in them—he seems to make a point of this in the ones where he casts himself, such as *Prénom Carmen* (*First Name: Carmen*; 1998), *Hail Mary*'s immediate predecessor, or, much later, *Notre Musique* (*Our Music*; 2004), even in *Histoire(s) du cinéma* (1989) with all the film images flying by, each with its own emotional weight. What *Hail Mary* involves us in is mind of an unprecedented sort, opening Godard out as much as it does us. (And *WR: Mysteries of the Organism* [1971] will provide as strong a case as may be of the film taking the bit between its teeth—a good thing, with a magic horse.)

The procedure of *Hail Mary* takes us to a remarkable realization of human female creativity in relation to divinity in some new, hard-to-box-in understanding of divinity. The effect on me of *Hail Mary* is like that of striking, involving religious art of any kind, Christian or other. I feel called on to believe it, as it is saying or showing what I have not heard or known before. I believe it all.

3

Earth and Beyond

On WR: Mysteries of the Organism

I FIRST SAW *WR: Mysteries of the Organism* (1971) when I was doing graduate study at Princeton, when the film was new and being widely screened and much talked about (organism equals orgasm, etc.). A screen was set up on the stage of Princeton's prestigious McCarter Theater, where the resident company presented Shakespeare and Ibsen, and, indeed, Sam Shepard, and where the visiting Cleveland Orchestra with Lorin Maazel performed Mozart and Mahler. One film series at that time included, besides *WR*, Pasolini's *Accatone* (1961) and Ozu's *Tokyo monogatari* (*Tokyo Story*; 1953). The mix of offerings seemed to dignify everything. Here was work that had deeply impressed people. Here was work to take in and think about.

WR, moving about unpredictably among diverse material, stirred and confused me, but stayed with me, haunting me until I could face it and think about it and write about it. The film offered, among other things, documentary material on Wilhelm Reich, a figure then unknown to me. The film provides all one needs to know, but it comes very fast and with much visual distraction.

WR also offers documentary material on aspects of the 1960s American counterculture, which might be seen as related to Reich's ideals, and material on the Stalin and Hitler cults, forces of repression. And there is a fictional story set in what was still Yugoslavia, centered on a young woman who admires Reich and advocates his teachings, but is killed by a sexually repressed lover at whom she has thrown herself. The film switches about frequently and abruptly among all its material, leaving a viewer not with a sense of structure or coherent understanding, but, at least at first—at least for me—with the sheer impression of strong images of sex and violence, flowing and blended without rationale—nudity, people actually making love, people exposing themselves emotionally in scream therapy, a man's erection induced and a plaster cast made of it, forced nasal feeding, electroshock therapy, a cut-off head coming to life and talking. The sense is of a wild mix, often worked up to a frenzy. And there is a strange high-handed good humor about it all, with cheerful music playing much of the time.

WR is visceral and at first impression chaotic—and a certain healthy sense of chaos about it never goes away, and is indeed the point: chaos is creative. There is not so much a sense of someone making points with this film, as of the material simply showing itself, exposing itself. This could be philosophy, provocative in some productive way.

Reich studied and worked with Freud, but broke with him over Reich's emphasis on the body and sexual satisfaction, tied to a utopian politics, calling for revolution. He settled in the United States at the beginning of World War II, eventually in Maine, where he operated a research and therapy institute, always writing and publishing books, sometimes venturing into strange areas such as the use of "orgone energy"—generated by copulating lovers—to shoot up into the clouds and affect the weather. Reich sold "orgone boxes," little closets where one could sit and accumulate orgone energy from the cosmos. He was prosecuted for advertising and selling improperly tested therapies and devices, and died in federal prison in Pennsylvania in 1957. Reich was very serious about his work, and had disciples who carried on and developed his therapy techniques in the 1960s and 1970s—we see a fair amount of this activity in the film.

By the time I came to contemplate writing about *WR*, I had some context. I knew Makavejev's films from Yugoslavia in the 1960s. *Love Affair, or the Case of the Missing Switchboard Operator* (1967) dealt with sexual repression and its relation to violence, and the film's free-spirited style appealed to *Cahiers du Cinéma* of the time. *Innocence Unprotected* (1968) mixed fiction with nonfiction and thereby explored human imagination: where it comes from, whether it draws from reality or contrasts with reality. Then there was *WR*. Later, working outside Yugoslavia, Makavejev made *Sweet Movie* (1974), also mixing fiction and nonfiction, and pushing further into the realm of the shock of liberation of the repressed—the regurgitative and excremental rituals of a Vienna commune, a woman's seduction of twelve-year-old boys—and further into the realm of the uncovering of the violence of history, digging up bodies from the Katyn Forest massacre that took place during World War II. *Montenegro* (1981) is a smart, stimulating fiction film, pitting a liberated southern European immigrant-worker culture against a Scandinavian bourgeois suburban world where there is a rebellious housewife.

Also, I had come to know Dušan Makavejev personally. When I was teaching for a time as a visitor in Harvard's film program, I came to know Makavejev, whose years as a visiting artist there overlapped with mine. Makavejev taught the advanced filmmaking students, whom he inspired with his great energy, open-mindedness, and love of experiment. He was argumentative, but in a thoroughly good-humored way—it was always aimed at getting somebody to think. He liked to teach film history and analysis as well as filmmaking. He gave a course on films whose titles had the word "angel" in them—*The Blue Angel* (1930), *The Exterminating Angel* (1962), *Only Angels Have Wings* (1939), and so on. He had a taste for surrealist juxtaposition, believing that it liberated suppressed truths. And in this instance he took an interest, as did Rilke in the *Duino Elegies*, in a superhuman order in a post-God age. Perhaps this is the very interest of film—those beings we contemplate up on the screen are angels . . .

Makavejev had the nature of a teacher, and was an artist with a widely inquiring, philosophical mind.[1] Having known him, I am the readier to take *WR* as an instructive work—instructive about what film is and what film can mean to, or do to, an audience—instructive about the human mind and the human condition. The film itself thinks, and offers in its unconventional way to teach—not by lecturing us or giving us anything intact, but by soliciting us to read it, to expatiate upon it, as it moves moment by moment.

I was not really involved in the counterculture, though I sympathized with its opposition to the Vietnam War and to moral hypocrisy in American high politics and big business. I was put off by a certain self-righteousness in the counterculture. Perhaps I was too timid. Perhaps being drawn back to this film is in part being drawn back to come to terms with a world I shied away from, a world all around me in my college and graduate school years. Like most any twenty-year-old, I was interested in guidance in the erotic life. But I did not want—and perhaps this is not unusual, either—to be overborne with images, either from the world around me or from a film. I got more from reading—D. H.

Lawrence, Norman O. Brown—where I could take my time and reflect. I had plenty of respect for film and its philosophical power, but *this* film was different—too much, too fast. Perhaps my being drawn back to it is being drawn to face the full philosophical force of film, film at an extreme.

For a time, history seemed to move beyond *WR*. With the end of the Vietnam War, sex, drugs, and rock music seemed to lose their political charge and become just consumer pleasures—we were in the world of *Nashville*. And just what had been *WR*'s attitude, anyhow? The film sympathizes with Reich, believes in Reich. But whether the film is celebrating the counterculture or making fun of it, whether it wishes to explode something and move on, is not easy to say.

I was able to begin writing on *WR*, fulfilling this something long brewing, after writing on *Hail Mary*, an equally dense film. Makavejev has said that he thought of himself early on as having much in common with Godard—the subversiveness, the making of odd juxtapositions, the development of an unconventional way of film editing—but that he sought to put more *body* into what was a relatively intellectual procedure in Godard's hands. Makavejev wants the images and junctures, Godardian in a way, to be more *felt* than in Godard. Thus Makavejev is addressing the power of film, drawing out a power of film's rhetoric, or of its nature, that Godard had opened the door to. Makavejev thus enjoins *us* to further address this power of film.

WR: Mysteries of the Organism brings to the fore a commitment to the body, a quality of earth, I would like to call it. The film insists on the body and the physical reality of what is before the camera, and it studies the relation of this reality to film imagination and to the imagination in general—the life we come into, out of the body, as it were; ideas and fantasies; the movements of history apprehensible to the intellect; thought and art.

The movement from body to more than body is epitomized in the film's treatment of the issue of male or female—which are we to be identified as? Ordinarily we think of male or female as the most body-determined of issues, but it is not so in this film. Makavejev identifies himself, as director/presenter, with a woman, the voice that narrates the early documentary part of the film, and it is at least suggested that this woman speaker becomes the lead character, a woman, in the fictional part of the film, who is in turn identified in many ways with Wilhelm Reich, the film's inspiration and first subject. Also, a human being of indeterminate sex, the New York transvestite or transsexual Jackie Curtis, takes over the film at crucial points.

The facing of the body with what is more than the body, yet not apart from it, is also figured in the strange facing of Earth with outer space and what may be out there and yet akin to us, maybe a source from which we are drawn. Early in the film Reich's speculation on his possible kinship with extraterrestrials is spoken by the woman narrator (it is *apparently* a woman's voice) as we move down a road through a Maine forest—Earth, home, to Reich—and eventually look at Reich's observatory and telescope.

There are three immediately notable aspects to the earthiness of *WR*: humor; people as real, unidealized people; and sex. These factors all work to ground things in the film, and in a way to comfort us. But they also work to unsettle things, to ready us for transformation.

Wilhelm Reich, the film's germ that gives it life, is not notable for humor or for his sense of people as people, despite his abundant presentation of case studies, as in *Character Analysis*. The case studies are very much case studies, conceived in the terms of Reich's theories. He does not have Freud's novelistic quality, sensitive to the unaccountable in people, the narrative of a (Freud) case always taking small unpredictable turns. Reich's other writings are general, theoretical, hectoring. And the impression one has of Reich in life, as from the very sympathetic biography by Myron Sharaf, who knew Reich, is of a certain crudeness, a regard for people only in relation to Reich himself and his theories. People who loved Reich and are grateful to him for liberating their lives, seem to feel the good done was by virtue of Reich's theoretical passion, something beyond personal consideration.

Reich *is* notable for his preoccupation, like that of the film *WR*, with sex. And here Reich works as an emblem for the body as this film conceives of it. Reich, by virtue of his preoccupation with sex, serves as the subject-germ for a film that in significant ways is not Reichian, or is more than Reichian—just as the body in this film's conception allows for, calls for, a going beyond the body. The funny thing is that what in the film is beyond the body takes us right back into the realm of earth and the body. The way up and the way down . . .

Humor begins at the start of the film. White letters—REICH, JOY OF LIFE—on a cheerful blue background ("the color of Orgone energy," the published film script informs us [Makavejev 23][2]) initiate a series of dissolves: REICH, JOY OF LIFE . . . ENJOY . . . FEEL . . . LAUGH. And a bit later: LUIS BUÑUEL AWARD/CANNES FILM FESTIVAL, 1971. The series of dissolves provokes chuckles in an audience, the quality of the chuckles changing subtly with each of those three words as the series goes on—as one may imagine: reread the words slowly, . . . EN JOY . . . FEEL . . . LAUGH. Just before this series the film has given us a paragraph identifying Reich as having discovered "life energy" and having revealed the "deep roots" of various fears, and as believing in a "work-democracy," "an organic society based on liberated work and love." The droll series of dissolves on words and the mention of Buñuel tells us that there will be nothing overbearing about the psychoanalysis and the projection of an ideal society in this film. We will not be overwhelmed by any fearful new future. That first paragraph of prose begins, "This film is in part a personal response . . ." The *person* behind this film—and one need not say it is Makavejev exactly—will allow for our common humanity. We will be left as we are, to the extent that we must be. We will be all right in the hands of this film. (Of course it is possible we are being seduced.)

In the ensuing sequence we contemplate a couple of dogs—life that is not human, always potentially humorous—and then the film begins to observe, or to collaborate with, a man who comes onto a slum street, puts on a mock-military costume, and begins parading around. (Some will recognize him as Tuli Kupferberg, "poet of the Lower East Side" according to the published script.) This man now provides the humor, as a street-theater satirist of regimes where war is endemic to the state institution. A voiceover (Kupferberg in fact) recites and then sings, roughly from Juvenal, "Who will protect us from our protectors? Who shall judge our police?" and eventually, "Very few poems get written. Fewer still get read." There are the controllers of society, "our protectors," then the liberator who is a further controller in a sense—a judge of things (such as Reich)—then the artist, a poet, conceivably a filmmaker, who is also a judge, and then ourselves, who become judges if we read (poems, films). All are conflated here, strangely, even as they are named and distinguished. In the written verse and the song the same energy seems to run through everything. Kupferberg's humor is Swiftian—desperate posturing to release energy in the hope of getting a general transformation of things. But the style of the film at this point is contrastingly calm and observing. The humor comes *into* the film, from Kupferberg. We are not sure how it will sit with the film itself.

We are not sure, in part because the film's second great quality has come into play, the presentation of people as people. Kupferberg is not a creation of the film just to serve its purposes, but a real man (like those real dogs), gawky, not conventionally attractive.

The voice recites, "He cannot clean his 'sockses' and says, 'The world is soiled.'" This man we see is, so to speak, soiled like anyone—not a movie-person, not a creature of imagination. But then with his mock rifle, tall, lean physique, and upright bearing, he is phallic. This and a certain dirtiness having to do with the black beard and long hair, as well as his humor, make him the perfect embodiment of the imperfect, healthful libido this film wishes to promote. He suits the imagination of the film. And of course he is an imaginative figure in the sense of being theatrical, always in performance—we never see a "real," nonperforming Tuli Kupferberg. Play between the real and the imaginatively suitable—even perfect—will become a major preoccupation of the film. The humor at this point, not being precisely the film's own, and the real-man/art-man question keep us in suspense as to where we are.

The credits sequence comes next, with written words over a close shot of an egg yolk being passed from hand to hand, and eventually a fuller view of the people doing this. The scene usually elicits chuckles, just as the ENJOY . . . FEEL . . . LAUGH dissolves do. Perhaps the humorous idea is "yes, this was really the sixties," or "yes, this is what all the progressive therapy or ideas about communal living boils down to"—we laugh with the film at its imaging of the silly essence of something. Perhaps we laugh at ourselves, or former selves. Of course we do just "enjoy" and "feel"—the yolk slipping around and eventually breaking and smearing engages us without thoughts needing to arise. We laugh as if physically tickled.

There is a disjunction here—perhaps it contributes to the humor, humor always depending on disjunction. It is that we recognize this sequence, interesting for what is "really" going on in it: play with an egg yolk, as fiction. Jaunty and loud, vaguely Oriental piping music, enough in itself to make us smile, seems to belong with a director's created scene. The lighting has the feel of a studio. The intimacy of the moving camera with the subjects looks choreographed. The people, when we see them fully, behave with a studied air that resembles acting. (How could we say for sure?) And they are young and beautiful, looking like movie stars, at least little ones, as compared with Tuli Kupferberg. These people are in fact the cast of the Yugoslav fictional part of the film, which begins much later on.

Is the yolk handling fiction itself, the very yolk and the sheer act of handling it? One cannot say absolutely what fiction is. The film will press this question again and again. If there is a real distinction between fiction and nonfiction in film, is it something inherent in the material, or a matter of how we see, or use, material? *WR*, with all its mixing, makes a great issue of how film is used. In the end, it is hard to say whether everything combined in this film makes a great fiction, a feat of imagination, or an essay on certain ideas, or a record of the film's times.

A final note of disorientation in this sequence is that with the appearance of the credit "Conceived and Created by Dušan Makavejev," the darker-haired woman in the group looks right into the camera, and then the others look vaguely toward it, following her lead, then look away before she does.

Perhaps this is the cast acknowledging the director. Or perhaps it is the director declaring himself, with the words of the credit, to "be" this woman whose eyes meet ours. The confusion continues in the next sequence, when the (seeming) woman narrator's voiceover begins. Is this the voice of the film? Of the director? Perhaps the credits sequence as a whole ought to tell us that the voice to come will be one of the group we see, if not the darker-haired woman. The voice we soon hear sounds entirely American, but the published script says it is Milena, who is the blonde woman in the group at the start, and who will be the lead character

in the Yugoslavian part of the film.³ Milena is identified continually with Reich by her speeches and actions; at the end, decapitated—"un-earthed"—but still alive and talking, her image is merged with Reich's photograph by a dissolve. She is identified with the germ—or egg—of the film, Reich, its director in a sense. Milena, the director Makavejev, the voice or intelligence behind the film, Reich—there is imaginative identification. Does this somehow amount to being real identification? Is there reality without a measure of imagination? I am using the interrogative a good deal because, in my view, the *film* uses it.

After what we have seen so far—an introduction calculated, good humoredly, to throw us off our bearing—the following part of the film (its beginning really) seeks to set out certain facts about Reich—but it does so by indirect, strange, and hurried means. We see the title "*Filme der Sexpol.*" Does this apply to all the rest of *WR* or just to what immediately follows? We see footage of a couple in a meadow, who are physically well formed, beautiful, and who eventually undress and make love. One cannot say absolutely whether they are doing it, as one can say with hardcore fictional (?) sex films and some documentaries, though we do see the man's erect penis at one point in the scene. All of this is multiplied into several images by a sort of kaleidoscope—perhaps a declaration of the camera, an extension of the camera's inevitable fantasy. Is this material with the lovers Makavejev's own footage? Is at least the kaleidoscope effect his? Are we conceivably seeing part of an old film of Reich's sex analysis and education group, Sexpol? The film soon intercuts another title, "*Internationalen Institut für Sexualökonomische Forschung (kopieren verboten)*," which looks archival. *WR* seems to want to identify itself with a production of Reich's—saying that *WR* is in a sense Reich's film.[4]

There is footage of Reich as a young man in a meadow with a young woman, and footage of the young Reich in a laboratory. A choir is heard singing the hymn-like "Communist Party my fragrant flower . . ." And through all this the woman narrator gives a fast commentary on Reich's ideas and his career in Europe and America, concluding with his prosecution and death in prison in Pennsylvania. The narration elicits laughs at a few lines: "fuck freely" (audiences must now think of STDs—of course "freely" does not necessarily mean "promiscuously"); "saliva is good"; Reich in the United States "eventually voted for Eisenhower." "Fuck freely" and "saliva is good" sound incongruous in the sober voice of the narrator. And with Eisenhower, the narrator seems not fully to relish who he is, merely offering his name as straightforward support for the idea of Reich's good citizenship. It seems that the speed and strangeness of what we have seen so far are meant just to give us a subject for the film, almost as a foregone conclusion. The film stirs things up as if they already mattered, without yet coming to what might seem its proper business of showing or telling us something directly. Probably by now we have got the couple making love, whom we could not see well enough, irrevocably into our heads. They stick. Sex—the earth—is compelling, despite the tricks of art and mind. But can sex and the earth exist without the tricks of art and the mind?

With the next material the film does seem to come to its proper business. There is a cut from the footage of Reich in his laboratory, with narration about his Orgonon Institute in Maine, to a moving-camera shot, approaching a shed or outbuilding, then moving through a room of junk to rest on one of Reich's Orgone boxes in the corner. Perhaps this is Maine (later information suggests it is not). Makavejev and his film crew are moving into the orbit of those who knew Reich, to get what information they can. The film now becomes pure documentary, if one likes, touching earth as nearly as it can. Dr. Myron Sharaf, alerted by Makavejev's voice, emerges from the accumulator, as he calls it, with a little boy in a cat mask. Has this image of birth been staged for the film? Just prior to the emergence we have heard Sharaf reading about Pinocchio—"'Hooray!' he cried, 'I am a real boy.' . . . Old Geppetto smiled . . . Pinocchio had much to learn before he could be a real boy." The reading from *Pinocchio* and the little boy we see in the mask stress the idea of metamorphosis and imagination and the hope for development upward, at the heart of all Reich's and Sharaf's realism about the body.

Sharaf talks with the film crew, casually and good humoredly explaining the accumulator. He is a stocky, swarthy man, who speaks with something of a city, working-person's accent. He is not an idealized figure. We are speaking with a real man about things that have to do with his life. With his vividly patterned cardigan—a link to the child's mask—and his city manner, he seems out of place in this country storeroom, if that is what it is. But he wants to be helpful and to be positive about Reich. He is less than fervid about the accumulator, and intercuts of photos of other accumulators and Orgone devices, with some solemn narration from the woman narrator, make all this seem a quaint historical phenomenon, at least a mystery—perhaps it is too fanciful. We have the feeling that for Sharaf, and for the film, the real story is yet to come.

But the interview we now go to with a former woman employee of Reich's underscores, on the face of it, the seriousness of Reich's work with Orgone energy accumulation. This plump country woman with large bare arms—perhaps a kitchen worker or cleaning woman—tells of once having had the bad bleeding of a cut finger suddenly stopped by Reich's applying a small machine to it. Here an almost disturbingly rough-hewn person attests that Reich's folly really worked. Perhaps she was fooled. Perhaps Reich was fooled. Are we seeing a bit of the fanaticism of the devoted? Who is this woman really?

We see the woman in profile from the waist up, tightly framed in the left and center of the shot, with another woman—her colleague, or alter ego—wiping down a car on the right in the background. The camera is fixed and a little above the woman as well as to her side, so that she acknowledges it awkwardly. She seems caught for a moment, and compromised—she is not the subject of the camera's flexible play, like Dr. Sharaf and many others in the film. I think most viewers, because of the context, will wonder about her sexual existence. Could she be reached by Reich's orgasm theory—that orgasms are the staff of life? Does she need to be reached by it? Perhaps she is a being of another kind than those whom Reich's theory concerns. The film is generally about the bridging or mixing of different areas, separate realms. The same currents seem to run everywhere—sex, politics, eastern Europe, and the United States . . .

The encounter with this woman makes a puzzle of whether people are really alike in some way. Who is reachable by whom or what? In this scene the issue of Reich's fancy about Orgone devices, with a real person testifying to its seriousness, turns into the issue of who, or what, a person is—especially in light of the next scene.

A meeting with Eva Reich Moise, Reich's daughter, is used with other material to tell us of Reich's trial and death. Eva is in Maine, outdoors, a middle-aged woman who is casual about her hair, clothes, figure. She looks as if she may have been working in the garden she shows us. She is fervid about Reich's work and bitter about his end, and the state of the world, her thoughts seeming to jar with her setting. She too raises the question of disparate sorts of people, or aliens. One cut to her begins with part of a sentence of hers that is never fully explained: she is addressing the crew, ". . . because you came from behind the Iron Curtain . . ." Does she mean that they cannot understand her, that they are too unlike her? She speaks very much like an American, but at moments shows traces of a foreign upbringing and education (which she in fact had), as when she pronounces "good state beings" (what children behind the Iron Curtain, she says—does she know?—are "manufactured into"), "good" rhyming with "mood," the consonants all forceful and distinct, spaces made between the words—"good. state. beings." This woman does not just serve to provide information about Reich. We are made to ask, Is she an alien? Alien to what? Who or what is she?

Between two sequences with Eva, the second seeming to continue the first, there is material with the Pennsylvania prison where Reich died and with the garbage incinerator in New York City where his books were burned by court order. Outside the prison the camera moves quickly, presumably in a car, down the long wall of the place, then zooms in quickly on the guard towers and on the entrance area, where some men are passing through the gates. All this is accompanied by a waltz for zither and accordion, reminiscent of the playful music for the egg-yolk sequence. One thing we feel immediately is that Makavejev and his crew are world travelers and artists. They can get away from Maine—shoot what they like, go where they like. The way the prison is shot has an antic quality. This seems to be filmmaking asserting itself—filmmaker's fancy. But of course this may be the only way the prison can be filmed: if Makavejev and his crew had not moved fast, they might have been accosted or arrested. The film may be as direct here with its real subject as it can be. The music may seem fanciful, but it is, like the music for the egg-yolk scene, down to earth too—popular music, folk music, one way people react to and cope with the realities of life. Maybe the humor of the music and camera antics dissolves for a moment any worry over the distinction between what is artificial and what is down to earth.

The music stops just before the end of the sequence, giving way to what is apparently the grinding sound of the prison gates we see. This sound blends with that of the garbage-moving machine at the New York incinerator, what we see next. The giant claws moving garbage about quickly over a long distance are fascinating to watch, seen at a distance from below and then above, and seen close up, the camera moving freely about this dangerous-seeming space, like the garbage machine itself. The woman narrator reads off the titles of Reich's books—*The Function of the Orgasm*; *Ether, God, and Devil*; *The Murder of Christ*, and so on—and there is a sense of outrage at these books being destroyed. Still, hearing the names as we see the garbage does make the books seem garbage in a way. And the fate of garbage does not look so awful, but intriguing and comic—to be the concern of this busy, hurrying machine, with no human operator visible. At any rate, the titles of the books, and presumably their essences, survive the destruction of all these copies. What is more than body comes through, while the body goes its natural, or fated, or arbitrarily unjust way.

For some time it has been common to speak of filming in terms of machinery—as automatic, possibly out of human hands, inexorable, artificial—and to note that film often makes metaphors of itself with trains and other machines, from the early silent period on (see De Lauretis and Heath; Rothman, *Hitchcock* on *Psycho*; and Cantor on *Shoah*). *WR* first identifies the prison gates with the garbage machine, by juxtaposition and an overlap of sound, and then identifies both with *WR*'s own filmmaking, as the camera moves about like the garbage machine. *WR* does something with—makes film of—Reich and his work, just as the state, the courts, the prison, and the incinerator did something with Reich. *WR* is hardly at one with the state and the justice system, but the film does show suspicions of its own apparatus and storytelling ability as distorting, even death dealing. We need more time to tell whether *WR* saves itself by holding its own fancy against a standard of being down to earth, true to a subject.

At the start of the prison material the film has given us a black-and-white still photograph of Reich, stout, well dressed, overcoated, handcuffed, being escorted to trial or to prison, an expression both sorrowful and a bit alarmed on his face. The alarm may be due to the presence of photographers, as well as to the judicial fate that lies ahead of him—the two are linked in our minds in a worrisome way. The film zooms in—not too fast—on the handcuffs. This moment is very affecting, which has to do both with the sorrowful state of Reich and with the zoom gesture itself. It seems that the subject matter of the film becomes fully gripping only when we reach the point of persecution and death, the passion. We feel for Reich, whatever we may think of him, and maybe full meaning is given to his work only in martyrdom. Eva Reich has brought up the murder of Christ and Reich's book of that name, saying Reich suffered "judicial murder" like Christ, and the garbage sequence has named the book again. The zoom gesture to the detail in the photograph is eerie, because a photograph is being operated upon by another photographic technique. We are far into the realm of the mechanical, the automatic. This particular gesture represents, with emphasis, what the film is doing constantly with its filming techniques and its use of old film. Reich in his passion is subjected to the state, and to film as well, also a great power.

Where will it lead? Perhaps the power of film is in fact the means for Reich to live, as the real man in a sense, and of course as transcendent of the fate of the real man in his body, in his life on earth. And if Reich lives in this transcendent way, it is so that he can reenter our lives as we live in our bodies, here on earth. This film helps bring the transcendent back into the body.

Part of the chill of the moment with the photograph is that it is suddenly black and white after (and before, we soon see) color segments. The film is constantly using this contrast—it is in color except for old material, but there is a good deal of this. With the handcuffs photograph black and white suggests death, making a *photograph*—a ghostly fancy—of what was alive and really there. But the black and white also suggests reality, truth, if we take color film as always a bit fantastic or unreal.[5] Film started in black and white, and its deep origin is felt to be the older still photograph, or the drawing (paint is too rich, *too* still). The photograph is the root, close to truth. Motion and color come later. The world's oldest art is objects, still images on walls, chants, prayers; later come elaborate narration and drama, complications of fancy. Do these take us *back* in their way?

When Eva Reich, in the second sequence with her, the return to her, criticizes the life in Communist countries, Makavejev asks her about the American dream, and she says immediately, "the American dream is dead." Whereupon the film cuts to what is seen by a camera moving in a car from the country into town and down the main street of Rangeley, Maine, the soundtrack giving us a well-known New York City radio station,

"It's a sunny morning, 79 WABC degrees" ("dee-grees"), then a chorus singing an advertisement, "Coca Cola—it's the real thing." This part of the film, which will include interviews with Rangeley citizens, might be taken as showing the hollowness and absurdity and backwardness of America, following on Eva Reich's suggestion—but only a cynic would so take it, one whose mind is fixed on certain ideas, not attending to the vitality of what is before us.

The film now becomes like a dream, to pick up Makavejev's and Eva's word. *Some* dream is here and alive. Or perhaps the film now becomes more of a film. It loses a certain quality of fooling around or just-before-getting-to-the-subject, and takes hold. The affectingness of the brief zoom-in with the still photograph is borne out—film really doing something. This really doing something is what will bring the film to blossom, or change, into fiction at a point not far down the road. The new dreaminess now in the film has to do with imagination—specifically film imagination—that is beyond the body, the earth, the real. And yet *WR* more and more will press the issue of whether the imagination is not the way to, indeed the very place of, the body, the earth, and the real.

I call the film dream-like now to suggest the absorption we feel: the feeling of things being weighted with interest beyond what we could ever explain; the feeling of curiosity as we move forward. All of which does not preclude a certain distance and holding back from what we see. I am not saying that we *identify* with the film—and one thing this film has to teach is that film is not there entirely to be identified with.[6] We often feel less than fully identified with a dream. The holding back or reflectiveness may come and go, in moments, in spaces, or may hover there constantly even as we are engaged—this is the transitional moment or field where, the Upanishads teach, all important knowledge comes in. Perhaps *WR* up to the point we have reached, being interesting but up in the air about its subject, has provided the moment or field of transition, the opening for understanding, that will now stay with us at some level as we more let go and live out the film.

We begin now with a camera in motion, taking in an Esso gas station, a purveyor of fuel for motion, a corporate presence in the wooded outskirts of this town. The camera takes in a view of a little bridge down a side road, then moves across a long bridge over a river. A good deal of time is spent here, looking out the side of the car, the bridge railing going by fast in a blur, while a railroad bridge is seen clearly and seemingly more "slowly" at a little distance up or down the river (one cannot tell which direction). This stress on images of bridges goes to the heart of the film's concern with juxtapositions, transitions, getting from here to there—with different kinds of film, different kinds of people, different places, the body as opposed to the mind or imagination, the self unhealed and the self healed or freed, "our sick society" (the narrator's words when she first begins to speak) and the world of revolution—WR: World Revolution. The blurry near railing might represent our sense deep down, anywhere in the film, or in life, that we are already on a bridge; while the more distant railroad bridge gives us a clear image representing something to aspire to, or representing clear and conscious recognition of where we already are or what we already are doing. The uncertainty of the direction of the flow of the stream might tell us that in bridging, not every consideration of measurement or having our bearings matters.

The poetic condensation of this moment of direct documentary filmmaking (is it that?) is compounded by the soundtrack from WABC, a New York station oddly heard way up here in Rangeley—considerable bridging there. Is this really what is picked up riding in a car here, or is it imported by the film? Is Coca-Cola (and Esso) harmless or dangerous? Can we feel free and all right, just a little dizzy, listening to the silly, sensuous commercial song? Or is it maddening, even if we do not recognize that it is? Is WABC itself dangerous? This station plays rock and roll (we hear some of it later in the film on this station), at least some of which in 1971 might be taken as crucial popular art, revolutionary, or healing. WABC dee-grees—*gradus ad parnassum*, maybe even the commercials.

We move down the main street of Rangeley and begin to hear in (apparently) a man's voiceover an account of a local mass uprising against Reich. People shouted, "Down with the Or-gies!" (hard "g," from "Orgonon"), "Down with the commies!" The narrator is identified by a title as Reich's son Peter, and he soon appears, dark, gentle, friendly, though nervously twisting a strand of his hair—a contrast to his somewhat self-righteous sister Eva, leading us to think about the different ways the germ of Reich, or any germ, could go. Is the film, moving down the road, an assault on Reich like that of the group Peter speaks of? An assault on the town like, in the town's own conception at one time, the assault on Reich and his foreign ideas? Perhaps the film is a therapeutic assault, on the subject matter before us, and on us ourselves? Peter is unsure about what actually happened in the uprising, as opposed to what he may have seen "out of fear." A little later the account we hear in Reich's own voice (the only time we hear his voice in the film) is painfully excited, as he speaks of stopping people with his gun and denying he is a communist.

We wonder if his view of these people is distorted, as Peter admits his own may have been.

Immediately now we meet, in interviews, two storekeepers and the deputy sheriff/barber, a big and frightening-looking man who is in fact peaceable and unassuming, and whose barber's gestures about his own head—to show how Reich liked his hair—are almost effeminate, certainly belonging to the world of dressers and cosmeticians. These townspeople knew Reich and speak amicably of him, though they found him "unusual" and "not like ordinary people." These men, or people like them, could have been among Reich's attackers. Or these men could prove that Rangeley has more kinds of people than those who wanted to attack Reich. Finally, we wonder about these men, as about the woman employee earlier, whether they are suitable for Reich's mission for sexual and social liberation. What would it mean to change a town like this? Was it right for the town to resist Reich violently, if that is what it did?

Just upon meeting these townspeople, the film shifts to a drive down a forest road with the woman narrator speaking words of Reich about possibly being the offspring of an extraterrestrial, and thus belonging to "a new race of earthlings," "an interplanetary race." This sequence pushes further the question of what a human is, what he is kin to, what he is suited for. Reich's idea about extraterrestrial kinship seems a figure for being transformed into a new kind of being by the power of ideas. (Reich says, as if describing how a poetic figure works, that his speculation about extraterrestrials may seem to be "irrationality," but that any irrationality will contain "something of truth.") To be liberated by ideas is to become of a new race—angels, in a sense?—yet a new race of earthlings, still of the earth. Liberation comes by partaking of what is beyond the earth, yet a teaching about the earth, essentially of the earth.

This sequence has a ghostly quality. The camera moves down the road as the woman narrator's voice speaks quietly. Because there is no road noise and very little ambient sound from the woods, the camera seems to float—we do not compensate for the absent sounds as we might with silent film, because we do hear that voice and just a little sound from the woods. The moving camera could be like the approach of spacemen in their soundless ships (soundlessness representing a stage of technology that is beyond us). If the spacemen represent what is beyond earth, which is taken into and transforms the earth, so would filming be an act beyond earth that comes to interact with what is of the earth. Film transforms its subject—and may transform its audience—but film allows its subject (and audience), in transformation, to be what they are, still of a race of earthlings—though now such really, maybe, for the first time. The play of film art—"concealment," it may seem—is after all "unconcealment." The "untruth" of film after all brings us to truth, to pick up Heidegger's terms from "The Origin of the Work of Art."

The ghost in the present sequence is the spaceman, or Reich's ideas, or the filming. Reich's teacher Freud tells us that the uncanny is the representation, the return, of our primary body-mind reality, which we do not want to admit. That is, the uncanny is a way of admitting this reality. The ghost—Reich's ideas, filming—seems unearthly, but it is really of the body, or body-mind. We find what is real by means of film, as we do by means of Reich's wild ideas. This is *WR*'s perpetual lesson.

Of course there is a discrepancy between image and soundtrack everywhere in sound film, even where we believe we are hearing sound simultaneously recorded with the image. How can we know synchronicity is the case? And what has the recording left out that we would hear if we were "there"? In the sequence just previous to the forest scene, we might ask if the WABC material, perhaps brought in unrealistically, should make the camera seem to float there too? I do not suggest that we question every sequence of film—a natural-seeming relation between sound and image is a real thing. But the Maine-woods/spaceman sequence calls attention to film's contrivance and to its not having, ever, a sure copresence of image and sound. Where do we stand in life itself with regard to sights and sounds? How do we perceive? There is contrivance, and a lack of certainty, even where we rightly feel presence and connection.

The eeriness of this sequence is due in part to being in woods, which are proverbially spooky. A forest shuts out the world; we feel distant from the world. We are amidst beings—trees—that are alive, but of a different kind of life from our own—nymphs or warriors or something unimaginable may be imprisoned in them. Being amidst or confronted with a different kind of life makes us think of possibly being changed. We might become that other kind of being. We might be assaulted by the other and changed. It might be glorious.

Ghostliness is there in the ensuing material with Reich's Orgonon estate, set here in the woods. We see Reich's observatory and telescope, and eventually an unidentified telescope-like contraption (a "cloudbuster" in fact, for drawing or projecting Orgone energy between heaven and earth). We see old footage of Reich outdoors and people arriving to confer with him. We see, back in the present apparently, Reich's large stone bust outdoors, presumably erected after his death, and here is where we start to hear Reich's voice, speaking of the local uprising. We think about living presence and disappearance, and the after-effects of old film and voice recording.

The camera enters the Wilhelm Reich Museum and drifts past tables with microscopes and other equipment, all covered with semi-transparent plastic—like film, it both covers and reveals. This laboratory, this scene of activity—of creation, perhaps—is now emptied of its workers, but we are here, moving about with the camera. Where is Reich? Perhaps he is here in *WR*'s film activity and our attentiveness to that.

The film cuts from a mystical picture on the wall, of two hands with a field of force of some kind running between them, to a camera movement down a hall and into an empty therapy room with a couch—is this the same building, or even at Orgonon? We hear what we take to be a woman's sighs—is this the breath of life? Reich, or his ideas, coming to life? There is a cut to another therapy room—where is it?—and what follows is a session with a reclining woman in a blue leotard doing Reichian exercises, guided by Dr. Alexander Lowen, as a title tells us. Time and space are obliterated in getting from Reich's laboratory, via that picture of the two hands, with a hint of the supernatural, to the living activity of Reichian therapy. We are brought to earth, to the therapy, by fancy. Earth and the body coming to the fore is a matter of ideas coming to life. The fancy of the film works as does the fancy of Reich's ideas.

The woman in this scene does deep breathing, moving her pelvis up and down, all aimed at "letting go," Dr. Lowen tells us. Lowen moves about the woman, giving her instructions, touching her, and making explanations to the filmers. Lowen's name is printed over the image of the woman, confusing identity as earlier in the film; the idea man and his patient are one in a sense. The flexibly moving camera contemplates the woman's body and also follows Lowen closely, getting his face close up in profile at times, his fingers close up another time. The filming takes part in the activity, the transactions, of the scene. There is strong sunlight coming in a window at the back—the energy of ideas? of film?—so that Lowen, or parts of him, appear almost in silhouette. The session seems a sort of rite, the elegant and dynamic Dr. Lowen a priest or magician or unearthly being.

Reichian therapy comes into its own now as Myron Sharaf, imaged with a river and bridge in the background, explains the therapy and recounts his own experiences with Reich (the scene looks like Boston and the bank of the Charles, and Sharaf is dressed as in the earlier scene in the shed, suggesting that scene was not Maine but Boston). Sharaf is less strange, more down to earth and comforting, than Lowen, but he starts us on a far journey. There are more filmed therapy sessions. A woman on her back, in underpants and an almost transparent bra, is guided by a voice—we do not see the therapist. The camera—standing in for the therapist?—moves back and forth along the woman's body as the primal spasms of the desiderated Reichian S-shape take her over. She is reasonably fit and attractive, but she definitely has a middle and hips and thighs and flesh that quivers. This is an unidealized human body. And this is what we see with all the people in these sessions, most notably in the large group session later with people screaming and some walking on others' backs. There we see fat and human oddity in all their familiar appearance.

In the present sequence the woman's head and face make only a vague impression, and this is the case too with people in all the sessions, and even with the present woman in the brief post-session interview, where she is smiling and speaking of her satisfaction. The head, face, soul seem to blur, extensions of the body and its experience. All this bears out Dr. Sharaf's final words in his scene of explanation, about an achieved "feeling of fullness and pleasure, and not empty feeling that you're just living in your head." At the end of the film Milena's severed head comes to life, and it may seem delightful or wondrous, or to come as a blessed relief—so that Sharaf's ideal picture of life is challenged, or reinterpreted. If the body and bodily experience become central, it is still by virtue of the head.

The film now begins to move fast, traversing material of various kinds in the moments leading up to the change to fiction. The film seems to press its boundaries, feeling ready to burst (as Reich says the body will feel like doing), until relief can come in a transformation into fiction.

The interview with the satisfied, bland young woman after therapy gives way to a brief meeting with erotic artist Betty Dodson, perky and articulate, as if to show that living in the head and being an individual can go with being liberated in the body. (Or is Betty Dodson liberated? Who is she, really? Perhaps an artist or theorist who can promote for others what she may not have attained.) Dodson discusses drawing models who masturbate for her, models who at first feel reluctant, but then find the experience freeing and joyful. And the subject of masturbation seems to focus or make pure Reich's emphasis on the individual's integrity in his/her sexual experience. It is for *you*, he says.

Masturbation also questions Reich, whether he is a cut-off, lonely pleasure, however intense, missing the dimension of acquaintance with another person. D. H. Lawrence writes,

> Masturbation is the one thoroughly secret act of the human being, more secret even than excrementation . . . In sexual intercourse there is a give and take. A new stimulus enters as the native stimulus departs . . . But in masturbation there is nothing but loss. There is no reciprocity. (*Phoenix* 178–79)

Still, Lawrence, like Reich, is for a wide social and psychological liberation that comes back to Lawrence's "very urge of life" (*Phoenix* 185) that is within one, within the individual. Perhaps *WR* critiques or extends Reich with its story of a complicated relationship, that between Milena and her lover Vladimir.

The meeting with Betty Dodson points us toward art—and toward the phallus. She speaks to us sitting in front of a large painting or color drawing of a black man on his back masturbating, his hand around his large erect penis. The camera moves in on the penis until at the end of the interview there is little else in the frame. The painting seems to represent the film, as if the issues that gave rise to the film had cried out for iconic realization: a film, like a painting. Let there be something we can fix on, contemplate. But let it be like the penis, penetrating, inseminating. Is art like masturbation? Is it a purer form of the broad reality it is connected to, or is it self-absorbed and isolated? Then again, masturbation, not isolated but in front of another person (or art with a viewer, poems with a reader) may not really be masturbation.

Why is the man black? No reason. Color (of persons—it has already happened in a more general way with color film versus black-and-white) here enters the film as a zone of flux, like gender. Color or gender is defined, but not absolutely. In a later scene in the *Screw* magazine office, a beautiful, shocking, naked black man with copious pubic hair appears and moves about, causing no stir, part of the group, as others in the office, all white, discuss transformation.

Dodson appears later in the film, interrupting the Yugoslav fictional material. She and her picture, this time of a woman masturbating, seem notably real in contrast to the now surrounding fiction. And this picture is more muted than the first, seeming less an art object, as if a woman's genitals are more real, less an art object, than an erect penis. Dodson speaks against women's having to depend on a male partner for orgasm—but her remarks are intercut with the image of lovers in the fictional apartment (Milena's roommate and her friend), locked in embrace and in high pleasure if not orgasm, seeming very happy. Who—or what—is able to tell us more, the fictional film or the painter and critic of real life?

The first meeting with Dodson, with her painting of the black man, is brief, just enough to give a fresh impression in the film and stir up questions. Now there is a cut to a woman on her back at a crisis point in therapy, screaming, "Give it to me! Give it to me! . . . It's *mine*!" as she clutches a towel held or attached out of our view. She seems to ask for the penis we have just been looking at as her right and her deepest desire. Perhaps she asks for art, for being filmed, which she is certainly now getting.

We cut to a moment with Dr. Robert Ollendorf, identified by a title, who stands near a railing with water and a cityscape behind him—he looks to be on a bridge (the script says it is the deck of a ship—a bridge in motion, we might say). He makes a very strange statement, and that is all there is to him: "If any sane man or woman would be produced by a doctor suddenly . . . he very likely would commit suicide."

The spoken emphasis seems to mean the *doctor* would commit suicide, but it might be the sane man or woman produced. Ollendorf means to stress the slow progress of therapy (speedy results would shock one into suicide), or the hopelessness, even the absurdity, of therapy, something the later Freud emphasized (and Reich fiercely rejected)? Or does he mean that "sanity" is not what we are after—that it is something else?

There is a cut to the streets of New York, and Tuli Kupferberg follows an older woman, respectable-looking, even stuffy. Kupferberg is helmeted and marching, his rifle held erect. The woman and Kupferberg start to walk onto what may be a bridge—there is suddenly a low wall beside the sidewalk, and we cannot see beyond it—and the woman notices Kupferberg and steps back to let him go ahead. She shows alarm as the two of them enter a bridge passage. The woman seems to think Kupferberg is dangerous or crazy. This is theater, making art of the issues of bridging and shock, in this case with an unwilling audience/participant. This is Kupferberg's art, which figures the film's art. Is this film dangerous or crazy? Does a bridge passage necessarily seem dangerous or crazy? Are we, the film's audience, unwilling? Now comes a cut to Milena, who is breaking eggs, with the sound of a sigh and more "Eastern" piping music. The fictional material begins.

In the moments leading up to this change to fiction—with Betty Dodson, Ollendorf, Tuli—the juxtapositions come fast and are agitating to watch. The thoughts stirred seem greater than the time given to the images. The film seems to be shaking its subject about, or to be shaken by it (as if the film is a dog, shaking its prey, or is shaken by a dog whose prey it is, a dog such as those we saw at the start of the film, now roused to life). The film is looking, out of necessity, for a new approach to the material, a new way to go, or a way out. The hints about art, with Dodson and Kupferberg, give the clue. The change to fiction then suggests that if film lets go, it becomes fiction. Fiction is the letting go of film. Fiction, fancy, is letting the dimension of earth, the camera's real subject, come to the fore and fully go its way.

Has the film forced this, or does the subject call for what happens? We know the film's subject through the film—where else? Does the subject call for what the film does in its effort to know or make known the subject? (Surely we can know a subject *through* a film and still feel that the film mishandles or misperceives the subject.)

Nonfiction, after some excited editing, turns into fiction. Nonfiction is always on the road to this, from the start. Would people in nonfiction film say and do what we see and hear, if not for the filming? Would people and places and situations be what they are on film—what are they?—but for the way they make themselves filmable and are filmed? Life creams itself this way so as to make itself understood, to be what it is.

The change to Milena and her story is like the change in Joyce's *Ulysses* from several hundred pages of more or less narrative prose to the big "Nighttown" section written as a play script (or film script, since what happens is hardly imaginable staged in a theater). "Nighttown" comes, too, just after the reaching about and mounting intensity of the "Oxen of the Sun" section, pressing the borders of prose with parodies of many styles, looking for a new way, at the maternity hospital.

With "Nighttown," the action of the book is suddenly made clearer, our vision allowed to be more direct. Or has the book shifted to a higher, more intense phase of artifice? *Ulysses*, like *WR*, gives the impression of extraordinary openness to the range of human experience, notably experience of the body. All sorts of things immediately recognizable from life just come in, it seems, as they like. But *Ulysses* also seems the most *written* of books, in its phrase-making, in its weaving of themes. The entire book is a crisis of fancy as against subject matter. The "Nighttown" section challenges the usual medium of novels, prose narration, challenges its validity. In *WR* the beginning of Milena's story asks us to think: What are nonfiction film and fiction film for? Ought one to cast the other aside?

The fictional story in *WR* is used to show us a number of things: Milena's dark-haired roommate and her friend from the army, who are a sexually liberated couple enjoying themselves; Milena herself, the independent-thinking Reichian Marxist, anxious to preach and promote her ideas; and Milena's encounter with Vladimir, a Soviet figure skater, proud and stellar, but repressed, very committed to the Soviet idea of the state above the individual (he means to be a "good state being"—he has Lenin's name, Vladimir Ilyich—is he what Lenin had in mind?). The locale is Yugoslavia—a title announces Belgrade and 1971, the year the film was made. We see a country that is not a utopia. There is a "bourgeois" bureaucratic class, which makes its appearance in a limousine in the first episode in the street at night. And there is a working-class element that makes demands only for its immediate sensuous interests, represented by Milena's raucous ex-lover Radmilovic. But this Yugoslavia is not the USSR, and it resists Stalinism. Milena and her roommate tell Vladimir that Yugoslavs care about "personal happiness" and do not blur that with state concerns. Yugoslavia is where Milena lives her Reichian life. It is a marginal or transitional place, in formation—in the 1970s and 1980s, still in relatively quiet formation.[7]

The fiction might be taken as carrying out ideas. The earlier part of the film has raised Reich's issues, and now there is the need to see them lived out and to see what opposition to them looks like (Vladimir). The fiction shows us the future in a sense, the world of lived-out ideas that is always a step beyond the world as it is.

The fiction also shows us something nearer than the future. These are real people in these roles, and real places and objects before the camera—even the sets are a reality, and the story does go on location and outdoors. The link in fictional film, of real people and objects and places, to story, emblematizes that we do live by or with ideas. We direct our lives by ideas and toward ideas. We live with a world of ideas in our minds, imagined as lived out, and we bring the ideas to the world we find ourselves in. There is a joining. This is reality. What is real before the camera takes us to the story, which is something that is there in real life such as we live it, life with ideas—life such as comes before the camera in the first place.

Milena's story is also allegory. Here it is not so much ideas lived out but people simply standing for ideas, the story being a drama of ideas. Milena's roommate and the roommate's lover are Reichian, but naive. Milena is consciousness. Vladimir is Stalinism, openly associated in the film with Hitlerism. In allegory we see not so much the world beyond or above us, which we might live out, as the world deep within us, the ideas we do live, purified of the chaotic details of life. (In allegory complications of detail are representative, not accidental, though the line here is fine.) Allegory can be very compelling by a power of recognition—the ideas and drama are right; we know them. Or allegory can seem thin—so much is pared away. Insofar as Milena's story seems thin, in want of more story—accidental, real-seeming story, rather than allegorical story—it calls attention to the rest of the film, the nonfiction, as *being* story. The fiction reveals the rest of the film, with its realism and also its film fancy, as perhaps being better story than this part. Certainly the fiction reveals the *whole* of the film, which includes the fiction, as being better story than the fictional part alone. (Similarly the "Nighttown" section of *Ulysses* can seem to run [brilliantly] thin after a time, to provide only images that represent ideas, and to need the return of rich descriptive prose—which comes.)

Perhaps all fictional film is allegorical in one aspect. Perhaps we take an interest in fiction only if things stand for ideas—this is what Aristotle suggests, distinguishing poetry from history. In life itself things do stand for ideas, or want to stand for ideas, actions for contests of ideas, so that allegory is realism, after all.

WR has Milena's story, and it has its nonfiction part. This film splits, for emphasis and recognition, what goes on all at once in other films. *Nanook of the North*, the ur-documentary, has a story like Milena's woven in it—a drama, an allegory, of life against the death-dealing universe. *Rules of the Game*, for many film lovers the supreme fiction, has drama and allegory in plenty, yet the story is continued or answered back to, developed at every turn, by the filming—the exploring—of a found and alterable reality. At the hunt there is real killing of animals in a bleak autumn field under an overcast sky.

Milena's story seems at first to add something to the rest of *WR*, to take part in what the film as a whole is doing. Yet one might feel that the film is really only beginning now. If we regard Milena as the narrator of the earlier part, this would make that, in retrospect, seem her own thought process or some of her proselytizing, which leads to her appearance in her own story. Also, Milena's story might seem the very point of the film when we realize that a long stretch of this story makes up the film's ending. At any rate, a short way into Milena's story there is a switch back to nonfictional material, and for the rest of the film we get a mixing of the two. What is contributing to, or illuminating, what? Which is the ground, which is the added dimension? What is really the subject of the film?

I have cited Heidegger's "The Origin of the Work of Art" in speaking of concealment and unconcealment, of film's allowing of its subject, or the real world, or the down to earth, to become plain through film's very acts of "concealment," its operations of fancy. I have been calling Milena's story a "world" in various senses (of lived-out, fleshed-out ideas, or of pure ideas, allegory). Now central to Heidegger's essay is his discussion of "world" and "earth." "World" and "earth" are in conflict in the work of art, in intimacy, in an unsettled, active relation that allows each to be what it is. "World," something "set up," has to do with meaning and values and human understanding. "Earth," something "set forth," is a matter of the "thingly"—the *material* of art, of its nature "self-secluding." The work of art has earth come forth to us to be acknowledged, while retaining its self-secluding nature. Earth comes into the art's setup "world." The work of art must be grounded, though the ground does not want to show itself—and this even though ground is only ground in being "set forth" in the making of a "world." It is all a wonderful circle, where the sides are not to be got free of each other.

In film we might conceive "earth" to be the real world that comes before the camera, or the real subject of the film, that forces itself onto film, even a body of ideas. Or, alternately, earth might be the material of film in another sense, the mechanism, the camera and celluloid and projector and screen, comparable to bronze, stone, paint . . . And we might conceive "world" as what is done with the real world, or real subject, or with the physical fact of film, its mechanics. There is what is done in shooting the real world, making selections and decisions, framing, and what is done in editing, putting parts of film together, sometimes in sheer exuberance with the medium, as in *WR*'s passage leading up to the change to fiction. And there is what is done in fictionalization, with scripting, staging, décor. Why should film itself come forth to be acknowledged, like stone, paint, bronze? Because it is a way, a path.

Milena's story in *WR* might act as world—a filmic setting up—to the earth of the rest of the film. This earth might be the real subject of Reich and his ramifications in people's lives, which is perhaps finally unfathomable (self-secluding), though one can look in its direction. Or earth might be the body, Reich's own subject, what he investigated and talked about. Or earth might be the segments of nonfiction film, the material Milena gathers about herself.

But if Milena, the created character, comes to seem the center of the film, its subject, then the nonfiction would be "world" in regard to Milena's story as earth. The nonfiction carries farther, or helps to bring out Milena.

The subject of *WR* cannot be said absolutely to be Reich and his effect in the real world—our sense of that slips once Milena's story gets under way. Nor, I think, do we want absolutely to call Milena the subject—there is just too much else going on. Heidegger says that it is "unconcealedness as such" that is finally the point with the work of art—the very way the work works, and our involvement with this. This matters more than any particular subject that is being made manifest—though the particular subject and particularity as such are crucial to the process. Carrying on thinking from *Being and Time*, Heidegger says it is process, motion in a sense, even motion within stillness, that matters essentially to people.

I suggest that *WR*'s elusiveness should bring us to realize that the subject or center or purpose of the film lies in just how it works on us. And here we are very close to the question of the political nature of the film. Meeting with this film, where are we, or where are we left? What are we sent away to do?

We do not get, exactly, a clarification of Reich and of the way the world works (or does not work) along Marxist-Reichian lines. Whenever we would bear down on something that is clarified, the form of the film, its nonfiction as well as fiction, its fancy, its editing, offers to cast us, almost unstoppably, into a state of meditation about reality, about the real status of what we see. The form of any film, carefully attended to, will cause this questioning.

WR puts us in the situation of making an approach to a clarification we finally cannot have. Just the approach, or the realizing of what an approach is, is a great deal. We are left in motion, or motivated.

Earth is what we are aimed at, but we would lose it if we attained it fully in the form of idea or art. Earth—the body, the new world or society of the body—is what we have in the "world," or the motion, of film, its constant starting over, its state of being as mind, Milena.

I want to look at two further sequences and what they bring to the film, and then at the ending. The two sequences come fairly soon after the start of the film's fictional material, where the transvestite or transsexual Jackie Curtis is introduced, and where China footage and Stalin footage come in.

Milena meets her ex-lover Radmilovic in the street at night and he raises a fuss, creating a roadblock for a Mercedes evidently carrying an important person, shouting at the car, "Down with the red bourgeoisie! Steak Esterhazi! Mitsuko! Marx Factor!" And here there is a cut to New York's Forty-Second Street, and on the soundtrack the programming of WABC radio again (no one we see is listening to a radio—it is, as it were, the radio sound in these people's heads). We contemplate a person who looks like a man dressed as a woman (identified by the script as Jackie

Curtis, whom one might recognize from Andy Warhol productions), as the camera backs down the street in front of him/her and a friend in male attire, with a few countermoves forward, curious or affectionate. This goes on and on, as the two walk toward the backing camera, eating ice-cream cones, looking about, having a certain amount of interaction with each other, never paying direct attention to the camera. "Marx Factor" is a joke on the corruption of Marxism into a "red bourgeoisie." And the transition to Forty-Second Street compares Yugoslavia with America to an extent, evoking America's makeup, which may be falsity and self-delusion. We hear ecstatic commercials for Maybelline "Hollywood eyelashes" and for Coppertone tanning lotion ("Who owns the sun? Coppertone.") and eventually we watch the crowds in New York moving about under movie marquees for pornography and shallow romance films—*Playmates, Without a Stitch, A Walk in the Spring Rain* (though the last is late Ingrid Bergman, so things are not so simple). In the midst of this is Jackie, conceivably a pathetic figure, part of this world but clearly somewhat edgy and ill at ease with the crowd around.

There is a positive side to the "Marx Factor" transition. The phrase reminds us that Marx or a true Marxist is supposed to be a factor, a doer or changer or enactor, and the joke points to the valid creativity or makeup of Milena, who would keep the revolution going on. Milena soon comes into her apartment, where she has an American movie poster (like the Forty-Second Street marquees) for *The Mating Urge* (1959)—presumably she makes good and healthy, not debased, use of what it represents—and she gets busy changing clothes and fixing herself up, positively costuming herself, in army boots, army jacket, and army hat, with bare legs, before going out to preach Reichian-Marxist ideas.

And Jackie Curtis is far from being a negative figure. There is an enormous weight given to her first appearance (let's rest with the feminine pronoun). We are only a short way into the fictional story when we get this switch to a lengthy meeting with Jackie. Perhaps it is the start of a fiction too, but it is shot in daylight in what looks like the true chaos of Forty-Second Street, and Jackie and her friend do not seem to be playing parts, beyond consenting to be filmed as they walk down the street. It is an extended meeting of the film with an interesting real subject. Jackie is right away a figure of charm, self-possession in spite of being ill at ease, and bravery. She is extraordinarily alive in the eyes. All in all an alter ego for Milena—a sister, or sister/brother.

But if we come to earth after a bit of Milena's fiction, it is with contemplation of an utter fantasy figure, with glittery makeup and *outré* manner, standing out against the (other) impermeably real people on the street. Jackie looks like a man dressed as a woman—something about the shoulders, stature, bones of the face. But for all we can tell, Jackie may have been born a woman, or physically changed into one. In her monologue later in the film she tells of her first sexual experience as a male and with a male, seeming to make clear who she is. But then she speaks of meeting this lover at a later time—"the next time I saw him I was a girl, and he couldn't get ready . . . he was used to sleeping with boys, which is a very limited view on things . . . I mean, since I was the same person, I mean literally the same person!" Has Jackie undergone surgery and hormone treatment to become a woman? We do not know her status really, only the fancy we see, and the appeal of her unassumingness and seemingly real feelings.

Jackie comes back into the film a number of times. She seems to make uncertainty about sexual identity, or to make sexual identity as fancy, a metaphor for the film's whole concern with the body—earth—as taking us inevitably into the beyond of creativity and imagination, a beyond that infuses earth. This is film itself, earth in relation with the beyond, a circle, restless starting over on and on, coming back but also paradoxically going on, opening out. Every real person is perhaps as strange as Jackie, living with uncertainty of status, calling upon fantasy, attempting self-creation. If only we would let go!

Later in the *Screw* office Jackie comments on her transformation—"glitter on the eyes, glitter on my lips, glitter on the hair"—and says, "unreal, you just don't see things like that," suggesting the impossibility of the—of course—actual. She picks up a framed photograph of the young Gary Cooper, elegantly suited, looking rather like Cary Grant, and shows it to the camera, saying admiringly, being very firm, "Just like you don't see things like that, you don't see things like that all the time!" If only we could! the film implies. What is encompassed in figures like Gary Cooper or Cary Grant, and the worthiness of this as a realistic ideal, is appreciated and argued by the deepest and wisest critics of American film, Stanley Cavell, Robin Wood, Victor Perkins, and others. Jackie Curtis, invoking movie stars, suggests that the film figures of *WR* itself, fictional, nonfictional, may be more than a mirror of life, or a field for thought—may be an inspiration. People are in fact made of inspiration.

After Jackie's appearance on Forty-Second Street, she gives a brief monologue in an indoor space, talking of her "marriage"—what is it exactly? how is it defined? we never know for sure—to Eric, whom she calls "the American hero." As she speaks, we suddenly see Tuli Kupferberg doing his street theater in front of Lincoln Center. Then Milena in her apartment, preparing to go out and speak to a crowd. It is as if Jackie has projected these realms of art—street theater, fiction film—to represent the creativity she talks about.

Milena's speech on the courtyard balcony and her interchanges with her audience there, like her conversations with Vladimir later, are full of pure doctrine, as if the film is moving, within the fictional story, to an element of greater realism. But soon Milena works up the crowd in a tribute to love and happiness, and her listeners lock hands and begin dancing in a long column up the stairs and around the balcony—the background music coming from who knows where—eventually taking up Milena, who dances with them as they all begin to sing,

> Without love
> Life isn't worth a thing.
> Nobody knows . . . Oh, nobody knows
> What tomorrow may bring.
> Life without fucking isn't worth a thing!

Then as if cued by "what tomorrow may bring," we are launched into one of the most intense and remarkable passages of the film, and the last to introduce major new material, Stalin, the force of death. There is a cut from the dancing column on Milena's balcony, to a massive rally in China with Mao and a surging crowd. After this we go to a Soviet fictional, adulatory film about Stalin, which we see a good bit of, and then to upsetting footage of nasal force-feeding and electroshock therapy, as if caused by Stalin, with Stalin material intercut, as well as a brief shot of Reich looking unhappy—a detail of the photo where he is handcuffed. All this issues into the prolonged scene of a large Reichian group therapy session with people of all shapes and sizes screaming, walking on each other, pulsating and thrashing about. This seems to be the Apocalypse, but we know it is all right and for the best—or do we quite? At least we know that this is honest nonfictional filming, as far as possible from the idealized Stalin film.

Nowhere in the film are we so aware as in this long changing sequence, of being involved in a film experience, of being in the hands of a film, abandoned—with our full consciousness—to be taken where the film will go. At the same time the film seems to reach more profoundly than ever into the real thing—the bodily element—it is all about. This last is strongly "set forth" (Heidegger, "Origin" 23) in the face of all the showy setting up of the choices and timing of the edited material. Nothing could be more conscious and idea-determined than such a series. And yet a physical force, something of the body, seems to generate it or to be brought alive by it. We feel this as we concentrate intensely on any one piece of footage, and then find ourselves stimulated anew and cast into another piece. From the dancing on the balcony we explode into China, and from there into the cold world of the Stalin film, and on and on—as sex seems to defy gravity.

The camera backs before Milena and her column of people, and the cut goes to Mao and other officials advancing in a similar column on a high platform or wall, toward a camera. Another shot, panning and high up, surveys an enormous crowd in Tiananmen Square. The singing of Milena and her people merges into the huge sound of the chanting and crying Chinese. It is as if Milena and her people are transfigured into the Chinese, people of the most world-historical political significance. The Yugoslav fictional characters in a sense come to earth in nonfiction, but it is an earth more glorious, more imaginatively charged than fiction. We realize what a sense of reality we have by now invested in the fiction we have been watching, because the change to the Chinese seems an escape or blossoming into an imaginative or fantasy world. This impression is given in part by the change from the highly realized filming of the Yugoslavs—which at first looked so much of the studio—to the faded color and ragged print quality of the China footage. The Chinese seem ghosts or spirits or demigods.

After some moments, the cut to the film celebrating Stalin makes the Chinese seem firmly real in retrospect. It is a stark contrast—with of course the suggestion that Stalinism and Maoism have continuities. The bluish black and white looks ghostlier than anything we have seen. The large formal room is like a tomb, with people standing in opposite rows as Stalin advances at the head of followers, all moving slowly, processionally. The open space seems dead because of the stillness or stiffness of the people, whereas the much greater space of the China footage seemed an opportunity for expansion, for life, even if hypertrophied life. Milena has explained to the crowd, as Reich explained (and she will say more later to Vladimir), that the craving for orgasm turns into politics, conscious and life-promoting, or warped and death-dealing. Stalin represents the warped and death-dealing—and we sense it through his regime's own fiction film meant to praise and idealize him. Death produces its own death imagination.[8]

With the asylum footage that ensues, almost unbearable to watch, apparently nonfiction, we might think about Stalin's prison-asylums, about the brutality that was the result of his elevation to power. But the political content and the fantasy-like movement of the film editing as well seem mainly to serve what this film does to our own bodies in the confrontation with force-feeding and shock therapy (and later a man beating his head against a wall). Politics and history, like film, seem fancies in contrast to pure awareness of the body.

With Stalin we see parts of two films, or very different parts of one, with Stalin dressed and coiffed differently in the two places.[9] In both places we wonder, at least briefly, if this is fiction or real footage of Stalin, perhaps Stalin playing himself for fiction filming. A zither plays "Lili Marlene," so popular with soldiers on both sides during World War II. Is this part of the original film, or added by Makavejev? Added ironically, to remind us that Stalin made a pact with Hitler, with whom he eventually fought? The song is reprised during the shock-therapy material. Is it to suggest the stoic, cheerful bearing of German or Russian soldiers whose work covered horrors? Does the film find stoicism and good cheer the only way to do its own work, which involves horrors? Is the asylum footage real? What country is it from? Is the force-feeding conceivably saving the life of someone whose not eating is not from political protest or from antagonism toward those who are feeding him (he looks unconscious)? Is shock therapy good or bad?

The long scene in the group therapy room, concluding the present montage, seems to show the real underpinnings for political-human advancement, for Milena's kind of politics and what might prevent Stalinist fancy. This scene brings the montage series to earth and seems to give grounding for the new departure into fiction that follows, virtually the rest of the film. In this scene we look and look at actual people—doing what they must, is it?—screaming, emoting without restraint, subject to spasms. We take our time. The camera moves here and there, and there are cuts, numerous shots. We see people in rows, in patterns. There are close-ups of distorted faces, close-ups of dental work. We have come to the element of the body as far as can be from any fancies. Or perhaps there is idea and will (even willfulness) at work in all this. Dr. Lowen is there directing things. Is there even self-delusion? Are American Reichian therapy sessions really connected to world revolution? We do not know. We are watching film here, for all it can reveal or occlude, as much as we are watching film in the brilliant, calculated, fanciful montage passage leading up to this. We acknowledge the body—there is no doubt—but there is no assurance what the body is.

Dr. Lowen comes on to explain expression through the body, or rather that "you are—you don't have—a body; you are your body," and he gives apt imitations of distorted postures and expressions, deriving from mental states. All this may seem plain realism and solid doctrine after the wild therapy session with the ambiguous filming-without-commentary there. Or Dr. Lowen's instruction may seem further fancy, a step away from looking directly at something real, a step into words. But the fancy of words can help point us back to earth.

Now a title announces, "The Moscow Ice Follies Visit Belgrade," and soon Milena meets the skater-actor Vladimir and takes him home—whereupon we see Tuli Kupferberg in Manhattan, discoursing on the phrase "bring the war home." The story line begins that will lead to the end of the film, with intercutting between Milena and Vladimir's life and the doings of Americans—Reichians and others. A woman in therapy begs for "mama," as Milena and Vladimir first feel attraction. A woman in therapy screams, it seems endlessly, upon mention in Milena's story of the murder of Trotsky and the imprisonment of Reich. Jackie Curtis appears briefly upon discussion of Vladimir's identity—"Who are you, really?" the Russian is asked. During the time Vladimir is imprisoned in a cabinet in Milena's apartment—from which he will eventually emerge blissful, as if from an Orgone box—there is the major interruption by Jackie's monologue about her earlier life, concluding with the emphasis on transformation and the picture of Gary Cooper. Is Vladimir, in the cabinet, being transformed like Jackie? To what extent? The concern with creation is carried on in the scene where real person (?) Nancy Godfrey makes a mold from Jim Buckley's erect penis to produce a plastic-cast sculpture (Godfrey and Buckley are identified by titles; we have seen Buckley in the *Screw* office with Jackie when transformation was discussed). The penis sculpture is shown just at the later moment when the Stalin film comes in again. Stalin equals prick, or creation, maybe evil creation, maybe necessary to destroy Hitler. In all this material there is constant play with the notion that common impulses, common realities—craving, horror, transformation—underlie politics and personal relations, the sick or cut-off and the healthy and growing, the concentration of the East and the abandon of the West. It is all a question of what we do with what is there.

Vladimir is freed from the cabinet, and soon the film's final episode in a park begins, introduced by two brief shots of Reich's cloudbusters being adjusted—the tools of his late attempt to link the universe to his work with the energies of sex. The film resolves itself now in a universe of fiction.

The snowy park setting for Milena and Vladimir's final time together is extraordinary for the fictional part, its first outdoor scene, a real public place. Lawrence's *Women in Love* likewise ends in a prolonged snowy episode, pitting the steely Gerald against himself and the book's women. Snow fits the spiritual death that becomes literal in both Lawrence's novel and this film. "The esoteric becomes exoteric," F. R. Leavis writes of the novel's last chapters (*D. H. Lawrence* 88). But the art works in opposite ways in the film and the novel. *Women in Love*, through many imaginative feats, has established a real England; then the book goes to a snowy world of imagination to play out inner concerns in isolated, exposed clarity. *WR* goes from the world of imagination of the Milena-Vladimir story so far, to a natural setting, as if that has called the story out, as if the story must be tested against this setting, as if Milena and Vladimir must live here if they are to live at all.

A kiss from Milena provokes a cut and a dreamier portion of film, with the outdoor background noise now muted. Vladimir, who had been at first fussy about protecting his life for his art, now begins, "I like being here . . ." A second kiss brings soundtrack music for violins and piano. Vladimir eventually slaps Milena, her advances just too much for him, and there is a cut to what becomes an extended stretch of the Stalin film, with a triumphant imaginative scene in Red Square, ethereal buildings in the distance, and the raising of a great banner in the foreground—it is as if projected by Vladimir, a Stalinist motive for his slap, or his bringing of his mind around to a bright state in his terms.

Vladimir and Milena make up, and there is long passionate kissing, going on and on, seen close up. There has been nothing like this between any two people in the film so far—except for a ghostly foreshadowing, seen briefly, when Jackie and her lover kiss in the back area of a station wagon, virtually in silhouette, close up, their feet and costume-like shoes propped up in the distance, the world seen rushing away through the back window. Vladimir and Milena's kiss is the felt reality, the letting go, that the film has been after—done at last by actors in a story—though a story that has come outdoors.

There is a wild image of pirouetting skaters—a bow to the unimaginable. Then, a scream or gasp—after an interval of time, it becomes clear later—indicates the murder of Milena. The film turns to horror as we see Vladimir rising up in the dark with bloody hands. And we go to a morgue where a man removes what is supposed to be Milena's head from a basket. The head is placed on a tray, and, after a cut (a trick to permit what follows and a reminder that film assaults, cutting like a knife—for our good, one hopes), the head comes to life and speaks soberly but not painfully of lovemaking with Vladimir and of his restlessness to go "further," into violence—"He's . . . a genuine red fascist." At some point, health is resting where one is. After a pause, Milena concludes firmly, with hope, "Even now I'm not ashamed of my Communist past!" It is like one of the steadier encounters in Dante.

Vladimir now wanders outdoors in the daylight and sings a song of asking to be remembered, as if needing help. It is a surprise that he can sing like this—there is more to him than we knew, or he has been transformed (in fact, the voice of a popular balladeer has been dubbed over the image). In a way, the scene seems done for the sake of another flirtation with real landscape, a few scroungers gathered about a fire, a loose white horse ("an old white horse galloped away . . ."). The scene goes on for a long time. The setting accents by contrast the quality of art or wish in Vladimir's song. Can reality and art or wish ever come together?

Finally Milena's head appears again, smiling, as Vladimir's song continues on the soundtrack, and there is a dissolve to the photo of the smiling Reich, from Milena's apartment—an element of Milena's imaginative world, and yet the photo of a real man, real as the character Milena is not, though the actress we see is—and the *character* Milena may be just one face of the Milena who is the voice of the film, or is the film itself, which is what Reich is now—where he lives. In this dissolve, worlds of persons, or of kinds or states of persons, pour through one another.

Vladimir and Milena have become real by this point. The fiction has penetrated, so that the fanciful concluding scenes in the snow and the morgue are straining against—and cooperating with—a reality now established of people as people. Fictional people.

Sex is a motive here, undeniable when we see the kissing (can this be acting?) and hear Milena's account of lovemaking, and the pathologists' talk of the "wild night of love," the "huge amount of semen, four or five times the usual" found in Milena's body. Sex is working with or against a most extreme transformativeness. Does sex induce the head to come alive and talk? Or Vladimir to sing? The film seems about to fly off into space. Has sex induced this, or does it anchor this fantasy?

Humor at last cuts two ways, or takes things in a circle. There is humor in the head coming to life, for all the horror, dissipating a bit the grim realism of the murder. We think of the live actress who must be concealed under the table. The film brings us to earth and lets us know things are all right. Yet we settle with the speaker into a certain

sobriety. We concentrate on her words, telling of her sad experience and her communist beliefs. And the smile at the end is sober, however uplifting. Milena's smile, dissolving into Reich's in the photo, over Vladimir's "Remember, I'm here too," is like the smile of the universe in *The Divine Comedy*, motion and stillness at once, or like the smile of the compassionate Buddha for those who are only what they are, a smile that would encourage them to more. This is not the humor derived from things being put together that are unlike. It is the humor of seeing all the array of things and realizing that it all might rise, as if against gravity—the humor of a spontaneous response to having seen this, as if being touched.

4

Blonde Venus

Experiment Successful beyond All Dreams

SOME YEARS AGO, I WAS AT A screening of *Blonde Venus* (1932) where several friends were present who, like me, were teaching and writing about film. My friends and I met on the way out of the screening and went off to have a drink or a sandwich. We were all smiling in spite of ourselves, somewhat inarticulate, tending to say things like "Just marvelous, wasn't it?"—"Amazing"—"I had forgotten how good film could be—just what it could really do."[1]

All of us there in this little group had seen *Blonde Venus* before, and we were familiar with Josef von Sternberg's films and with Marlene Dietrich in her many roles. We were used to talking about these things. But somehow the occasion of this screening in 35 mm, on a large screen and with a large responsive audience, mostly of students seeing the film for the first time—somehow in all this we were taken by surprise, at the wonders of this particular film and of film itself.

What in *Blonde Venus* could provoke such a response, or be the focus for such feelings? Certainly, one thing is Sternberg's way with the physical world and light. There is the sense of a world of palpable things that is really there, revealing itself in a fascinating new light before the camera, and there is at the same time the sense of a world created, a world of fantasy or imagination, made out of pure light and shadow. Always shadow impinges—not bluntly as in the world of "film noir," but complexly, in small places, giving the sense of three dimensions, and also being the means for fantasy, the play of light and shadow seeming to embody the will itself, the power to recreate, or to modify one thing into another. This double sense, of a world of real objects and a world of imagination, is endemic to film, and is perhaps more acute, or is pushed farther, in the films of Sternberg than anywhere else.

Then there is the theatrical inventiveness of *Blonde Venus*'s musical numbers—Dietrich emerging from a gorilla suit to sing or sauntering in white tails and top hat along a platform through the audience in a huge Paris theater. Or there is the inventiveness of the staging of the exotic life in a southwestern border town, toward the end of the film. We delight in these things, confronting them as being in some sense realities—how could we delight in a nonreality? Yet we never seem to wonder how we can be seeing what we are seeing.

And the film makes astonishing gestures of self-consciousness about being film, about its own film personality and ability to utter film thought. How else can a film know so much of what is going on with it? Because without doubt *Blonde Venus* as a poetic creation is conscious of itself, as in the final image, where a child's fingers, huge on the screen, fondle a revolving toy in the background, as if fingering the screen itself and therefore as though in a condition where the screen is opening to being fondled this way—the lost child who has recovered his mother. Here flesh and blood of the world seem to reach out, or up, for contact with the world of film's imagination. Soon, but not too soon, we will meet the Greek poet Pindar and his words about the poetic (I say filmic) imagination.

And of course, there is the presentation of such a figure as Dietrich. She is given to us, but she is not to be possessed. She has the interest of a remarkable being who is there, really before us, but the film does not have the effect of exhausting her interest or "packaging" her for viewers. Perhaps the final wonder of this film is that it works the open-ended and nonpossessive process of our getting acquainted with a person. And yet, she is a movie star, a movie *being*.

Considering the real world of objects in Sternberg, and the approach to Dietrich as to a person, I want to say that even the first wave of excitement about this film—about such a film as this—is not a matter of giving ourselves over to a purely artistic, filmic, artificial world. To be struck by this film and to confront it, and reflect on it, is to become aware of its connections with life, with our own lives. We become aware first or last of an intelligence about life—as in knowing how to go from one thing

to the next and knowing what is good to aim at. Whose intelligence is this in *Blonde Venus*? Sternberg's? Dietrich's? The screenwriter's? The very medium's, the Hollywood film's own—the way various interesting forces could be brought to bear organically in the case of at least certain films? If transcendence is at stake in *Blonde Venus*—transcendence we might associate with glamor, or events rising, so to speak, into the shape of melodrama—it is transcendence such as we see and move within our lives every day. This film makes us think about transcendence.

One reason *Blonde Venus* seems connected with life is the impurity of the film. It does not have the consistent exalted style of Sternberg's *Morocco* (1930) or *Shanghai Express* (1932)—only in stretches does *Blonde Venus* sustain the intense filmic-imaginative feel that runs from first to last in these other films. All the Sternberg-Dietrich films are emotionally profound. But usually one has to work one's way back into life from a world of pure steadily held central emotions and symbolic actions and images. The obsessive love and the cynical, desperate love in the desert cities of *Morocco*, or the high resentment and the forgiveness in *Shanghai Express*, on an exotic train journey amid a political revolution—all this takes us far outside ourselves, and we must reflect after the fact to recognize these rarefied and intense states of being as kin to our own feelings and lives. We are carried away in these films, and there is a pause, or gap, before recognition comes.

Blonde Venus lets in a good deal of familiar life—it is set in a recognizable modern world, and it has its familiar-seeming low-key exchanges among characters. Or perhaps one should say, *Blonde Venus* usually lets in familiar life in narrative film's conventional way—as opposed to Sternberg's way—of dealing with such life—and of course it is a question how one is to tell the difference between life and the conventions we accept as conveying life. Or again, *Blonde Venus* lets in a current of common myth, as opposed to having complete originality. *Blonde Venus* is the story of a woman performer (Marlene Dietrich) who takes her child on the run from her alienated husband, suffers many trials, and comes finally to a strange sort of reconciliation. It is the story of a suffering, wayward, wife and mother in the modern world—like many popular films and popular novels of the 1920s, 1930s, and 1940s.

Sternberg and Dietrich here open themselves to the power of genre. Stanley Cavell in *Pursuits of Happiness: The Hollywood Comedy of Remarriage* has described a body of impressive Hollywood films of the 1930s and 1940s, a set of comedies about marriage, human change, possibilities for happiness in intimate relationships, individual couples in relation to the larger society—such films as *The Philadelphia Story* (1940), *The Awful Truth* (1937), *It Happened One Night* (1934), *His Girl Friday* (1940), *The Lady Eve* (1941), and others. America of these years seems to carry on a great public discussion in these films, pressing to ask how a man and a woman can talk to each other and attain equality in their relations, and pressing to ask, if indirectly, what personal happiness has to do with the larger world, the polity, suggesting that personal happiness sets a standard for the polity. There is a generation of film actresses here—Katharine Hepburn, Barbara Stanwyck, and others—who virtually demand treatment as "new women." To tell these stories film draws on its remarkable ability to reveal change in human beings, bringing us so close to face and voice, and indeed to reveal more than change, a "best" or "further" self in a person at any given stage, even a self that runs counter to gender identity. Clark Gable as "mothering," Cary Grant as passive and leadable, even while they are something else. And of course the women, while being women of a certain society, are seen as newly forward and active. The glory of these films is the rendering of American *talk* at what seems a high point of development for humor and warmth and exploring of possibilities for life, specifically, possibilities for breaking through to another person.

In his subsequent book *Contesting Tears: The Hollywood Melodrama of the Unknown Woman*, Cavell describes a dark set of films complementary to the remarriage comedies. *Blonde Venus* of 1932 is named as the first of these melodramas, the originator of the genre we might say, a group that includes *Stella Dallas* (1937), with Barbara Stanwyck; *Now, Voyager* (1942), with Bette Davis; *Gaslight* (1944), with Ingrid Bergman; and Max Ophuls's *Letter from an Unknown Woman* (1948), with Joan Fontaine. *Camille* (1936) and other Greta Garbo films are closely related to these. These films focus on unsuccessful marriages or bad romantic relationships, isolated and suffering women, and the forces in the world and in the mind that defeat the impulse to converse, to break through to another, to make a good life of relations with those closest to one. A child or child-substitute figure is typically present, a burden, a hope. The central women in these films might reach a remarkable inner self-development or self-realization, but it is sadly disconnected from the world about them. The women here characteristically come to speak in an ironic mode—think of Dietrich, of Davis—as if speaking to themselves and to us, cluing us in. The ironic mode taken by an actress is a mode that film is wonderfully suited to relay and bring its audience to be intimate with. It is the audience to the films that is brought to some beginning intimation of who these women are, and some beginning of an intimation of what it would take to converse with them. Such is our world, and the way of working of the art of film.

Dietrich in *Blonde Venus*, with her desires and difficulties and changes, would seem to be the woman and the created character who opens the door to the series of women in the films that follow. Dietrich here asks to be rethought—by Hollywood and by Hollywood's public—as will Stanwyck in *Stella Dallas*, Davis/Charlotte Vale in *Now, Voyager*, Bergman/Paula Anton in *Gaslight*—and perhaps as the comedy heroines as well.

From where does myth derive—these repeated stories of a woman and a man coming to terms and embarking on adventures together, for example, or these stories of a woman turned away by the world and soaring off into her own realm? We make myth, or dwell on myth, just beyond or below the life we live every day, and in connection with that life. We picture what can inspire us, or caution us by its horror—in either case we envision a working of life up into myth, or a working back from myth into life. Art that opens itself to myth in fact opens itself to life.

But for all the talk of myth and pattern I would insist (as Cavell does, it seems to me) on the importance of the individual film or play or story. The ways of myth, and questions of the borders of art and life, will be clarified by looking closely at a particular work, such as *Blonde Venus*.

As will emerge in the pages that follow, much about the film suggests that Dietrich the person, the potential film being, determines in a significant way the form the film takes. Can the Dietrich we see have been made up or created except out of recognition of who she actually is? Can the story of the film, and the form the film takes in every respect, be anything but made in answer to recognition of who Dietrich is? Alternatively, what would it mean to conceive of Dietrich as other than she is in the film? Where is this other Dietrich? What matters, after all? The question is like that of Heidegger's "Origin of the Work of Art": where, or exactly what, are the "real" peasant shoes we are tempted to measure against those we see in Van Gogh's painting?

To watch this film with some openness, and to rewatch it and think about it, is to be brought up short by this question—is not this the real Dietrich, virtually generating this film about herself? This question is there in the images and unfolding of the film. The film will not really allow prejudgment to get anywhere—prejudgment about how films are made, and how people are used in film.[2]

Near the beginning of *Blonde Venus* there is a family scene in which the parents, Helen and Ned Faraday, played by Dietrich and Herbert Marshall, tell and partly enact a bedtime story for their small son, who asks questions and gives a few instructions from his child's bed. The story subsumes in fairy-tale terms the first meeting and courtship of Helen and Ned. At the end of it Dietrich sends her husband away and sings a German lullaby to the boy, to words of Heinrich Heine:

> Leise zieht durch mein Gemüt
> Liebliches Gelaüte.
> Klinge, kleines Frülingslied,
> Kling hinaus ins Weite.
> Zieh hinaus, bis an das Haus,
> Wo die veilchen spriessen.
> Wenn du eine Rose schaust,
> Sag, ich lass' sie grüssen.

> *

> A sweet sound of bells
> Peals gently through my soul.
> Ring out, little song of spring,

Ring out far and wide.
Ring out till you reach the house
Where violets are blooming.
And if you should see a rose,
Send to her my greeting. (Stokes 227)

As she sings, Johnny seems to be already asleep—it is as if she wishes to enter the boy's dreams, or to sing the lullaby for herself, or to us, the film audience.

This bedtime scene is very strikingly repeated at the end of the film, when Helen, estranged, and after many adventures, returns to see her child, Johnny (Dickie Moore), and the boy prevails on his parents to go through the story again. The doing of this reconciles Helen and Ned, and they determine that they will live together again. Helen sings the lullaby again, this time with Ned present, and the film ends with this music welling up in symphonic scoring on the soundtrack, as if this woman is identified with the film itself, which wants to sing a lullaby to us all. We see the boy's fingers now, huge in that surprising close-up, fingering the revolving toy, or fingering the screen. (I think of the little girl at the end of *The Philadelphia Story*, muttering to herself about the reconciliation of Tracy and Dexter, "I did it. I did it all.")[3]

The question is strongly raised: have the forces of home drawn Helen and Ned back together, overcoming hostilities and whatever joys Helen may have been taking in her life apart? Does the film declare that home is the most important place, and that it is the destiny of a Helen Faraday—great performer, cynosure, adventurer, as she turns out to be—incarnated as she is in Marlene Dietrich—to be brought home; brought back; perhaps we would say, brought down? Destiny gloriously happy in spite of all. Or just destiny irresistible, inevitable. As if home is the *reality*, so to put it, so that at the end of the film we (and Helen) are just where we were in the bedtime scene early on, no real change, all the intervening fun, pain, and compulsion being, as it were—if not literally—a dream, a game of the mind, unmattering.

Metamorphosis is occurring, one would almost say rampantly, in this film. Or perhaps it is not really metamorphosis, just the illusion of that. We see Helen in many places, many sorts of costume, many roles. But she makes her journey, and undergoes her transformations, only to enter into her original marriage and to come back to that first scene of storytelling with the child. Or perhaps it is not the same marriage, and that same scene of storytelling.

Dietrich is named Venus—"the Blonde Venus"—when she becomes a performer in a New York club early in the film, and one thinks of the story of Venus being born from the foam of the sea, and Venus's significance as a figure of transformation. Venus is imbued with the power of love, and she imbues others with it. Love transforms, and creates. Sappho, the great poet of Venus, or Aphrodite, tells of love in her own life and implores Aphrodite and at the same time creates Aphrodite, giving us the Aphrodite we have. Helen is Venus or Aphrodite, and is—if we can think it—also the poet who gives us her own life and her self. Poetry sometimes takes form in what seems other than poetry: prose, life itself, film. Sappho has a claim to being, along with Homer, the inventor or origin of poetry. In Homer wide experience and wide fancy come to clarity, with a transparent-seeming, tried-and-true-seeming right language. In Sappho narrow, special, or strange experience, which goes deep or wells up and takes over all of life about it, seems to have the poet invent every word anew, or bring the word forth trailing roots of the thing the word was attached to in some prelinguistic, or prehuman, realm.

Dietrich's original—true—name in the film is Helen, before she is renamed Blonde Venus, and the story is told about the classical Helen, that she was hidden away in Egypt while only a phantom of her was carried to Troy by Paris and fought over in the Trojan War—"the face that launched a thousand ships." This story of the phantom is the inspiration for Euripides's play *Helen* and in our own time for H.D.'s [Hilda Doolittle, American poet] late long work *Helen in Egypt*. There hangs about Helen in any place or appearance the question, Is this the real or true Helen? She states in Euripides, in fact summing up in a sense what happens in the play over and over,

> Hera . . . in my likeness fashioning
> a breathing image out of the sky's air, bestowed
> this on King Priam's son, who thinks he holds me now
> but holds a vanity which is not I,
> and a bit later, in grief,
> I wish that like a picture I had been rubbed out and done again.

H.D.'s long poem sees Helen's existence in Egypt, a faraway world with mysterious sources of divinity and creativity, as containing or actually coinciding with, her life "in time"—her down-to-earth life and trials and affairs with men (H.D. plays with T. S. Eliot's words—his concepts—"in and out of time" [*Four Quartets* 39]). Helen is outside of her life, but also generating it and living it through.

The story of the phantom Helen first appears for us in fragmentary lines of Stesichorus [Greek lyric poet], one of those figures we discern, and discern as great and significant, only in fragmentary remains and in what others said about him. Virginia Woolf makes the point in her essay "On Not Knowing Greek" that Greek culture altogether is something we think about and know only from fragments, where there is so much we do not know—yet this world is something we know vividly (she goes on), and which matters to us very much. How many worlds do we know only in a sense from fragments? Are the world and the people about us now, and here known in fact only in this way, by portions that we perceive and react to? Film seems especially suited to reflect and to reflect upon this situation, bringing us to know real persons—real in a sense not easy to define—by means of fragmentary scenes and actions rendered as shadows on a screen and as recorded sound.

Dietrich in *Blonde Venus* is also identified, to my mind, with Athena, patroness of weaving and crafts. Dietrich is so identified by the images of her at her sewing machine and later embroidering, in the New York apartment with her family—images so conspicuous and odd as to start speculation. These are not just housewifely tasks; they are singled out—we do not see Dietrich cooking or housecleaning. Athena is a figure of wide powers and interests. Her spinning and weaving suggest a bringing to bear of art and craft upon life itself. Her image associates itself with all those women—Fates, Norns—who appear sewing and embroidering—like Helen herself back home in Sparta in the *Odyssey*—and who seem, as they work, to be forming the life about them and the course it will take.

Athena is a figure of transformation, like Venus or Helen; she is born full-grown from the head of Zeus. And both Athena and Venus—and Helen too, if thought about H.D.'s way—suggest self-creation, instant transformation under one's own impulse to come into being or identity, or a new identity. This is the image that has stayed in the human mind, despite cause-and-effect rationalizations about Venus's sea foam having come from the severed genitals of Uranus, or Zeus being pregnant with Athena after having swallowed his wife. Self-creation may be amazing and may have utter integrity, though origins, we know, are never from pure nothing.

Dietrich's changes in *Blonde Venus* are notably external, with the many costumes, the presentations of her—self presentations, are they?—in diverse settings. She keeps her bearings through all this, always Dietrich, who seems able to go anywhere and face anything and still be herself. There is something of the impressiveness of Elizabeth I's *semper eadem* about it. It—Dietrich's deportment—is so much different, at least at first seeming, from the dramatic inner life that shows itself right on the surface in the face and gestures and voice of Davis in *Now, Voyager* or Bergman in *Gaslight*.

But the view of external change as contrasted with inner change in these films is problematic. First, to see the costumes and settings and action of *Blonde Venus* as representing what Dietrich herself does not show, is to think of Dietrich as a stick—as less than a person, or less than an artist. One simply does not want to do this; one is impressed—from the start of the film, and perhaps inevitably from other films and from life outside of film—with the sense of Dietrich as a remarkable personality, as being very much a person. Surely the key to *Blonde Venus* will lie in a *relation* between Helen the imposing person, and the flamboyant changes of setting and attire and activity that the woman may be projecting as symbols of her inner life.

Then, too, Helen's deportment does change in the film from her good-willed and compliant and apparently happy bearing as wife and mother in the first part (which well might invite our questions about what she really feels) to the high-handed ironic manner she assumes, and seems to enjoy, when she enters the world of nightclub performing—quipping, for example, to her surly dressing-room companion who introduces herself as Taxi Belle Hooper, "Do you charge for the first mile?" The character has become Dietrich.

Then there is the unease she shows—the unhappiness, I would say—in her affair with Nick Townsend/Cary Grant. And later the hard contempt when she says to the detective who is in the border town, and to whom she is going to give up her child, "What does a *man* know about mother love?" Or the hard ironic stance when, drunk in a flophouse, she gives to a suicidal woman the money her husband has given her—as he meant it—virtually in exchange for the child, and repeats bitterly his exact words to her: "In this envelope are fifteen hundred dollars. It represents my life work. Had I had time to exploit it properly, I could have made a fortune." At the end, coming back to Ned and Johnny, Helen/Dietrich is almost bafflingly wide-eyed and straightforward—asking the audience more emphatically than ever to think, What is really going on with her?

Dietrich's perhaps small-seeming, but unmistakable, changes ask us to ponder and respond to the life of a self, which may be as florid a life as that of Charlotte Vale/Davis or Paula Anton/Bergman; just as the small-seeming changes in anyone, if we will notice them, ask us to ponder and respond. But what have the expression and changes of expression of Helen/Dietrich to do with Dietrich the imposing personality and Dietrich the unusual great beauty, and with the floridness of the film, of the surfaces before us—the floridness, if you like, of Sternberg? Here is the gap, or terra incognita, of film—the strange area to which we must give ourselves up, or to which we must give over our thinking, without our thinking's ways of preparing us to know where we are. We must give ourselves up to a coming-all-at-once of "incompatibles"—story and role, Dietrich's way of playing, the film's surfaces and events, and Dietrich herself—the phenomenon. We must give ourselves up here if we are to gain access to what matters in the film.

There is more in the problem of inner and external in these films. Davis's or Bergman's impressive emotions are to be pointed to only in the surface of the face and in the gestures that we see, and in the voice, the words and sounds that we hear. Yes, the visible and audible here are generated by the woman—not, as you may say, like costumes and settings and the motions of plot and filming. But the face and gestures and utterances of Davis or Bergman are to some degree scripted and directed, whatever that latter function may involve; the face and gestures and utterances are in a sense part of the plot, part of the director's art, part of the film itself. There is really no distinguishing the integrity of the actress, the person, from the integrity of the role, what is in and of the film. On the other hand, Dietrich's costumes and settings, and all the paces the film puts her through, so to speak, can be seen as generated by Dietrich—by her participation in the creation of the film, whether that amounts to her speaking up in the conventional sense, or to the film's—Sternberg's, the very art-of-film's—taking inspiration in a grasp of who Dietrich is and what she asks of film.

The question of inner life and outer showing, of the experience of a person versus the trappings and outer events of life, comes to a crisis in film—or rather, comes to a different crisis in each film that commands interest—film, with its documentation of face and gesture and voice, and its constant suggestion of something behind what we see and hear. We do not know what inner and external, in general, exactly are—only that it is not possible to deny either that there is the inner, or that there is the external. In film the question comes into a crisis of art. In *Now, Voyager* or *Blonde Venus* what may seem external, seems to belong to the domain of the director, or of the art of film: the woman must be elsewhere. But then, in just what way is the real woman subject to direction? Does she live for art? Is she more of the artist in her film, generating it, than we might suppose? Art here seems—if we will see it—to share ground with the real person.

In nonfiction film the faces, gestures, voices, surfaces, might seem the area of non-art—the camera records what is indisputably there in the world. But the faces and surfaces and sounds are subject to direction in a way—subject to the filmmaker's sensibility in looking and choosing, and putting together the film. When a person appears in nonfiction film, the real person cannot be disentangled from the film person, the person as a being in film.[4]

Art is involved in our lives, whether one is a projector and creator in one's life, or one merely deals gracefully, creatively, with what occurs—taking direction in a sense. As Thoreau puts it,

> It is something to be able to paint a particular picture, or to carve a statue, and so to make a few objects beautiful; but it is far more glorious to carve and paint the very atmosphere and medium through which we look, which morally we can do. To affect the quality of the day, that is the highest of arts. (Thoreau 83)

Leontes says in the final scene of *The Winter's Tale*,

> What fine chisel
> could ever yet cut breath?

He implies that the supposed statue of Hermione, which he sees before him now, must be a woman, something beyond a work of art, such are the signs of life about her. (Hermione is the name of Helen's daughter.[5]) But Leontes implies more deeply—the play implies, Shakespeare implies—that to "cut breath" is a wonderful aim for art, which we can actually consider possible—art making life. To "cut breath" may be to kill, but it is to create as well. What is at stake in art—conceivably—or in morality welling from so deep a source as creation, is to die into life.

When Helen in Euripides's *Helen* wishes she had been "like a picture rubbed out," she uses the words to mean a portrait picture, originally a *statue*—as with a statue dedicated to a deity or great person—is "disanointed" or "un-anointed." Helen in the play comes finally to a surprising, joyous, earthy reunion with her husband, Menelaus. With Helen as with Shakespeare's Hermione, what is in question is a desacralizing, in a sense, and a bringing to earth, to life, of a woman made into a statue, an image—a woman put into a corner of the mind. Could the unearthly seeming ending of *Blonde Venus*, with ritual-like movement and abundant music, perhaps, amount to such a coming to earth, to life?

Blonde Venus will take us to a new realization of how art and life stand to each other. The film is to be surrendered to provisionally, in the way of a possibility to be seen. This might, if we will allow it, modify the standing of art in our own lives—how we think, how we live. We are given the seed, we are touched. Are we to fear this? We cannot know. The line between sympathy and judgment is the hard-line concern that criticism must tread if it is to save us. It is a hard line to walk.[6]

Metamorphosis is going on rampantly in Helen's story in *Blonde Venus*. The energies of it seem to generate the course of the film, the woman's adventures, throughout. But giving it only a second thought will bring one to realize that the film deals with the external forces driving Helen only conventionally, or as a given of this *kind* of story. The emphasis of the film—the real oddity that demands a response—is Helen/Dietrich, odd being, in motion in stillness, conjurer with her own destiny.

Conjurer even of the ending, the reconciliation or submission? The scene looks strange, perhaps with the promise of life. It brings the film to an end as if bursting with implication that cannot be shown. As Eliot puts it in *Four Quartets*,

> . . . the end of all our exploring
> Will be to arrive where we started
> And know the place for the first time. (208)

We are in the realm of what is "unknown, remembered." We have been told that "[h]ome is where one starts from," starts as at a beginning, put into the past as one moves on, but also "starts" as if in fear or wonder, at every point up to the end and beyond, embarking at last upon what is so strange, albeit familiar, that it cannot be represented, not be made part of a story (as happens with the ending of Chaplin's *City Lights*).

From *Four Quartets*:

> We must be still and still moving
> Into another intensity
> . . . in my end is my beginning. (189)

The idea that what happens to Helen is at once her creation and her destiny would accord in its doubleness with the nature of Sternberg's filming, at once highly artificial and imposingly thing-y. The material world we are so sensible of in Sternberg, was once there before the camera, a beginning for the film—a world there in the past. Now, as we watch, we are caught up in film imagination, where the material world is forever a new beginning for the *meanings* of the film, the directions it takes, for our own responses and thoughts. What happens to Helen is the world's imposition and also her own imagination and willing, if we are able to see her as a film being, a being made of film, of the nature of film in its doubleness, where reality and groundedness (home) and the markedness of time are also, at once, a beyond-reality and a beyond-groundedness and a readiness forever to be reread. We are all beings of film in this sense.

Someone will say, isn't it a delusion to think that what the world hands us, or compels us to, is our creation? Isn't this just a way of cheering ourselves up about what ought to be minded—hated—seen through—and changed? I say just that we have to look at the case at hand. We have to go with Helen/Dietrich through the story of this film. Energies are at work to make the final scene seem strange, energies that are perhaps bound to force change in any imaginable future. Whose energies are these? Sternberg's? Who is Sternberg—not the man, nor anyone's definition of a director, but the director at work, now, in this film? Sternberg is famous for the Flaubertian remark (also sounding like Cathy in *Wuthering Heights*, speaking of Heathcliff), "I am Miss Dietrich; Miss Dietrich is me." How is this so, if it is so, in the film?[7]

The film has opened with a shot down onto a water surface, with Dietrich's name and the title of the film superimposed.

The rest of the credits follow, as the shot of the water is held. Tree trunks and branches are reflected on the surface, as from the bank of the water, at the bottom of the frame, and we clearly see in the water a small circle of strong light reflected as well, perhaps the sun, but possibly a filmmaker's lamp. That the first thing the film shows us is a surface reflecting light and recognizable images ought to tell us that film itself is a subject of this film. And the confusion, if we press it, about the sun or the artificial lamp, is part of this larger issue—are we in the natural world, or are we in a film studio or on a film set? What exactly would be the difference? Is the natural world, unlike what is filmed in a studio, there anyway—there not necessarily to be filmed? But film exists now. Can we really say of the natural world that it is not there to be filmed?

At the moment the last of the credits disappears, a woman emerges swimming through the water, from the lower left side of the frame. She has blond hair, so she may well be Dietrich and the "Blonde Venus" of

the title, Venus who is born in water. She is apparently nude, a little under water and obscured. She and the water surface are only a short distance away from the camera, so that her body comes to fill much of the frame, and her swimming motion is enough to destroy all the surface reflection of trees.

This woman emerges from the area we take to be behind the camera setup, the place of the director, so that either she is sent forth by the director from close to himself—perhaps is a part of him—or is herself the director, coming from behind the camera into the film, making literal here the way directors commonly enter or become their work. Thus, the story of Helen that will follow would be her own presentation of herself, her own film of herself. The fact that the swimming woman obliterates the "film world" of trees reflected on the water surface suggests that a real woman now wreaks havoc with the supposed art of film—that we move a step closer now to a real woman and her world than film usually—perhaps ever previously—has allowed us to do.

There is the suggestion of a birth here—the nudity, the start of activity in the water, the shock of the swimmer's disruption. Perhaps the birth is that of an idea—the idea that the woman is in some sense the director, that this film is a woman's film. But by birth, I mean not just

the proposal of a notion, but the becoming flesh and life (on film) of what is more than a name or a definition.

The idea that the woman is to be identified with the director is an idea the film will tell us more and more about. We have to see more to assess this idea. But the film will never reach the point where what it has to tell can be summed up and translated into words. What we know, we have as a film experience. Words and thought, one hopes, can help to point us into the experience, or remove what holds us up, or away, from the experience—or help the experience to develop and flower.

We have seen the words "Directed by Josef von Sternberg" up on the screen. And we have, in 1932 or now, some idea that at least some film directors are artists who observe the world, and reflect, and work and create in the medium of film with integrity, with character identifiable from film to film. In 1932 in America, one might have thought of Griffith, Erich von Stroheim, perhaps Lubitsch, perhaps—with their special situation as performers—Chaplin and Keaton. If one were cultivated in film, one would have known about Eisenstein, Murnau, Lang. Sternberg himself, with several silent films, *The Blue Angel*, and a few early Hollywood talkies, would have held a place somewhere between the well-known entertainer-producer-director, such as De Mille, and the more artistic Germans, noted for mood and style and the making of a dream world or nightmare world.

We do not know now—and we did not know in 1932—what a film director entirely is, what measure of responsibility belongs to this figure decidedly present to our minds in the world of film. We do not know where to see a director as between observer and contriver or imaginer. (It's the same, really, with a dramatist or novelist or poet.) In *Blonde Venus* a woman comes from the place behind the camera, shattering the reflecting water surface. Does a director enter the film, conceivably at every moment, so as to shatter what we might think had been set up? Is this event, or perpetual event, like a nude woman swimming before the good-humored eye of the camera, to strains of Romantic ballet music (what we hear now)? What is all this to us, just now, in the film? Perhaps the answer lies in the quality of Sternberg's, and Dietrich's, humor, characteristically life-and-death serious (ironic, trenchant about the way of the world) and at the same time above it all, ready to propose any fancy—any—as on a par with what we are accustomed to take seriously.

A passage of Sternbergian humor begins to unfold. There is a long-held shot of a group of women swimming at a distance, behind foliage which we see in the foreground—the group presumably includes the lone woman we saw emerge into view just a moment ago. This new shot seems to make the camera a spy now, an outsider. Or perhaps the shot just projects a picturesque view of the swimmers, a scene at a distance, emanating from the woman the camera has just been close to, or identified with—all this a view inviting intrusion. In any case, there is a cut to a group of men hikers, with the camera moving laterally to keep them in view.

One of the men is being led by a dachshund, out front and straining at its leash. The film seems to acknowledge the phallic interest of

the observer-intruder, conceivably the film's own phallic interest. This shot, like the view of the lake, too may be the projection of the original woman, summoning up the men—but perhaps that would not contradict the idea of Sternberg acknowledging his phallic interest—such is the mystery of what we are faced with. From whatever point of view the shot comes, the dachshund looks a bit silly, and the dog's master is a wispy man with a comic hat, and a high-pitched voice as it turns out, who behaves ineffectually throughout the ensuing scene, though he very much desires the women—or acts as if he does.

The men learn about the women from the driver of a taxi incongruously here, they note, "in the middle of the Black Forest." The car is serving the women and comes to serve the men by providing information. Perhaps the taxi, as a machine, represents the camera and all the apparatus of film intruding in this world of nature, or faery romance—or would the taxi be the incongruous heart and source, or generator, of this world? The men come to the bank of the water to look at the women, as if sent by the women's movie apparatus, the taxi (the next Taxi in this film will be a woman, Helen/Dietrich's colleague in the nightclub dressing room). The men are now seen from a camera position out in the water, as if by the women, though the women have not made it known that they see the men. The women have been called by the taxi driver "actresses." Perhaps they are acting unawareness. The men make a noise, and the women become upset, showing that they see the men. And now Dietrich appears for the crucial first encounter with Herbert Marshall, which will round out the forest scene. Her face appears in a close shot, seen from the bank.

Her hair is disarrayed, perhaps a little wet at the ends, but her face is dry and her make-up fresh—a situation suggesting something of the goddess, or at least the imaginer or dreamer in her own realm—we all see ourselves in dreams or fancies in a way that could not really be.

Dietrich is quietly outraged, amused, and interested all at once, as Marshall talks her into making a date for later. She has authority. But Marshall has, as we keep cutting back to him, a force of his own. Clothed and hatted, substantial in face and body, older seeming than Dietrich, speaking his beautiful English a little off into the distance, he seems not just a man but a being of another kind than Dietrich, jarring to imagine as a partner for her. Their suppressed smiles bring the two together. They are interested in what is happening between them. But she tells him he ought to be ashamed, and he replies, "I am."

There is something traumatic, unnatural while yet natural—regrettable, though it is the way one wants to go—about the meeting of women and men. The difficult but forward-looking feeling of it, captured at the beginning of *Blonde Venus* (and perhaps at the end), is something Sternberg films study in the odd pairings of Dietrich with Emil Jannings in *The Blue Angel* (*Der blaue Engel*, 1930), with Victor McLaglen in *Dishonored* (1931), and with Clive Brook in *Shanghai Express* (1932).

The serious questions about Dietrich's origins and her role as imaginer-creator, and the serious note in her meeting with Marshall, focusing upon ashamedness, are caught up in the above-it-all humorous unfolding of the film, with visual wipes and light music and archness in the playing, as if the humor is an attitude to life, that can admit anything. Every element

of the scene, sparkling or sober, stands in a context of other elements of varied mood, so that the world seems not to have to be warped all one way. *Blonde Venus* at this stage might possibly turn into *Gaslight* or *Letter from an Unknown Woman*, or become a mythic celebration of a goddess, or a festive comedy like *The Lady Eve*. The humor we share in—this way that we come to know the matter of the film—amounts to an ability to contemplate something, or conjure a mood, while keeping in mind other things than the one that is momentarily singled out.

I am virtually giving T. S. Eliot's definition of wit (in his essay "Andrew Marvell," 1921). Surely it is no mere coincidence that an interest or enthusiasm modern literature finds in 1921 should be met again in the sophisticated Hollywood films of Sternberg in the 1920s and early 1930s. What the human spirit wants, or looks to, is to be found in various forms and places all at once. Another temperament that suggests itself here is Stravinsky, tender and distanced—Sternberg's memoir, *Fun in a Chinese Laundry*, read remarkably like Stravinsky in his reminiscences and chats.

The striking and thought-provoking, though also smile-provoking, continues in *Blonde Venus* in order to get us out of the opening scene and into Dietrich and Marshall's domestic life. The kicking feet of Dietrich and then those of another swimmer, as the women depart from the shore in a huff, dissolve to the kicking feet of a child apparently in a bath. The little boy, as he now appears to be, emerges into view, his skin luminous and remarkable to contemplate, as he talks to his mother (out of view) about being a crocodile, and plays in the water. All we see around him is water, milky white in Sternberg's lighting. Where are we? Is it someone's imagination? Then this image dissolves to a view of New York Harbor, with the boy in the bath looming large in the dissolve against the skyscrapers of Manhattan, plenty of the harbor water visible in the foreground. The boy's bath is now New York Harbor. Is this *his* imagination? Whose, then? There is a cut now to the boy in a bath again, this time surrounded by an apartment setting, far from glamorous, with Dietrich at the side of the tub, talking to the boy and washing him. We have gotten from the courtship in Germany to the home life. *How* have we gotten here—what is the film telling us about how we have gotten here?

The images of water, repeated and varied, at the start of *Blonde Venus* are striking, unaccountable-seeming, inviting to thought, letting oneself be touched by the film's imagination, letting oneself go toward what is brought before one, as we find in the opening of Pindar's First Olympian Ode, "Best of all things is water . . ."—*Ariston men hudor* (what an odd word *hudor*, water, is—think of it, sound it)—when the poet will go on to talk about things very much other than water: public games, horses, the correction of myths, honor to the gods. But then an important element in the Pindar will be the love and favors of Poseidon, god of the sea; the poem's principal mythical character, Pelops (who will win a horse race, like the contemporary victor celebrated in the poem), goes down to the "grey sea" in his time of need, and cries to Poseidon, and is answered and helped. The sea is, or figures, one's source of strength—the expanse or depth one can conjure from, and project one's life forward from.

In *Blonde Venus* the reflecting water surface at the start suggests the film's screen, and Dietrich's birth to herself there is like the director's coming to be or coming to life in his (her) medium. Film is a way of doing things, or it figures the imaginative way of doing things that is there in life itself. Dietrich's birth turns into the boy's birth, through her film-like imagination or will, or film-like destiny, pictured as water. Water, milky in the first image of the boy, as if stirred with potent substances, suggests the universe of powers where we passively, as it were, before them (Poseidon, film as an institution, child bearing and family, language or imagination as an institution . . .). But the reflecting surface, and the way it takes different shapes from moment to moment, suggests activity, sparked by will, one's own or that of the friend one can call forth and direct.[8]

Pindar's First Olympian is haunted by—its mythic story in a sense motivated by—the erotic interest Poseidon takes in the boy Pelops; the poem first names Pelops as he who was desired and carried away as a child by Poseidon. The film image of the boy in milky water focuses our attention on this boy's skin, his nudity, without at first providing any narrative to interpret or channel or civilize the erotic energy put into play.

And of course Helen/Venus/Dietrich will eventually carry the boy off from home, like Poseidon. Has she an erotic interest in the boy? Like that of any mother? Both the poem and the film have something elaborate to make of the raw material of the desirable boy, but neither work ever neutralizes the elemental suggestion of erotic interest in a child. Perhaps such a wild card as this passion is necessary for imagination, enabling that as the way of getting forward in life.

Here, or with *Nashville* (1975) and the Donne poem cited in chapter 1, it is wonderful, the resonance films have with poetry, as if poetry and film belong to the same greater imagination, or poetry prophesies film, or is its unacknowledged legislator, as Shelley would have it. Creative engagement is the way to make the acknowledgement and enhances the power of the work.

The young Pelops in Pindar is said to have "a shoulder gleaming with ivory." This may be said figuratively, but perhaps—Pindar wants to be ambiguous about it, the story is so awful—the ivory refers to a repair for the boy's having been cannibalized in his father Tantalus's plot to serve human flesh to the gods. In any case the suggestion of ivory has us objectify Pelops's skin, and also think of what is not in fact ivory, what is living and human in the skin of a boy. Similarly, Sternberg's image of the boy in milky water—the human being put on film, the Sternbergean lighting both linking the boy's skin to the water and distinguishing between the two—has us see the child as object and as living non-object at once. The poem and the film ask what seeing and seeing as are. In life we have difficulty settling what it is we see, and we are caught up in love or attraction nevertheless. Perhaps this situation drives imagination forward, to get us beyond the stage of confusion, or to keep recapturing it.

Pelops in Pindar's poem is first noticed by Poseidon when the Fates lift the boy from a cleansing or purifying cauldron, *katharou lebetos*—shades of the prophecy scene in *Macbeth*. This lifting from the cauldron may mean just being born, or may mean a purification from cannibalism. Perhaps to be born is to undergo such purification, or to begin the process of purification, from the cannibalism of our being given fleshly identity with others. We are born already consumed by others and need make our way free.

In *Blonde Venus* the boy's birth into the film, like his mother's a few moments before, takes place in a cauldron of sorts. The women's swimming place becomes the boy's mysterious milky cauldron, which becomes New York Harbor as cauldron, which becomes the actual bathtub in an apartment, where a conversation can begin—a new life. The series of births is perhaps a series of purifications, or beginnings, leaps into new life. This is at least a wish, what drives things forward, on the part of the woman, the child, the fashioner of the film. Sternberg in his memoir likens his work as a director discovering and developing Dietrich to the Angkor Wat wall sculpture picturing the god Vishnu churning a sea of milk to bring forth a remarkable woman.

Virtually Helen's last words to the boy, before retelling and enacting the fairy-story courtship with his father at the end of the film, are, "Would you like me to get you nice and clean for bed?" And we then see her moving about the apartment with a basin of water. Cleansing for life, as earlier in the film, becomes cleansing for bed or the realm of dreams, which will generate the ending of the film, or ending-beginning. But of course dreams may have generated all that has happened so far, so that one kind of dream is now cleansed away for another.

Near the end of his ode Pindar comments on the progress from dream to dream, with a pragmatic conclusion about it all. He notes that wonders (*thaumata*) are all about us, and that what people tell (*phatis*, or *pheme*—fame—which turns into *mythoi*) may be a lie and may deceive, and he notes, ambiguous as to how he feels about it, that grace or beauty or charm—*charis*—can make the unbelievable believable (the *apiston* is made *piston*). Pindar resolves what he has stirred up, just by looking to the days to come—they will be the witnesses (*martyres*) knowing the most (*sophotatoi*).

Where Pindar starts out, "Best of all things is water," I read him as also saying, "best of all things is poetic imagination." Poetic imagination, which is also film imagination, transforms poet, audience, the present and past, the world. All is transformed, but there is a test of reality, of the days to come. In the last lines of the poem the poet's song is called *sophia*: insight, skill, craft, good sense, wisdom, philosophy—or what philosophy loves.

The start of *Blonde Venus*, with all its water, says, "Film is the subject here." Perhaps it must be the subject, or be one of the subjects, in any intelligent film. As Stanley Cavell insists, as I noted in connection with *Nashville*, film imagination figures, and also sometimes inspires—gets into, motivates into being—imagination by which we know and live. *Blonde Venus* will go on from its start to test film imagination against recognizable life, as life is available to film—and it is so, very strikingly, for all one must be cautious about this. The documentary power of film—what this sets us thinking about, testing image against experience—is the witness for film imagination. Helen/Dietrich is a strange being. Can a woman be *this* being?

Maurice Bowra writes about Pindar, "His guiding and central theme is the part of experience in which human beings are exalted or illumined by a divine force . . . the enhancement of consciousness which his athletes enjoy in the moment of triumph . . . the joy beyond ordinary emotions as it transcends and transforms them" (xvii). Pindar is a distinctive intelligence. But to give his picture of transformation, and to bring his audience into the experience, Pindar allows himself to be written, so to speak, like *Blonde Venus* in a way, by the images and myths and concerns of the world about him—the wonders at large, we might say. And Pindar writes choric odes for public performance—events like attending theater or a film. The form seems to have been invented by that Stesichorus who gives the alternative story of Helen.

Film can be a picture of, or an invitation to come into, or come into understanding of, transformation, transformation in a world recognizably kin to the world we know, as we lead life. Life is transformed in the very coming into being of films, life becoming film. And transformation comes in the particular unfolding of each story, with all the aspects of film that convey the story, notably, in Hollywood, in the comedies of remarriage and the melodramas of the unknown woman described by Stanley Cavell—and think of transformation in films of Griffith, Chaplin, Ford, Welles, as well as all the directors I consider in this book.

It is the great contribution of auteur criticism of Hollywood film to recognize that an intelligence generates the images and shapes the actors' performances and the stories in the most interesting films—and this is not to say that the director as a person is solely responsible for things.[9] The director gives ground to the ideas and work of others, and to the power of the world to project itself on film. There is a Pindar-like intelligence at work in a good Hollywood film—what Heidegger identifies as the poet in all forms of art and making—bringing, with wild and ever-new coherence, something into being. The poet in film is identifiable, as it were, personally—we have no other term for it—and a Ford, a Lang, a

Chaplin, does mark a film, and follow out and develop concerns from film to film. But the intelligence is finally the film's own, the *occasion's*. There is something in the film person-like but not literally of a person that we draw toward and discern and think about. Part of recognizing the intelligence of a film like *Blonde Venus* is to see that it can talk to, can be illumined by, a poem of Pindar's.

We desire gods, or desire to be transformed and made god-like; at least we are *interested* in these things. The "unknown woman" and her fate, or her creation of her life, compels us, like the athlete carried beyond himself in dizzying accomplishment.

We come to the New York domestic life of Helen and her family, where the film's background music stops for a time, and we pay attention to daily life rendered with a certain realism. We see the boy in his bathtub, various toys and implements around the rim, Dietrich kneeling on the right side of the bath, busy washing the boy. A modest kitchen is visible through an arch in the background. This is the same boy as in the milky water and New York Harbor images; he is being directed in the same way—behaving in the same way—his earlier "I'm a crocodile" becoming now "I'm a fish." But the open imaginative quality of the boy in the milky water and New York Harbor images turns into an ordinary boy in his bath, conversing with his mother. The boy is his mother's—his mother's creation—his birth in water an extension of her own birth in water, but the boy has an individual existence and begins to make his own claims. In the transition now we are made to feel that the mythic or open, and the everyday or down-to-earth, are strongly tied, are in a sense the same, while we are made sharply aware of the different ways these realms appear—their real differences, perhaps.

Dietrich is business-like, even brusque, hurrying the boy and saying his father will be home soon, but she is at the same time a good mother, entirely poised, and considerate of the child. To his "I'm a fish" she replies, "Oh excuse me, I thought you were a boat," engaging with him in a tone that does not really challenge or upset him—the boy remains relaxed, happy-seeming, malleable. Dietrich firmly removes toys to the side of the tub, including a bugle the boy blows right into her face—but she is not hectic or combative. Dietrich appears here made-up and beautiful and very much Dietrich, but dressed in the modest white blouse and skirt and apron of a housewife, her hair plain and a little disheveled, entirely believable for the role. The strange being from the start of the film may be thought of as tamed and confined in the mother's role. But she seems unharassed here, though busy, and she has an air of enjoyment and of a superior way of being amused—as of a superior being—which Dietrich is so good at conveying even in her submissiveness in any situation—"Oh excuse me, I thought you were a boat." Her domestic incarnation is real. But the touch of enjoyment or superiority links to the rush of energy and the suggestion of creativeness in the opening of the film.

Seeing *Blonde Venus* for the first time, it is hard to tell where the film as a whole is going for a time as we are given a succession of scenes centering about the family's home life. The ambulatoriness here seems to imitate the tensions and relaxations of an ordinary life that may go nowhere, except into suffering due to lack of money. But when we have once seen the film, we realize that the place it is headed now is the "Hot Voodoo" number in the nightclub where Helen will soon go to work. This is the decisive poetic scene the film wants to get to, and in light of it the homelife scenes begin to take on a shape: they seem Helen/Dietrich's means of getting to where she wants to be.

When Dietrich is bathing the boy and tells him they must hurry because his father will be home soon, there emerges from the right side of the screen, by means of a wipe, a new scene where the father visits a doctor's office.

The scene is as if conjured up by Dietrich, the wipe associating her with Sternberg, or with the director of the earlier part of the film, executing wipes, who may of course be taken as Dietrich there too. The father, the Herbert Marshall character, is a research scientist, and he thinks he has terminal radiation poisoning. He has come to a doctor to "sell his body," as he puts it, to provide for his wife and child. This is a fierce thing to imagine Dietrich as imagining, or projecting upon her husband—some sort of revenge? For what? His having fathered the child on her? His possessing her as if it is *her* body that has been sold? But of course, if Dietrich is imagining/creating this, she is also imagining a way out: Ned will be told of a cure if he can raise the money to get back to Germany, and Helen's going to the nightclub to perform will be the means to get the money.

The doctor's office scene is presented very conventionally; taken by itself, it is one of those not especially poetic scenes done the way Hollywood almost automatically performs a given narrative task—the sort of scene that sometimes occurs in *Blonde Venus* and seems to make it impure as a Sternberg film. A distant shot gives us Marshall entering the large, unremarkable set of the office, and meeting the doctor. The camera moves slowly in on the doctor as the conversation starts to get interesting, and then there is cutting back and forth in a series of close-ups of the two men as they talk. Finally, there is a medium-length shot as the doctor gets up from his desk and moves closer to Marshall, so that the two men finish talking both in the same shot, now closer to each other in understanding and sympathy. The scene is not short, and the dialogue and delivery is stagey-formal: "I want to sell you my body." "Why do you particularly want to sell it to *me*?" (slight emphasis) . . . At the end of the scene the doctor is playing with a human skull he picks up from his desk, as if in heavy-handed unconscious suggestiveness.

All of this takes on a different cast if seen as Helen's projection. Then the very idea for the scene is the important thing. And because the idea—revenge, if it is that—is severe, grotesque, a distance is kept between the idea and full filmic realization. The scene is, as it were, a whim of Helen's which she would not peer at too closely.

I do not propose that the doctor's office scene is just Helen's imagination, or even a "real" scene—just—in which she has had a plotting hand. (How did Ned get radiation poisoning? Through work Helen drove him to? His laboratory is at home—did she spill something or leave something uncovered?) The whole film can be taken as Helen's dream, or her act of will. But this is only a possibility which renders the whole truth more interesting. What the film suggests is that the scene is dream and will and at the same time what happens, what comes to Helen the dreamer or willer from the outside. (Shades of *Hail Mary* [*Je vous salue, Marie*, 1985]!) That we see a filmed encounter, with Ned and the other man actually there and saying certain words, weighs for the scene being outside Helen—real, if one likes. And the mixture of styles in this film—Sternberg-poetic, and conventional—weighs in this same direction. We keep seeing the characters and their activities in different stylistic lights, which argues for the persistence and actuality of everything through the twists and turns of the film style. But in the world we live in outside film, we can never separate absolutely what is there outside ourselves, and what is willed or will-colored. Film insists on this—it is the very basis of film. In a sense, we never live in a world outside of film. We never did, even before film came about. The doctor's office scene is there on its own—one would not deny it—but the way it is filmed and placed, suits the working of Dietrich's will.

This scene is followed by one of Dietrich, Marshall, and the boy at home in the evening, sitting in their living room. The one shot, of all three of them, is held a long time, until Dietrich rises to carry the boy off to bed. The frame is crammed with decor and quiet activity, with views at the back out the windows to walls and buildings of the city.

The richness of the image, different from any we have seen in the film, suggests a symbolic weightedness to things, meaning that we can sense but not make out clearly, as if in a dream. There is almost too much to take in, so that we simply accept it as a world, reality, while we feel the weight of shape or depth below or beyond. Ned, facing us from an armchair, reads a book, the large kind held in two hands, like a magician's or priest's book. In a moment he will call the boy by name—Johnny—for the first time in the film, as if exercising a patriarchal right. Dietrich, her back to us, bent over a bit, sews at a sewing machine—an ordinary task, but also the first suggestion of Athena, a suggestion that Helen is stitching out life, or stitching out a strip of film, not yet putting her face into the life or film she is setting up.

The boy shoots a popgun in our direction, or in the camera's direction, aiming at a toy bird that hops up and down on a table in the foreground (it seems to be a giant goose, with someone, perhaps a witch, riding it—altogether a figure from fairy tale, or Rabelais—an artist who makes *use* of fairy tale). The boy is Helen's, and inventive mechanical toys, and toy masks, will be associated with him throughout the film, emphasizing that he lives in a medium of imagination. He is created by imagination, and he is creative himself. Mechanicalness links the toys and imagination to the idea of film. Toward the end of the film, the toy bird *becomes*, as it were, the strange, plump real birds that sit and move about in Helen's apartment in the border town where, accompanied by the boy, she is playing director in her most seemingly Dietrich-created environment. (Pindar tells us in the Fourth Pythian Ode that Aphrodite worked her powers by means of a "maddening bird" she brought forth pinned to a wheel and spun on. Sappho says to Aphrodite, "Beautiful keen birds have brought you / Whirring their dense plumage / Over the black earth . . . and you / Had a smile on your deathless face" [transl. Terence Du Quesne]. The first shot of *The Blue Angel* gives us chickens in a yard, and birds and eggs become a running theme in Professor Immanuel Rath's journey to ecstasy and humiliation with Lola Lola.)

The boy shoots his popgun toward the camera, which has some claim to be Dietrich's camera—she who is momentarily turning her back to us, as if hiding, perhaps as a director always is. The boy shoots at his mother, the camera, as if shooting film back at her shooting film, acknowledging he is her creation and extension, an artist in cooperation with her—and perhaps also resisting her, asserting his integrity. The boy shoots toward us, the audience, reminding us that we may be being created by the film, ourselves film subjects. Our role is to be receptive, like the camera, and also, like it, creative.

This brief scene, all one shot, is a real enough picture of family life, but meanings that have to do with creating life as if creating film are there to emerge—meanings that tie in with clear and imposing declarations made at crucial junctures of the film. All this—loud declarations at certain points, with seemingly throwaway passages that bear out meaning if one looks closely—is typical of how good Hollywood films of the period work.

It is said to be time for bed, and with a cut, we see Dietrich carrying Johnny piggyback into the bedroom and putting him into his crib. He wants to hear the "Germany story," and in order to tell it Helen summons her husband, Ned, naming him for the first time, as if to answer his naming of Johnny just before. A shot follows of Ned rising in the other room to come in—the camera here seeming very much at Helen/Dietrich's command.

Ned can be seen throughout the film in a way this moment gives the clue to—that is, as subordinate to Helen, at her command, and thus a means in her plan for herself, or in her unfolding of herself. He can be seen this way even when he is difficult or dangerous. People impinge on us, but they are also what we make of them. This state of things film renders back to us, explores, and of course leads us further into—for better or worse, depending on the intelligence of the film, and on whether we will be awake to it.

During the telling of the story of the parents' fairy-tale meeting and courtship in Germany, Helen is at first subdued, the business-like but kind enough mother. But she becomes imaginative, stressing her own activity in her past. In her reactions, during the cutting around among the three of them as the story proceeds and everyone speaks, she seems moved and made happy when Ned speaks of meeting her and then seeing her magical appearance in the theater. She herself stresses the erotic in the story, starting out, "I had spring fever," as if this was the motive for everything that ensued, and eventually she gives Ned what looks like a very serious kiss, when the two of them are acting out the part of the story where they did kiss. Dietrich walks her fingers along the crib's side to illustrate walking, and they look very bare and leggy and bold, stressing her activity and initiative, past and present. Finally, Helen ends the scene, having sent Ned out, by singing the German lullaby, using a little music box carrousel, stressing her art and linking voice and song with a machine, the imaginative-mechanical—a pointer to film.

With a close-up of Johnny's face, asleep, the film dissolves to a new scene for Helen and Ned in a new sitting room, or new part of the sitting room we have seen previously. Because of the view of the boy asleep, the new scene might appear as his dream or projection, he who has been identified already as an extension of his mother, or as her colleague in imagination. In the new scene we see Dietrich walk in and sit on the left side of the room, facing us, fairly close to us, and she begins to embroider on a large frame set up before her. Her identity as Athena-like artist-weaver is stressed, with perhaps a pun on embroidery frame/film frame. Marshall is sitting on the right, his back to us, working at his microscope, smoking, surrounded by a chemist's flasks and other laboratory instruments, cooking something up in *his* way. With the two of them sitting at their respective work, the scene mirrors the previous living-room scene, just before the bedtime story, and underscores the symbolic quality of that earlier scene. Perhaps the scene now will lead to another artistic episode, as the first sitting-room scene led to the bedtime story and song.

Helen, rising and approaching Ned, asserts she will go back to her "old work"—we assume she means the stage, though larger and more mysterious things may be hinted at—to earn money for the treatment Ned needs back in Germany. It is as if the two of them are at work together in this laboratory to produce the life that will follow—a dimly lighted laboratory, the human figures unnaturally bright in the context, as if to suggest unseen possibilities or uncomprehended powers in the background and setting, all in contrast to the "normal" brighter, more complicated lighting of the first living-room scene. This collaboration in the laboratory is recalled later when, after the long episode of Dietrich's nightclub performance, we see Ned again in the apartment, collapsed in a chair as if exhausted among his instruments and bottles—as if he has had a part in doing the nightclub number, conjuring it up from the home setting, and has spent himself. The present conversation about going back to her work ends with Dietrich moving her head and eyes and upper body about energetically, looking ready for action, and full of thoughts. And there is a long dissolve to the kicking feet of a chorus line (recalling the swimmers' kicking feet earlier) with jaunty piano music playing—all of which represents only what this woman has in her mind, maybe: the kicking feet are not visually part of the scene we go to next, or of any actual scene in the film, though the music and the sound of dancing feet continue in the next scene, as if it is all happening next door.

The shot of the kicking feet dissolves in and then dissolves out to a shot of the reception room of a theatrical agent's office. Is this an "actual scene" or, like the kicking feet, an idea or wish-image—if that is in fact what they were? Both scenes are actual and wish-image at once, the film asks us to think. The actuality is stressed as the scene goes on and we learn that Helen is here to take steps that will lead her on into her world of work and all the ensuing parts of the film. Or do we want to regard all the rest as dream, or mere wish embodied?

We see Helen in the foreground with other figures, including the receptionist. She is now elegantly dressed, with a showy fur collar and smart hat—a new woman, we might begin to think. The dialogue is poetic—like all the dialogue of the film, of such a film—rendering an immediate situation, but pointing also to a deeper situation or transaction:

> RECEPTIONIST: Have you come to be placed?
>
> HELEN: Yes.
>
> RECEPTIONIST: What's your name?
>
> HELEN (quietly): Faraday
>
> RECEPTIONIST: What's that?
>
> HELEN: Helen Faraday.

This is the first time the woman is named in the film. "Faraday" suggests science, recalling Michael Faraday, and Helen seems to declare herself a scientist and at one with her husband, as the previous laboratory scene has suggested. "Helen" is the woman's own name, unlike the surname that belongs to her husband, but we cannot say whether "Helen" was given to her by her parents, or whether she gives herself this name. (Has she parents? Of course, like all of us—but in a sense, like all of us, no, she is an original.) Helen has come to be placed—she is placing herself, though "place" is an inadequate word for the process, perhaps endless, that is set in motion.

The image here is symbolic, just as the words are. Helen is in the foreground with a few others, all in deep shadow; the bright office with more people opens out behind this shadowy group.

The camera's view on things, with this lighting, is conspicuously odd, perhaps to suggest that this woman's going out to earn extra money for her family is in fact an odd thing, a strange adventure. Helen and those she is dealing with close up are virtually shadows, transfigured

persons, and conspicuously, film figures—what they are, or how they appear, being very much the result of camera placement and lighting. Something like film imagination is involved in the step Helen is taking into a new life.

These figures are black, as if in a sense they have become Negroes, to use the polite, respectful term of the time. Actual black people are about to enter the film in the next episode, at the nightclub owner's office to which the theatrical agent will take Helen, and black people will come more and more into the film as it goes on. There is the stuttering bartender in the nightclub, set against the eloquent women performers impersonating tribal blacks on stage—though the bartender does get said what he wants to say, and he is addressed seriously, and listened to, by a woman at the bar. Then there is the babysitter, Viola, in Helen's hotel in Norfolk, when she is on the run. And most important there is Helen's servant/companion in the border town, Cora (Hattie McDaniel). Cora and Helen seem to have a relationship quite as equals, different as they are. McDaniel is forthright: Dietrich is, as always, very much Dietrich and staying somewhat within herself—but without superiority here, giving. Each of the two women attends entirely to what the other is saying or doing, or showing, with no sign of suspicious distance kept.

Throughout the film there is a blurring of black and white identity—by the receptionist's office image of shadow people, for example; and by the coming of black people into some prominence when there is no narrative need for it, as if the black people are just people encountered accidentally by the camera. Then, of course, there is the "Voodoo" number. In the film, the blurring of black and white goes with the blurring of male and female identity—enterprising woman, fused with a son; woman in man's clothes—and the blurring of activity and passivity, director and subject, director and star.

This is a black-and-white film, a film of a certain era. We look into, or enter into, a world of black and white. In a way we easily accept this world, recognizing it, yet it is transfigured, so very strange. There is a tension here—*is* this a credible world, or is it nothing, just ghosts?

This tension is played on exhaustively in Griffith's *Birth of a Nation* (1915), the first—great, is it?—film, the scandal of film. The world and the course of history depicted here—a beloved world at first, which comes to run horribly mad, the film seeming to assault the world it has made—all of this seems to reflect, or embody, the attraction and repulsion of the audience to film itself, not knowing what it has before it, not knowing what to do with it. D. W. Griffith said he was inspired to make *The Birth of a Nation*, being haunted, driven, by the image to be created of massed riders of the Ku Klux Klan charging in their white robes—white men transfigured into ghosts—so they intended—more white than ever to lord it over black people who are—the film makes it clear—mostly whites in blackface, *ideas* of black people. What are we to believe of this world? Perhaps the film is screaming at us not to believe. Perhaps *Blonde Venus* is trying to restore the sanity lost of *The Birth of a Nation*, with, now, real black people who come more and more into the life of the film—a film that, with all its wild energy, draws toward calm.

Blonde Venus's reception office shot of foreground figures in shadow, contrasted with a different-looking, opening-out background, recalls the views we have had through windows in the apartment living-room and laboratory scenes, out to city buildings and rooftops and tenement laundry lines. In a few minutes, in the nightclub owner's office we will get a background view through a large window, of black people talking in a courtyard. In all this there is the suggestion of a world beyond the foreground one we are concentrating on. This world beyond is perhaps more real, more ordinary. Perhaps it is the world from which the foreground story arises, as if the ordinary world, really concentrated on, will yield a strange story. The central "Hot Voodoo" number arises from familiar, for the times, African American dance band music that we have been hearing for some time when the number starts. And yet the background world in the film is seen framed and, as it were, screened, in the windows and in the distant-light/near-shadow contrast of the reception room. So the background world is in a sense a film world, suggesting that even the ordinary world comes to us in the aspect of something like film imagination. Film imagination is how we attend to things.

The beautifully made reception-room scene goes on as the agent enters from his inner office and the camera presses forward with him through the crowd, the camera—Helen's still?—siding for a moment with this man's authority and forwardness. But the movement through the crowd is interrupted by a cut to a close-up of Dietrich, as the agent, naturally, singles her out from the others. The close-up shot jars, with its simpler lighting and the only sign of people around Dietrich a blur.

The shot seems made in a different place from the room we have been in. It might seem a bit of narratively logical but conventional filmmaking, to give the agent's point of view, the film's creativity relaxing into standard practice. But the textural incongruity of the shot makes us realize there is something of a shock, or jumping of a gap, in the agent's noticing of Dietrich—the film technique gets at something in the mind, or takes the mind where it has never been. The isolation of the close-up gives the uncertainty, the indefinability, of who Helen/Dietrich is.

Helen has a meeting with the agent in his private office, and then both of them go and meet a nightclub manager, who agrees to give Helen a try. Both men are crude in manner, and both imply they are used to getting sexual favors from their women performers. Helen is compelled to show her legs while insisting she can do the job, is quiet and deferential, and not at all aggressive about money—"Anything I can get—it doesn't matter." Does she relish getting into this tough world? Is she simply desperate? Perhaps she cares more about having work of any kind than about the circumstances of that work or even the need for money for her husband. Perhaps she realizes that her inherent worth will show itself and eventually get her a job with good salary, and will take her far—which turns out to be the case.

A brief scene at home precedes the nightclub appearance. Helen is excited and nervous, moving about and packing her things—as if for a real departure—not looking anyone in the eye until goodbyes at the end. She is in the world of her own thoughts. Johnny presents her with a toy bear, "for luck," keeping alive his and his mother's imaginative bond—after Helen's performance, the Blonde Venus wig is seen atop this bear's head in the dressing room. And now Helen leaves her husband and child on the apartment-house landing and hurries down the stairs as if to the lower world, the camera looking up at them all from a low angle, as if inviting Helen, the one on the move, to come down—the camera placed or projected where it is by Helen to draw her and give her her fate.

We get a shot from above of the lighted show district of a city—a shot made with models, announcing a fantasy world, and not recognizably New York, as was the case with the earlier harbor shot. Already we hear nightclub music, large jazz-band music, high-energy and raunchy, such as Mae West likes to play on the gramophone in *I'm No Angel*. What we hear turns out to be the music for the voodoo number Dietrich will perform later. In a sense the number has already started.

Next, we see the nightclub sign, letters formed out of lightbulbs, which begins to flash on and off: "THE BLONDE VENUS—COME EARLY—STAY LATE." The reannouncing of the title of the film suggests that the nightclub number is the essence of the film, or that the film as a whole is virtually this nightclub number. The sexual suggestion of "COME EARLY—STAY LATE" is confirmed by the performance to follow, and other transactions in the nightclub, and by a shot of the nightclub sign later, when the bulbs are being unscrewed and handed down, the letters disappearing—an image of flagging or detumescence after Helen has left her job at the club and begun what turns out to be a barren private relationship with her wealthy patron Nick Townsend (Cary Grant).

We now see Dietrich before a mirror, so easily in film a symbol of the fragmentation of a character's identity, or of the remaking of identity. Dietrich is busy remaking her face, her hair tied back, her dressing gown disarrayed—altogether a picture of being-in-transition. The sexual motive of what is going on now in the film is borne out by the dialogue when Taxi (Rita LaRoy) introduces herself to Helen and gets the response, "Do you charge for the first mile?"—Dietrich smiling wickedly to herself in the mirror, becoming a certain Dietrich we are familiar with, for the first time in the film. Taxi says back, "Say, are you trying to ride me?" There is antagonism between the two women; Taxi has been acting resentful and difficult, and Dietrich is needling her in return. But Dietrich's surprising new spirit of fun is not just malicious or defensive—it is part of a "high" as she enters the nightclub world, and it might be seen as offering the other woman a real opening.

The lesbian undercurrent of Taxi's slang, about being "ridden," starts a vein—unless it was already started by the women's nude swimming scene at the beginning—that runs through the film. There is Helen's encounter later, on her flight from home, with the woman club manager in Norfolk (Cecil Cunningham) wearing men's clothes, her hair cut like a man's, her voice like a man's, her club having, at least at this moment, in the daytime, the ambiance of a world of women. Women sit about looking at ease with one another and not concerned to make a front or appearance for—men, it occurs to us. The club manager helps Helen against the law, out of sisterly feeling—or is it a little rush of sexual attraction—who can draw the line? Then near the end of the film there is Helen/Dietrich's appearance in drag—white top hat and tails—on the stage in Paris, with her affectionate chucking of the cheek of a chorus girl. Men's gossip, in a scene just before the stage appearance, suggests that Helen is now living a strange, detached life, from men's point of view. Is Helen living privately in a lesbian world? This is what she suggests onstage, where the audience can laugh it off, or, in an odd way, accept it.

Certainly, it is possible to feel that Helen's appearance in Paris represents her highest aspiration, her purest self, the perfect realization of her "work," the life far away and yet natural to her that she has wanted to get to. She leaves this Paris life, and goes back to New York; the film suggests there is something vital missing in the Paris life. Her work in the largest sense wants not just purity, but to include impurity. But this is not a comment on lesbianism, if lesbianism was there. We do not directly *have* lesbianism in Paris, or anywhere else in the film. It is a possibility, one dimension to a swiftly passing scene, something that may seem perfection just out of view.

Compare the situation of the possible homosexual affair in Thomas Mann's *Doctor Faustus*, that uncertain, multiply ironic tale of the development of an artist in our time. It is not clear whether the protagonist composer, Adrian Leverkühn, has an affair with the brilliant young Munich violinist, Rudi Schwerdtfeger—there are strong but uncertain suggestions that this happens. Whatever is between the two men, ends. Life goes on another way for both of them, and for Leverkühn this appears to be for the best, or to be inevitable—his work continues, and grows stronger. But then the musical work seems to draw from, to include, something positive but unspecifiable in the episode with the other man. The reader is left able to imagine homosexuality, to suppose that it is there, and to feel that it is not renounced, even though the tale, and Leverkühn's life, move on from it, and away from it.

Helen's return to her husband includes, so to speak, lesbianism: the return to Ned, being with him, invents itself as including lesbianism, made up of that as something that moved Helen on toward the return to Ned. In another story, another life, lesbianism might include heterosexuality. This is how we live, isn't it, by inclusion—unless we deny and violently contradict ourselves?

From the perspective of the whole of *Blonde Venus*, with its lesbian vein, we might look back to the border-town episode shortly before Paris, and wonder about Helen and Cora (Dietrich and McDaniel were both the subjects of Hollywood gossip about lesbian activity). Here is the only case in the film—unless the beginning, with the actresses swimming, is such a case—where women are together talking and living in a settled situation over, it is suggested, a period of time. Are Helen and Cora, so different but so at ease with each other, erotically involved? The film has us ask this question, conceive of this possibility.

The lesbian images and moments and possible story lines in *Blonde Venus* perhaps offer a connection for members of the audience: Dietrich in her character as Helen, or seen apart from her character, realizes and affirms the erotic interest of women for women. Helen, and the film, is indirect and playful. But about this Dietrich is, as about most things, at ease and self-possessed. Dietrich suggests an abandon she can fully handle. Love of women for women can perhaps exult in this film. So some women critics have said.[10]

The question of a (male or female) audience member's actual desire for Dietrich is a complicated one. Looked at one way it seems ridiculous to speak of desire for a figure onscreen. But photography, and especially film, has a way of relaying a person to us; we have a sense of the person who was there before the camera and with whom we might conceivably have contact—this is felt, oddly, even with persons from the past. Moreover, figures onscreen, like those in other kinds of art—though perhaps it is more emphatic in film—can represent the imaginative or fantasy grasp we do have of other people in life—an imaginative grasp that may be for ill or for good, for self-deception or for the precise perception of what is real and important, but delicate and fleeting and difficult of comprehension. Imagination may cooperate with a delicate reality, not just distort or obscure it.

Dietrich on film may make us feel, if not desire for Dietrich the person, *something like* the desire for some actual person—a general or freely directable desire—the fact that we desire at all. Women's desire for women, something general, may awaken here, as men's desire for women may. And Dietrich on film may make us feel, once and forever, the Dietrich-like in what it is we desire, wherever our desire may go.

Now it is difficult to separate desire for Helen/Dietrich from identification with Helen's own desire; as in life it is difficult to separate desire for another person from feeling at one with that other person's own desire, or capacity to desire (see Proust). A feeling is brought to life, that seems to run over boundaries. So another possible awakening in the face of this film is a man's desire to be, at least temporarily—provisionally—a woman, a woman interested in women's love for women, as well as a woman interested—is she, this one?—in men. A man may feel at first desire for Dietrich, but the roots begin to run here and there.[11]

In the story of *Blonde Venus* Helen's sexual activity is not specified. In a way it is hard to believe she has slept with Ned—they seem such a mismatch—the child seems in a way (like the child of Godard's Mary) just the mother's own. But of course, in another way we do accept the union with Ned, and Helen's desire for it—the paradox and mystery of this union becomes the ultimate interest of the film. Those who are matched are also always mismatched: it is amazing that people, always of different *kinds*, looked at one way, do match. Isolated images and events in *Blonde Venus* point one way, to incompatibility of Helen and Ned, but the whole film points to a scary, perhaps miraculous reality of their conjunction.

With Nick/Cary Grant, Helen has her great affair, which precipitates her break with Ned and her flight with the child. But there is something sour about the affair all along, evident in all Dietrich and Grant's scenes together after first meeting at the club: Helen constantly appears unhappy; there is a tomb-like atmosphere, spacious, empty, and cold, to the apartment we see Helen settled in at Nick's behest, reminiscent of the setting of the Stalin films cited in *WR*; there is the falseness of their vacation speedboat ride, with its back projection loudly calling attention to itself; and a falseness about their posed, overdressed break from horseback riding in a scene by a river when they say goodbye. Their reunion in Paris is not warm. Taxi complains to Helen in that first dressing-room scene that Nick has not asked her (Taxi) for sexual favors—"I wish he'd ask me . . . " she says. Perhaps he does not ask women for favors after all—perhaps this is the source of Helen's disillusion in the affair with him. At least, Taxi's comment might signal us to think about some sexual disappointment when we see things sour with Helen and Nick. (Taxi is altogether something of an alter ego for Helen. There they both are in their dressing room. Both are "good lookers," the club owner says. Taxi has an alto voice, like Dietrich's. And Helen replaces Taxi as a star at the club, and then as the woman in Nick's life—and Taxi is called to replace Helen when she leaves the club.)

And again, with women, Helen shows positive interest at moments, but what more goes on, we cannot say.

Physical involvement would seem to be a definite enough fact. People touch or they do not. But is eye involvement physical involvement? Dante and Petrarch say so (Christ said, "When he looketh on her, he hath committed adultery"). Can thought be considered physical? Is thought involvement physical involvement? Certainly, thought and imagination—mind—are present in physical experience and activity. This is the very basis of art, and art's perpetual point of insistence: here is the physical, but it is the evidence, and effect, of mind. Film emphasizes this point specially, as the medium for relaying an actual physical world and actual action, but itself a series of shadows of uncertain physical status—pure mind in a sense, a flow of mind or imagination.

Blonde Venus is full of hints about Helen's sexual activity—and for the character Helen the child would seem to be hard evidence, more than a hint, though for Dietrich, who to an extent rises above the film in her own identity, the child is a fiction, a pointer to what she might have experienced. With the hints *Blonde Venus* in its way goes as far as film ever goes. Film always, however explicit about sex, stays within the mental or imaginative—the image, even if it is a recorded image of actual activity. Film cannot give us sex. Film, like other art, gives us surfaces, pointers, perhaps really recognizing sex and feeling its force, convincing us that sex is taking place, or has taken place. It is a matter of convincing us, a matter of conviction. Much of life, perhaps all of it, gives us but surfaces, pointers, so that reality comes in fully only in our response.

In another way, *Blonde Venus* may be seen as studying the component of the potential in activity, sexual or other. Rilke meditates on this sense of the potential, in the *Duino Elegies*, responding to Picasso's painting of acrobats, *Famille de saltimbanques*. Helen in her story altogether may be seen as dwelling in the area of the potential, playing out a thought experiment or emotional experiment over the whole film, which leaves her at the end just where she started, though at once a world away from where she started. The woman Helen and the film itself seem to know the paradoxical importance of the potential, its persistence in the actual—persistence *as* potential. The woman and the film know, as in Lao Tzu, the way the potential has of overcoming or outdoing the actual—force that is not force, that tells or matters incalculably.

It is the nature of film, so this film indicates, to hold us in suspense from reality or action that might be reached—like a woman experimenting in her thoughts, or swimming in water she projects "of that wide water inescapable," as Wallace Stevens has it in "Sunday Morning."

Taxi shows Helen a bracelet gift from Nick Townsend, worth fifteen hundred dollars she says, and this arouses Helen's interest, that being the sum her husband needs to go to Germany for his cure. Then the actual performance scene in the club is begun by a transition from a close-up of Helen/Dietrich looking thoughtful over the bracelet—finally shutting her eyes as if to dream—to a shot of Nick and his table in the club, as if conjured up by Helen, with Taxi. Throughout the ensuing musical number there is business with Nick and his group, finally shots of Nick watching intently, cut in as Helen sings, this interest of Nick's leading to their meeting backstage after the performance. Maybe all this is conjured up in those moments of brooding over the bracelet.

The business with Nick and his group is rather flat, in the acting and staging and shooting. Cary Grant is a good-looking man here, with self-possession and authority, a certain kindliness, and a distance on things, staying somewhat within himself, a little like Dietrich. But he is not the rich figure he was to become in films a few years after this—*The Awful Truth* (1937), *The Philadelphia Story* (1940), *His Girl Friday* (1940), *Notorious* (1946) . . . There is a rhetoric about his dealings with people here—and always about his dealings with Helen—that marks him as a superficial figure, or one whose depths will not connect yet with another character or with us.

The scenes with men in the club, and the incarnation of Nick/Grant in particular, take on a subordinate or two-dimensional quality as compared with Helen/Dietrich and her performance in "Hot Voodoo," as in the film as a whole. The shots of Grant watching Dietrich sing do not determine our view, as audience, making us into conventional men who look upon and desire, and feel dominant over, the woman on view—as some film criticism suggests of all scenes with men watching women. Quite the reverse happens here, it seems to me—we feel at one with Dietrich and her performance, in regard to which Grant watching is an effect, as if summoned up by the performance. In art we tend to feel at one with the centers of energy and seemingly endless suggestion, not with the relatively dull or flat or predictable areas.

The "Hot Voodoo" number is astonishing in its conception. There is the chorus of women not clearly black or white; wearing make-up, but who can say to what extent; carrying spears as do primitive *men* conventionally; the unkempt hair and somber faces suggesting the drudge or the truly intent ritualist rather than the usual chorus girl. Then there is the gorilla on a chain, who goes with the chorus out among the club guests and upsets people. And there is Dietrich emerging piece by piece from the gorilla suit to sing—at first, for a moment, she is only a bare hand and forearm. It is all a picture of unidentifiability and of a state of change. Black is brought into white, the beast into the human, male into female. Are we to imagine the gorilla as male or female? Are the women who circle and bow to it, engaged in phallic worship centering on a male animal? Or is it mother worship, or exaltation of female strength? And there is the glamour—the coordination of everything into an act with music; the lavishness; the spangles; the focus eventually on Dietrich and her talents, letting go at last. With this element of glamour the beyond-human or above-human is brought into the whole uncertain and exciting mix.

But there is always the question whether art with all its constraints can mean what it says. Either one is interested in art, finding that it does mean what it says and does, or one is a skeptic—uninterested in art, really, or able to focus only on the constraints. Is Pindar less free as a poet than, say, Shelley, since Pindar wrote poems to order for patrons? Art is a certain reality, speaking and acting, which constraints, though they are there, paradoxically do not necessarily touch. Sternberg says in his writings that his principal purpose in making films was not to entertain or make money or please his producers, but to pursue something marvelous and new in what film as an art could do and could convey (he does not spell this thing out in words—only in film could he spell it out). Do we believe him? He did wish—and he admits it—to make money and to be celebrated and to keep his status in the world he worked in. So did Shakespeare and Dickens. Purposes can be contradictory, looked at one way, and yet work at one with one another.[12]

What is a nightclub act? Dietrich's lesbian interest, which is taken seriously these days (and likely always was), finds a crucial moment in *Blonde Venus* in the gesture with a chorus girl in Paris, done onstage as part of an act—as is the famous woman-to-woman kiss on the mouth in *Morocco* (1930). In both these instances the stage act goes beyond the stage, and beyond the film. Perhaps we ought to allow all elements of a stage act in a film leeway to go where they will—not block them with prejudgments about what an act and a film can be.

The astonishing *conception* of the "Hot Voodoo" number—the idea of the images and sounds of transition, of metamorphosis, of letting go—is only a beginning, a way in, a way to open us to a film experience that is finally deeper than, or beyond, and more immediate than, the stage act itself. This film experience is a being brought close, and more than close, to Helen, where the art of this film at its most splashy and self-assertive is in utter cooperation with this woman, who is more than the art of film could quite invent, or can contain. The cooperation of film with Helen will strike us like lightning, if we will let it, with the realization that she, as much as anyone, or anything, has generated this film—generated it to realize herself and put herself across.

We see O'Conner, the club owner, who says, "All right, Jimmy, let's go—trot 'em out," and a moment later, just after the music starts, there is a view of the Black conductor (Jimmy?), elevated and surrounded by a waist-high circular wall—is he projected, in his own world? confined?—as the chorus begins to come on in the background while the conductor waves his arms. Both O'Conner and the conductor are director figures, thus figures for this film's director, Sternberg. O'Connor's unprepossessingness and the conductor's obscurity—he has no part in the film except to be seen here for a moment—tell us that official directors, or producers, may not be what we think—that perhaps real directorial authority is to be sought elsewhere. We are pointed to Dietrich. A bit later, after the dance of the chorus and gorilla, and just before Dietrich begins to come out of the gorilla suit, there is another brief shot of O'Connor, watching from the side, looking awkward and insignificant. Of course Sternberg is reminding us that there is a little man (himself) behind Dietrich and what we have been seeing, and what we are going to see. But the film makes clear that there is much more to Dietrich than the man on the side can compass.

The camera observes the chorus come on from fairly close up, so that incomplete bodies, mostly legs, fill the frame, and the broad, rhythmical step-marching of the women seems to jostle against the boundaries of the frame. It is a view at the bidding, we might say, of the dance itself—a view unlike that of any club audience member, unless he or she were possessed of film imagination. Soon there is a more distant shot, making a wide pan, more like the club audience's point of view, getting in view the whole chorus and the gorilla moving across the stage. Then, as the dancers and gorilla come off the stage into the audience, there is a series of closer shots again, with slow camera movements different ways, all the shots at higher or lower angles than a straight-on view. We see for a moment the women's body-length shields all in a row, for the first time showing the shields' monstrous design of faces with huge teeth. We see confusingly—only in part—the swirling of the dancers about the gorilla. Eventually the camera moves at a high angle to follow the gorilla as it moves about disrupting tables of guests. The disruptive gorilla seems identified here with a moving camera, the machine itself, which is famous for having to have people and properties snatched away as it moves through a set.

This is a sequence with so much going on, and such infectious music to listen to—strong drums, brass, and large-band woodwinds—that it is hard to be conscious of the filming and editing as such. We are just brought close into the mood and the heart of the dance—all the time retaining a little consciousness that we are seeing something most strange, the last thing, we might think, we would find it easy to be brought close to.

The sense of cooperation between camera and subject—the sense that the camera is controlled or motivated by the subject—reaches a high point as Dietrich begins to shed the gorilla suit. We watch her straight on at medium distance. She sways, and removes the suit bit by bit. The chorus behind her sways in a different rhythm. Finally the camera sways, more or less with Dietrich, but really in a third rhythm still. The camera seems to have come unhinged here, to be a part of the dance rather than an—even very sympathetic—observer of it. Dietrich's Helen begins to sing,

Did you ever happen to hear of voodoo?
Hear it and you won't give a damn what you do!
Tom-toms put me under a sort of voodoo,
And the whole night long
I don't know the right from wrong . . . [13]

We look at her from a low angle—respectful, impressed, if you like—close enough so that we see her only above the legs. She wears a spangled suit over the trunk of her body, is bare-armed, and has a sort of fur bikini bottom placed over the lower part of her spangled suit, suggesting pubic hair, and fur epaulettes on her shoulders, suggesting underarm hair displaced, as in Buñuel's *Un chien andalou* (1929). On Dietrich's head is a huge frizzy blonde wig (which she placed there) with arrows shot through the hair. After a time there is a view of Nick watching; then the camera is back on Dietrich, but now far enough away to see all of her—she is bare-legged, the new image of legs perhaps suggesting what interests Nick most. The outrageous brief costume and wig contrast with the bare, true flesh of legs (even shaved legs) and the bare arms and the real woman's face, though the costume, like anyone's costume, can seem an extension of flesh and the real person.

The point of view on Dietrich as she sings is something like Nick's or the club audience's in general, though always literally too close for that. The camera moves slowly in on Dietrich once she is seen legs and all, eventually showing just her face, and then backs up—and even this might seem to mimic the audience's bringing to bear of attention, and then letting it go a bit, under too much intensity. During this song an audience point of view is not abandoned for the sake of the film cooperating with the spectacle itself, as during the dance. The audience point of view is there. But it is virtually the same as—at one with—filming that is done for the sake of the subject. With regard to the latter, one could not ask for more. The film brings us close to Dietrich—indissolubly so, I want to say—but still allows us to remember that we are ourselves—at the moment, an audience.

Dietrich is haughty but relaxed, proud but giving away a secret. Her eyes are at first heavy-lidded, as if she is working in a trance, in her own world, but later she opens them more and looks about, as if she has decided to make more direct contact with the world. A smile plays about her face all the time, of the order of, "I know more than you, and I love being here with you." She is not at all to be demeaned by the occasion, her costume, her off-color song. The smile and the integrity in her manner are not at odds with the song and the whole spectacle—the smile and her integrity show precisely that she means it all. She impresses us as a higher sort of being—freer than she has seemed in the film so far, more self-possessed and more capable of enjoyment than people ever seem to be in doing something possibly demeaning. Dietrich's quality as of a higher being is something she realizes *here*, in doing *this*. The occasion is the way up for her, or the way forward, or the way out—it is what she wants, her "old work."

We feel her conviction when her so far merely flickering smile breaks out into a big, genuine, irreversible one as she sings the drawn-out word "cave" over several notes—"ca-a-ave"—in "I'd follow a caveman right into his cave." She would like to go with a man into what the song says is his domain, but it is an interior space traditionally associated with women or thought of as a woman's domain. The subject arose here with *Nashville*'s opening setting, that womb-like recording studio. John Ford's film *The Searchers* (1956) contemplates such space from the first shot, from inside a house looking out, whence a woman steps out into view as if from behind the camera, a director, and on to the crucial use of a cave in the scene near the end when John Wayne has found the lost Natalie Wood, now a grown young woman whose adulthood and foreignness he must face. The film's concluding shot repeats the opening one, but with the woman now stepping back into the interior. Male and female are confounded in Helen's song, as she makes a high moment of the word "cave." The big smile is almost fully repeated on the long-held word "vacation"—"va-ca-a-tion"—in "My conscience wants to take a vacation." Confounding male and female is a matter of letting go of conscience, or "my" conscience, a certain conscience.

Helen's performance expands and expands, as film makes it effective for audiences through all eternity—will it not be so? All is felt to be one, as we enter into this performance, the genuine smile breaking down the barrier between audience and Helen/Dietrich, audience and work, in the way the poetry of poetic drama and the words set to music in opera break down the barrier between audience and work, and the barrier even of a sense of self.[14] As lovers turn into love, so we feel *in ourselves* the work and creativity that must go into Helen's performance. What we feel is the result of the power of film to convey a Helen, her work, such a smile. All this happens though Helen is doing her nightclub act, and Dietrich is doing her Hollywood job, and, we may suspect, the smile is directed by Sternberg—Helen takes identity for us *in* her work—because the work is so good, so overwhelming. Emerson: "Do your work and I will know you" (Emerson 264). Keats is not the man who suffers, but the mind which creates, as T. S. Eliot would have it in "Tradition and the Individual Talent."

The words Helen sings declare what she is doing with her life, and project what the rest of the film will be: "My conscience wants to take a vacation," "I want to be bad," "All night long I don't know the right from wrong." She wants to enter a night where conventional attitudes are cleared away, a course of life or a state of mind beyond good and bad, right and wrong—a place she might remain, presumably, if the life of right and wrong proves impossible, less than life, or a place where she might prepare for a life of new right and wrong, right and wrong newly conceived, newly felt.

Helen's words stress the heat of hot voodoo all along. We hear the word "hot" over and over, and, "that heat gives me a wicked sensation," "hot voodoo's burned my clothes," "I'm aflame"—perhaps like the phoenix, who will re-emerge. She finally sings, "I'm going to blazes," and this seems to project exactly the late episode in the border town, the filmically rich episode where she comes to the fore stronger than ever as director/creator. It is clearly hot here, in every frame, and Helen leads the detective who pursues her, but does not yet recognize her, to a cafe where everyone is smoking and great clouds of smoke are rising up—"blazes" itself, it might be. Conversation begins with the man saying, "Terribly warm today, isn't it?" and Helen replying drawlingly, "Warm? It's *hot*." She accepts a cigarette from him and smokes with conviction throughout the scene—earlier in the film she had refused a cigarette and declared that she did not smoke. When she plays at guessing the detective's occupation, he tells her, "You're gettin' hot." A bit later he says of Helen Faraday (whom he still does not recognize in the woman before him), "She leaves a hot trail behind her."

This "blazes" is a hard fate for Helen, a poor life, with the giving up of her child imminent. But this is also a place where she takes control and leads life where she would have it go—at least provisionally—seeming to spin her environment about her like a web, or a cocoon. Her "Hot Voodoo" number has been poetry not just of the kind which is created, but which itself creates or projects, and projects into a state where creating goes on and does not cease.

Voudoun, says extraordinary filmmaker Maya Deren in her book *Divine Horsemen: The Living Gods of Haiti*, is a worldview and a practice aimed at bringing human beings into touch with what is beyond them.

With drumming and song and invocation, one can become possessed by a god; other people learn from the god who is present for a time in the cynosure. A film star is a god in a sense, it is often remarked, or a person like the rest of us who is yet irradiated for our sake with the *quality*, as Deren puts it, of a god. The gods come from the deep, Deren tells us, a beyond signified by an expanse of water, whose surface is a barrier or border, a crossable one, between us and what is beyond, as in Cocteau's *Orpheus* (*Orphée*, 1949). Film images itself as a water surface, I say. The screen is at once impassable and possible to cross, both ways. (The border and the beyond are also seen in *voudoun* as a mirror—a mirror with illustrations and writing on it will fill the background in *Blonde Venus*'s next to last episode, in Helen's Paris dressing room, where she starts to decide to move toward what will be the end of the film.) Deren writes about the goddess Erzulie,

> *Voudoun* has given woman, in the figure of Erzulie, exclusive title to that which distinguishes humans from all other forms: their capacity to conceive beyond reality, to desire beyond adequacy, to create beyond need. In Erzulie, *voudoun* salutes woman as the divinity of the dream, the Goddess of Love, the muse of beauty. It . . . regard[s] her (like Mary, with whom Erzulie is identified) as mother of man's myth of life—its meaning. (160)

Deren tells us of "La Sirène, who is understood as an aspect of Erzulie . . . specifically related to Agwé [god of the sea] . . . she is said to steal children and take them to the bottom of the sea or of a stream, but also is known to bring them up" (like Pindar's Poseidon, and this film's Helen). Erzulie's manner has an "insistence upon 'fraicheur,' coolness" (342).

There is a "sense of innocence which emanates from [Erzulie] that makes her identification with the Virgin Mary somehow seem truer than her promiscuity, than even the fact that the devotion of prostitutes makes of her almost their patron saint" (165; Helen will be tarred as a prostitute). One might think of Godard's Mary as well as of Helen, as Deren goes on:

> To call Erzulie virgin is to say that she is of another world, another reality . . . To say she is virgin is to say that she is . . . the loa of things as they *could* be, not as they are . . . She is the divinity of the dream, and it is in the very nature of

dream to begin where reality ends and to spin it and to send it forward in space, as the spider spins and sends forward its own thread . . . the labor of Erzulie is as endless as the capacity of man to dream and, in the very act of accomplishing that dream, to have already dreamed again. (165)

One thinks of Spenser's powerful virgins in *Faerie Queene*, and of his inspiration, Queen Elizabeth. Helen in *Blonde Venus* is possessed, we may say, by the "quality" of Erzulie or is it Sternberg? Our involvement in the dream of this film can make a way for us seriously, gaily to draw from this quality.

The last words of Helen's song are "I want to be bad," and the next words in the film are Nick's, to his companions, "Not bad, eh?"—he seems to have picked up, and to be carrying on, the Nietzschean playful/serious disruptive spirit. He and his party decide to go backstage to see Helen, and they are seen departing the room with the orchestra conductor in the foreground—they are, as it were, summoned backstage by the story's real conductor. Nick is played along by Helen ("I think I'd rather go home alone . . . Will I get a bracelet?"), as she jauntily dons a soldier's parade hat with a plume—looking and acting Dietrich-like, more than she seems just playing the role of Helen. The scene ends with the image of a large check being made out to Helen. Later there will be other images of the written word—a cable, police reports—and perhaps this first one ought to clue us in that they are all the products of Helen's will and efforts, though later ones seem to constrain her, or seal her fate, or go against her.

Turbulent music on the soundtrack resolves itself into the folk song heard at the very beginning of the film, and throughout associated with Helen's home, as we go now quickly from the club, via a car ride, back to the apartment, and Helen goes in and finds her husband collapsed in his chair. She prepares him for departure to Europe, explaining that she has sufficient money in an advance on her salary. And Ned's departure is enacted in a long elaborately staged sequence with crowds at a ship, and then images of the ocean, all accompanied by a German lovers' folk song in full orchestration. It is all as arbitrary-seeming as the images of water at the start of the film. We are in the realm of the poetic, the self-declaredly staged, the logic of music, film form and procedure declaring itself, the beyond as it can give energy and shape to earthly life.

Helen now enters on her odyssey—if she has not done so already. At any rate, the odyssey comes before us now in external, unmistakable terms, and moving fairly quickly. Helen spins off into external events, as Kierkegaard says in *Diary of a Seducer*, as young women will do. The poppy explodes and scatters, as D. H. Lawrence says of characters, women particularly, in the novels of Thomas Hardy—the character turns into events, to make clear what has to be made clear, or what the character wills to make clear about herself. In film, Sternberg and Helen/Dietrich anticipate Maya Deren. Deren's *Meshes of the Afternoon* (1943) gives the interplay of inner and outer experience, the force of will acting upon what comes to one, and the subsequent films *At Land* (1944) and *Ritual in Transfigured Time* (1946) bring Deren's central woman (herself, in fact) into linear, open-ended, more external-seeming adventures.

The story of *Blonde Venus* now is that of a woman's suffering, of her being driven before fate. The film continues sometimes Sternberg-like and inspired, sometimes more conventional-seeming. The more artistically intense moments suggest Helen's power as creator and desirer, or reformer—not just sufferer—of her fate. In the interplay of conventional and inspired, in the logic that begins to develop going between these, Helen/Dietrich's identity takes form, or comes clear, as much as possible.

The inspired and artistic involves itself with the ordinary—or throws itself, through the ordinary, onto a higher plane of the inspired—or the ordinary pulls the beyond to itself. The mixed quality of the film, like Helen's uncertain experience itself—to think of it psychologically, from her point of view—continues until the extended border town episode, pure artistry, which precipitates the final scenes.

Helen is sad or depressed, at least seems decidedly bothered, in her scenes with Nick. One might say she is torn by her feeling of responsibility to her husband, or by her affection for him, her affection for her home. But there is little sign that she takes any positive enjoyment in Nick—there is nothing to be torn about, on this side. She is where she is by virtue of a flash of desire, or a confusion about how to get money to help her husband, or an accident, events moving too quickly for her—it is hard to say, hard, I would think, for her to say. She is in a state from which she has to move on, for her life. It is one of those minor deaths—what may feel like death itself—which we suffer and get out of, without being able to spell out clearly to ourselves where we are, what is happening. The tomb-like opulent apartment where Helen and Johnny are placed to live, by Nick, is cold and empty except for flowers; it suggests a death.

The apartment image is significant, but simple and maybe a bit awkward—what we see not as full and intelligent as the sheer idea behind it—as is the case too with the scenes of Helen and Nick's vacation later, the silly boat ride with back-projection, and the mannequin-like waterside scene with the two in riding clothes. Helen, though, is not just in a bad state; she is in a rudderless and awkward phase of life, where she does not know what she wants or where she is going. She is where she cannot *see*, so to speak. It is a phase for which the awkward images are right, if we see Helen as the seer of the film, identified with the director, as with us. What we see is where we are. This phase of life for Helen, and some of her later wanderings too, is the chaos that must precede concentration, and that moves concentration—a letting go in muddy life, confused, or numbed, in preparation for art, art-in-life.

We may be near the fallacy of imitative form here, but valid art often is. One must consider how things go in the individual case. Popular drama and narrative perhaps take greater freedom here than do other forms. Such is their need in order to wield the great powers they do, of involvement of the audience, and of all-encompassingness in the life material taken in. Sandra Gilbert and Susan Gubar in *The Madwoman in the Attic* defend narrative awkwardness in Charlotte Brontë as phenomenological, the right depiction of a woman confused or confounded, where the writer, or the book, is identified with the experience of the woman character. R. P. Blackmur earlier gave a similar account of the middle portion of Dostoyevsky's *Idiot*. Things begin to happen which, in themselves and in the style in which they are presented, seem fortuitous beyond the bounds of art—fortuitousness being what the book wants to take up in this middle part. (Helen in *Blonde Venus* is close in a way to Prince Myshkin in *The Idiot*—in her force, her strangeness, and in the reaction on our part, in thinking, she is meant to provoke.)

Just before the tomb-like apartment scene, and just after a brief, empty scene with Helen and Nick in his office, Helen comes forward for a moment as the artist of her life—forward out of the chaos, so to speak. She shows she has the imaginative momentum, the very identity that way, to get through the empty life of the scenes that surround this moment.

She goes to her old apartment to collect mail, and we wonder right from the start, is that all it is for? We hear the music earlier associated with home, in the minor mode now. This music suggests the poetic aspect of the scene—that poetic power is at work, or is being represented. Just reprising the musical theme suggests the deep interest, the pull, of home. The minor key harmony suggests something amiss, or something new, in home—something mysterious which is now being faced or followed. The minor suggests suspense wanting to be resolved.

The room, with long, shaded windows muffling the sun, is dramatic-looking just in its light, definitely a part of the Sternberg world. Helen comes in beautifully dressed, with a hat—not just as a woman well off in a love affair, but Dietrich, the star, someone to contemplate in a moment set off from everything. Her expression, determined but relaxed, is sufficient unto itself, not necessarily connected to the story at this point. Her movements seem deliberate and also sufficient unto themselves, as if it is all done for the sake of her enjoying—and our contemplating—an abstract gracefulness. She walks in and raises a shade, one might think for light—but she lowers it again almost immediately. It is as if she is giving a signal; at least there is an air of ritual about it. The apartment and her being here become a center, sheerly by virtue of artistic realizedness. Things must be done *for* this moment, this appearance of Helen, this place. Here is the poet in her poem.

The importance of this moment is borne out by the echoing of it, and expansion of it, first when Ned comes home from Europe while Helen is on a trip with Nick, and then when Helen and Ned meet here. Helen's story is being created here, just as earlier it was created in this same home as laboratory and weaving center. In the second apartment scene Ned comes in and finds his unreceived cable announcing his early return, and this cable momentarily fills the screen, headed, "EXPERIMENT SUCCESSFUL BEYOND ALL DREAMS." This statement I take to characterize the whole story, Helen's life, this film, film itself. That the statement has great importance is indicated by the cable's filling the screen a second time when Helen herself discovers it just before meeting Ned in the third of these apartment scenes. We are given two remarkable full-face confrontations with this statement: "EXPERIMENT SUCCESSFUL BEYOND ALL DREAMS."

With the overtones of scientist and magician and witch about Ned and Helen, "experiment" seems a fair description of what they are doing with their lives. And they invoke shots, plan scenarios, and try scenarios out, like those who make films. Film itself, still in 1932 and still perhaps now, is fairly called an experiment. Sound film in 1932 is certainly still an experiment. Popular art that is poetic drama, is an experiment at any time—the time of its origin or any time it is received—if we think of the perpetual question of how it is to be taken.

Film, this film, and Helen's life are like a dream, letting desires be played out, putting us and putting the film character—Helen here—in touch with a new world, where new motives take over life, and a new logic seems to operate. That is to say, Helen is put in touch with a new world *if* we conceive of her as somehow, at some time, *out* of the film, apart from it, there before the dream starts—more of this in a moment. Pharaoh dreamed and was put in touch with a new world, needing a Joseph to explain and help to bring the dream and life into accord (film asks for criticism). Helen is her own Joseph, explaining to herself, or turning what is within her outward, into images we see and the film she lives out. She is her own source of dream, like God who gave the dream to Pharaoh. Helen's dream is always occurring, right from the start, coming from herself to herself—unless, of course, what comes to her comes from Sternberg, or cinema, or the genre, or the way of the world. This opposition—she as source, against the world—will never be solved. *This* is what the film has to convey.

"BEYOND ALL DREAMS"—in this film, in film itself, in the "experiment," dream comes to life, or becomes film, a new life beyond dream and life both. Helen's dream becomes her life, or put it the other way around—at any rate we are on the ground of a new kind of life. The documentary power of film renders what we see—however strange as a plot with characters and settings—as something undeniably there, once, photographed by the camera, now there forever on film. Actual people and objects and places did take the form of this story, this film, so we see that in a general way life *can* take such a form. Film imagination gets into life. Dream is a way to this.

Is Helen/Dietrich conceivable apart from the film? We want to conceive of the subject in any work of art—a character, a situation, a pair of peasant shoes, as somehow there apart from the work, having justification by itself. We may want to think this way, though we recognize perfectly well, as Heidegger says, that the subject apart from the work is not really to be seen or held or pointed to. We want to see the art as doing something with a subject. This is a way we have to help ourselves get close to the work done, the activity, in the work of art. The activity draws us. But to let go we want a grounding. The work, with our cooperation, posits a subject for itself, and then seems to be what happens to the subject. *Blonde Venus* is quite self-conscious about this, with the film's strong suggestion at the beginning that Helen/Dietrich creates the film, or imagines it, in a burst of water—so she must, it would seem, have been there before—yet she is Helen/Dietrich, or Helen/Sternberg/Dietrich, a figure of film.

Ned is said in the cable to be "completely cured," and we may infer that he has been put on the way to some new kind of fitness for life with his wife and family. It is perhaps Helen who is not quite ready for family life. In a sense she has sent Ned away and now brought him back, and she will go on to precipitate the quarrel and break what sends her traveling. Could she have handled the quarrel scene differently than she does?

When we first see Ned returned, in the second apartment scene, he enters and follows the round of gestures we have seen a moment before from Helen—bending over to pick up the mail, raising a window shade, looking behind a doorway hanging to see into the next room, circling back to the table in the middle of the first room. That Helen has just done all of this suggests that Ned is summoned up by her, or is summoned by the same power that summons her, or that he is part of her, or an alter ego.

When Ned and Helen meet, the two circle each other like gods; then, as they quarrel, the scene devolves into two sequences of cutting between the two, each person more or less in close-up, Ned becoming a terrifying figure as it were imagined by Helen more than simply perceived. In the first series of shots Ned's face is half masked by a band of shadow from his hat brim, and in the second series almost wholly masked, when he has moved to put his back to the light, the sunny window. Ned is a monster here of light and shadow, in a sense Helen's film creation, her work of light and shadow, to give herself the obstacle and challenge she at some level wants to propel her life elsewhere and along.

Helen was here before Ned arrived, and when she first hears him approaching, there is a strange shot of her in medium close-up, her body turned screen-right, but her head twisted around to face the camera, half of her face hidden by her hat and her large fur collar, one excited eye peering out at us. It is an image of texture in a bath of light contrived just for this shot. In the isolated shot Helen is momentarily as if from another world, which suggests that the world of the apartment quarrel that will follow is apart from her, perhaps her projection. The sense of the apartment as an uncertain world is further given by shots of Ned walking into the inner room where Helen now is, and later shots of Helen exiting this room, where the direction of walking for each person is reversed from shot to shot. Where are these people going? Where are they?

When Helen explains what has been happening in her life—her affair—and then says she is here if Ned will have her, he snarls, "Go on as before, eh?"—which is exactly not the point: they must go on in some new way. She says, "I love you," which is hard to interpret, something for him—and perhaps her too—to think about for some time, through trials. He rejects her now and demands custody of Johnny, and she says

she will bring Johnny here—and of course at the end of the film she in effect does this, sending Johnny back and then bringing herself, and we have the three of them back in this place. But first there must be an escape, a desperate adventure, at least in the mind—a warp in time, perhaps. This adventure is a fate that happens and a melodrama, and also a representation of contemplation—a getting of Helen's mind and that of Ned, and perhaps even Johnny's, to the place these three can come together and be at home, at least for a moment, in a provisional ending—perhaps an endless moment, ever renewed.

The image of Helen as she speaks of bringing Johnny back dissolves, as if in her imagination, to the scene of a railroad station where she is hurrying with Johnny to a train car bound, so a black train official tells her, for Baltimore. With a cut, the camera moves in dramatically on Ned as he deals with what has happened, seeking help at a police station to find his wife—and the great amount of police help this relatively obscure man gets in a nationwide search for Helen and her child, suggests it is all a projection of someone's fear, or of a desire for a provocation to move on. Immediately now the camera moves in, in the same dramatic gesture as with Ned, on a missing persons poster with a picture of Helen/Dietrich as the Blonde Venus, with wild wig and arrows through it. The repeated camera movement, in on Ned, in on the Blonde Venus, suggests an identity of Ned with Helen, or a realization that they are subject to the same pressure, or formative force. The use of the Blonde Venus photo—surely there was a more natural one available, or this one could have been cropped?—suggests that we are in a realm of mind. Helen sees herself pursued as the Blonde Venus. Or the Blonde Venus is simply who Helen is, this film says. The world is not after "Helen," but after this outrageous—what?

The Blonde Venus photo gently dissolves, as soft big-band nightclub music begins, to an image in lights, of a star (indicating what precisely Helen is), which in turn dissolves to the words in lights, "Star Cafe" (identity is one's work), which then dissolves to Johnny obscured behind a fanciful mask on the side of his head; Helen's Johnny. Then the camera backs up, reversing the pressured gesture in on Ned and then on the photo, releasing now a world to look at—of fantasy, reality—a dressing room with Johnny's mother doing mysterious things with a burning candle on her table, like a sorceress. This sorceress is at the heart of the series of dissolves we have seen, getting us from New York to here.

In a moment Helen will go into the club and sing the music we have been hearing already for a few minutes. She's walking, progressing, as the camera tracks with her—her camera, presenting herself, obscured at times by foliage from potted plants—an image typical of Sternberg films. The intention seems to be to have the audience strain its attention, and perhaps imagination, thus getting all the closer to her. Her song might be taken as erotic self-expression with indirection and verbal avoidance: "You so-and-so . . . You've got me you-know-what . . . I ought to take you out and—how have you been?" Of course, as Dietrich sings it, she *knows* she is being indirect—she is playing at being indirect. Is she addressing Ned, whom she has just told, "I love you"—now having her private thoughts while she lets her audience think what they please? Her art of song seems to reach back through everything that has happened from the quarrel to now, in the series of dissolves.

The escape, or flight under duress, continues. There is right away the Norfolk encounter with the helpful club owner of ambiguous sex, in a seeming world of women,—a lesbian bar?—so that the lover addressed in Helen's song just previously might seem to be a woman, or of ambiguous sexual identity: "you so-and-so," "you this-and-that." The song might seem to have found its object now in the new club or to have conjured it up.

Ned's last words before departing on the boat for Germany earlier had been an injunction to Johnny to learn to write, and in their Norfolk hotel room Helen is teaching Johnny just this, showing something of a bond with Ned, as the word "father" is written. But the word is also taken apart, showing a certain rebellion against the father, against writing, and against conventional values altogether. The idea of father is being thought about still, uncertain. Johnny writes "F-A-T," turning our attention to, say, the body as such. Then a mechanical toy is set off, bouncing its bottom across the writing table—an interval of play. Then Johnny writes "H-E-R," making us think of woman, and specifically of his mother. Mother—her—is in father. Mother and body pull apart. What is Johnny learning, exactly? What is on Helen's mind?

A montage of speeding train images suggests escape, and the mechanism of driving fate, and also the mechanism of film, Helen/Dietrich's creative medium. This suggestion is confirmed by the immediately succeeding image of Helen peering toward us from outside through a large window, which suggests the screen, what we in fact always see her in or on or through. It is the window of a restaurant, the camera already inside, as if drawing her into a film world. Or the camera stands in for projector, with Dietrich up on the screen, so that she comes down off the screen and into *our* world, when she enters the restaurant. The camera oddly contemplates a wall telephone as Helen and Johnny walk in—a mechanical means for relaying one human being to another, like film—and a mechanical piano is seen, and plays throughout the episode (Orson Welles perhaps recalls it with the mechanical piano in Dietrich's scenes in her dive in *Touch of Evil* [1958]). This restaurant is ambiguous as between being an imaginative world and reality—like so much on film, and in reality. The restaurant provides real food for Helen and the boy—perhaps we should take it as food for the imagination too. And the restaurant faces Helen ineluctably with sex. When she cannot pay the bill, she says to the owner, "I'll wash dishes, clean up—anything," and this man, at first angry—and fat, full of body, linked to "father"—smirks and says, "You gonna wash *my* dishes?" and mouths a cigar. Lapse of time. This scenario of humiliation and sexual exploitation is at once a shock of reality for Helen to endure and a role to play out.

In a New Orleans court hearing she is accused, tried, and convicted of vagrancy—read, prostitution—and ordered to leave town. Then she is seen leaving her hotel, carrying Johnny, the camera—her own, let us say—tracking her ominously close up as she backs along a wall with fear clearly on her face, like Peter Lorre, harmer of children, stalked by the camera in *M* (1931). This fear—self-induced? to some extent?—is a raw energy that will jolt us to what follows in *Blonde Venus*: the border town and the film's final flowering. This fear is the spark across gaps that carries us ahead, as in *Macbeth*, moment to moment, word to word. There is wonder about what *can* conceivably ensue, and a frightened willingness to submit to anything, even as one recoils. This procedure of mind can go the way of Dante—down and then up and up—as well as the way of *Macbeth* or a Fritz Lang film. Fear is what Helen must be suffused with, suffuse herself with, submit to, as her means for creating a next step.

We have been traversing a mix of material. Certain things looked at in isolation may seem conventional—perhaps the montage of speeding trains looked at just for itself. But more importantly, the very *mix* of things may seem conventional, as in a carelessly made movie. The speeding trains, the highly atmospheric restaurant, and the more ordinary New Orleans courtroom look as if they belong in different films. We are in Helen's submission of herself to chaos, to movement as such. And because this part of the film represents, more than any other, a woman's melodramatic fate, her being driven before the storm, careless-seeming or even the quotient of the conventional—the montage of speeding trains, the villainous restaurant owner and judge, the rainy street—should indicate that a woman's fate is not—*may* not be—her deepest or most real experience.

The fear on Helen's face as she flees New Orleans, dissolves to the image of a file drawer and then a missing persons report saying Helen has been seen west of Galveston, but then lost, and this image dissolves quickly to that of child's toys and a chicken walking about on the floor of what turns out to be Helen's quarters in the border town. The intense feeling of fear in Helen seems to provoke, or to fuel, her imagination of the police pursuit west and south, and then the final setting of the chase, where she will give up the boy.

The fear is still alive at the start of the new scene, as Helen's servant/companion, the black woman Cora, reports a strange man who has been "browsing around" the street, and Helen and Johnny are both anxious for a moment. But then Helen takes over the management of a scenario, showing assurance. She goes out to engage the man in the street and take him to a bar, to have fun with him and humiliate him a bit, and at last to give up the boy, in her own way and her own time. The fear that might imagine something awful turns into a poetic, positive, active sort of dreaming—at the same time, awful things do happen to Helen.

The whole setting here is a richly imagined one, with the live, heavy birds all about the seedy apartment; the new element of the character Cora, and Hattie McDaniel's vigorous performance in the part; and the elaborate décor of the street, with its vendors, pedestrians, trees and lattices, and the sounds of foreign words; and then the romantic seedy bar or café where Helen takes the man. There is strong light everywhere, as was the case too in the New Orleans courtroom—Helen, going south, has been moving more and more into a region of strong light, which might be to say, onto a movie set, into a movie. We enjoy seeing her in these late settings of in extremis (including the next one, the dark, hellish women's flop house), and not, I think, because we like to see the woman suffer—Helen shows amazing pluck in these situations, and a great part of their interest lies in Dietrich's quality of being able to go anywhere, do anything, and rise superior to it. The settings have beauty and a poet's imagination, so we feel either that the gods have transported Helen into a heaven of the spirit while they deal her her worldly suffering or that Helen has projected the settings herself. The imaginative quality of the settings shows her *way* of going through what she will go through.

The suggestions are many that Helen is making her own film now. She comes outside in order to find the detective, and moves along a wall, projecting her shadow very dramatically onto a lighted blank area, as a filmmaker may be thought to project himself/herself into the settings and characters of film. The camera regards her in a flattering middle-distance shot, appreciative of her pose and hat and shawl, as she leans against a wall. It is not the detective's point of view—he is not looking.

The camera looking at her is intimate with her, serving her—it is her camera. Now from Helen's point of view, this camera regards the detective from the back, as he stands in the fork of a tree trunk as if framed in a director's viewfinder. Then he turns around to see her, as if at a telepathic signal, a director's signal, what audiences do not see or hear. This detective has intruded into Helen's life, but also she has summoned him up.

Mexican music accompanies a dissolve to the place Helen leads the detective, the cafe—the place is as if created by the impulse the music represents. The two of them sit at a little elevated table with a balcony, as if in a theater box. They are, as it were, at the theater, surveying the scene of the town they are not really part of, perhaps surveying—imagining—us who are out here before them, part of the nonfilm world, those on whom the gods look down, and with whom, it is said, the gods sometimes get involved. But we realize looking up at them that they are on stage in their box, too. And beyond this they are onscreen, in Helen's movie. The white shuttered doors filling the space behind them suggest the screen,

as closed shuttered doors will do a bit later, back in Helen's apartment. Helen and the detective are bodies just *in front* of the shuttered doors, suggesting the resistance and integrity there are about subjects we might imagine quite as in or of film.

The dialogue now, as I have noted, seems to put these two in the world of the voodoo song—heat, blazes—a script now come to life. Moreover, the two communicate in terms of movie phrases, self-consciously it seems, at least on Helen's part (she is the director, knowing what a movie phrase is). The man does not recognize Helen, having his mind on whoring, and she draws him out on his pursuit of the runaway woman, asking, "How do you know she's in this neck of the woods?"—saying "neck of the woods" very archly. He says, expansively, "I've got the whole border covered," and, with some pride in his *bon mot*, "She took 'em [men along her way] like Grant took Richmond" (a possible reference to Cary Grant, taking Helen?). There has not been much talking in the later part of the film, and suddenly there is this ongoing conversation with movie-character poses and modern-seeming wisecracks, familiar from westerns and gangster films and the popular books these are drawn from.

And, too, Helen/Dietrich becomes ironic, which is to say, she becomes Dietrich, this woman of film, or rather, this woman who is able to be the woman she is—only, is it?—by way of film. Her delivery is overemphatic and thus ironic, as if she is inventing the words and at once realizing she has found clichés—stupid cover-ups of the things that matter. She seems to be playing a critical game with a foreigner's language. She starts questioning the man: "What are you doing down here, big boy?" a little overbrightly, especially on the "big boy." She tells him she expects he is a "go-getter," dwelling a little on the words, and, raising the pitch of her voice slightly, she says she knows every day of his life must be "active and exciting." The irony is obvious, but not enough for him to get it. She pretends to guess his occupation, with the old jingle, "rich man, poor man, beggar man, thief," doing a little aria on the "th" and "f" of "thief," smiling knowingly on the word—he will steal her child. He tells her she doesn't look like the other women in this place, and she says, drawling it, "Give me time." He says the runaway woman with the child is not practicing "mother love," and she asks witheringly, but not exactly of him, "What does a *man* know about mother love?"

Helen indicates continually, in her manner, that she is thinking about what her interlocutor—and perhaps everyone else—cannot know. The irony puts her in a world apart, of sensibility and consciousness—a situation her film audience, at least, can savor, even if not knowing her thoughts fully. She is devastating, but she remains approachable, with a sincere smile coming and going on her face—she is able to be amused. She remains sensuous in a way, open to life, seemingly life-loving, if only, if only . . . as Lisa puts it in *Letter from an Unknown Woman*.

With Dietrich's irony, as with Bette Davis's very different, more excited, more on-the-attack irony ("Some man to make me happy!"), one is tempted to say, these women have come into their own—it is something wonderful, enjoyable in a way for them and for us, valuable in its disturbingness, instructive. If suffering has produced this, so be it—the women are strong, are fully there, only in reaching this stage. But at the same time, it is the irony that brings us as far as possible into sympathy with these women (there is still distance, of course). So that more than ever we are against the idea of suffering brought to bear on the women. The irony states their suffering, while the energy of the irony shows the women's appetite for life, their capacity for happiness.

We do not wish the fool in *King Lear* any different from what he is, and we value Lear's own ironic, knowing manner when he takes over the fool's role in the later part of the play. At the same time, we wish for an undoing of the life that has brought the fool and Lear to where they are.

With Dietrich or Davis we have feelings not only about the fictional characters they play. We may feel as well, sorry, and glad, that film puts these women through their paces. How can we not feel concern? How can we, in the face of these films? The films, like tragedy, will not resolve the at-loggerheads situation of the two ways of taking what is here. The films are deeper than the kind of thinking—one or another—that would make up its mind.

In *Fear and Trembling* Kierkegaard ponders Abraham and the injunction to sacrifice Isaac. Abraham is faced with double experience: faith in God, and unavoidable thinking about justice, thinking about ethics. Abraham says to Isaac, "God will provide a lamb," and Kierkegaard comments that irony is the way of speaking forced by the situation of experiencing incommensurable realms.

Helen has her own crisis over giving up a child, and is faced with two realms, the world where she must function and deal with people who think they know who people are and how things are done and the world of what she knows which no one else can know—who she and Johnny really are. She speaks irony, and she creates her film fancy. Perhaps her creativity, going back to the start of the film, even to the bringing to birth of Johnny, is a version all along of speaking irony, her creativity—and Sternberg's, or film creativity itself—coming from an unsolvable double experience that will not issue in words of resolution, which would be avoidance.

Abraham is found in a sacred book, a history of a sort. If we do not believe in Abraham and God, the story does not matter so much—who could be torn by it, worrying over it as Kierkegaard does? But then it is not clear and definite what belief in such a story is. Even if we are not believers in the Bible, we might say that the story of Abraham is something beyond, and different than, what we call fiction. Film characters have their own way of seeming more than fictional—Dietrich, Garbo, Chaplin, and others. In books and plays many of those characters who stay in the mind as more real, more of the earth, are those involved in a thinking process, a crisis of thinking—involved not so much in a clearly outlined crisis as in one that will not come clear, and that invades our own thinking—Abraham, of course, Julien Sorel, Madame Bovary, Tolstoy's Pierre, Hamlet. Dietrich is thinking, in her depths, as is Garbo, as is Chaplin's Tramp, faced with the world's incongruities.

Helen/Dietrich's film continues when she escorts the detective home to her apartment. He asks about her bedroom, and she leads him across a balcony to shuttered doors—an image of the screen, which will be life itself for her, where her film/plan plays itself out. With a cut, the shutters fill the screen, and we see Helen's fingers in close-up scratching at the surface, giving a director's signal—and prefiguring the image at the end of the film, where the boy's fingers finger the screen. At Helen's signal the detective, suspecting something, says, "What are you trying to do, frame me?"—calling attention with the pun (unconscious?) on "frame," to the film imagination at work here. And he suggests the link of this imagination to revenge, aggressiveness, and blackmail—as well as to sex, what *he* thinks the present encounter is all about, his line recalling Taxi Belle Hooper's earlier one to Helen, "Say, are you trying to ride me?"

Helen reveals the boy, Johnny, and states her intention to give him up, making fun of the detective for not so far recognizing her—"Sherlock Holmes . . . What a brain. . . ." "I'm no good," she says, seeming to bear out—in a new direction, going deeper—the words of the "Hot Voodoo" song, "I want to be bad." "No good," she says now, "except to give up the boy. . . ." Did she all along at some level wish to be brought to give up the boy? Does she want to triumph in Paris without him, as will occur later? Does she know already that they will come together again?

At the town's outdoor railway stop the giving up of Johnny is played out. A shot of the shuttered bedroom doors dissolves to a vivid low-angle shot of a train rushing into the station: the doors, an image for the screen, are merged into an image for the whole mechanism of film, as trains so often suggest the film mechanism, and as they have done in this film already more than once (in *Shanghai Express* Dietrich's passive/active reconstruction of her life is projected into a train journey, using life, using the train, as if making a movie). The present station shot recalls the Lumières' *L'arrivée d'un train en gare de La Ciotat* (*The Arrival of a Train at La Ciotat Station*), at the origin of film. The film-like imagination motivating the scene at the apartment is linked by a dissolve to the train shot, to the imagination motivating the new scene. Now we see Helen with Johnny, and he rises to watch with interest the arriving train, the thing Helen has put in motion to take him away, as the way to the future.

Ned steps out of the train, and a shot from Helen's point of view takes in the boy and his father embracing ardently, as Helen and Johnny will do when she finally comes back home—Helen and Ned are linked here. The boy and his father are seen buying train tickets at a little window, suggestive of a theater or movie box office—they are getting their tickets to enter Helen's film. Then Ned goes to Helen and bitterly repays the fifteen hundred dollars she had provided to save his life, and he enjoins her to stay away. She is silent; her cup runs over. Or her feelings and answers are there in the actions of those about her, which she has set in motion.

Ned sends Johnny to tell his mother goodbye, and we see her hand him his stuffed toy, one of their many toys from throughout the film, counters of their imaginative life. Johnny wags the toy like a bell clapper, just as a bell is heard ringing, and a new train from another direction begins to come in, the one which Ned and Johnny will board. The train is summoned up by Helen, through Johnny, with the toy and the bell. Of course, it is also just a train arriving from elsewhere on schedule, as everyone expects.

Throughout this scene Helen is mostly seen from the back, or side and back, at a distance, as she sits, her face partly concealed by a hat and the weeping branch of a tree near her. The film keeps its distance, respecting her grief and pain, allowing the grief and pain privacy, perhaps fearing them (as Murnau keeps his distance, across a room, from Nosferatu at the end with his lover/victim Nina). Helen is imaged as exhausted after, or in the face of, her work, what she has wrought or is wreaking—like Ned earlier collapsed in his chair in the laboratory. In some shots Helen looms lifeless, like a corpse set up, prefiguring the image of Mrs. Bates, the mother, in Hitchcock's *Psycho*, sitting up with her back to us in the cellar—the source of that film, of the destruction and the creation in it.[15] At the end of this scene in *Blonde Venus* we see Helen still sitting, now in the left middle-ground of the shot, and the background is filled by the blank-wall sides of passing train cars as the train goes away, and then blank sides of still cars on a farther-away parallel track, after the moving train is gone. It is a very lengthy shot, asking us to ponder what we see. The blank car sides suggest the screen, and we begin to think of a woman sitting before a movie screen, perhaps a director in a screening room—since she is alone—surveying her work, what she has wrought, and the realm where she may work more at the end of *Morocco*, the blank rising desert in the background as Dietrich walks forward, suggests a screen. Amy Jolly contemplates it, thinks, enters it, and disappears into it, over the horizon, to make a new life. At last now Helen walks out decisively, moving her hands and arms a good deal as if to reflect emotion, and she stands between the tracks, identifying herself with a camera in a way, which moves on tracks. Her long scarf—representing the soul as in Bresson's *Une Femme Douce*, or as a balloon does in *M*—blows up and out. Helen is now very much a human being, caring and alive, for all her identification with the deathly source, and the mechanism, of film.

The succeeding women's flophouse scene is a descent into hell. The camera tracks Helen from the side as she walks into this place, and then a bit later tracks her as she walks back out, the formalism of the track-and-reverse suggesting the ritual nature of what is happening. The place is dark, the human forms hard to discern, as if not fully alive. Between the camera and Helen are large hooks hanging from the ceiling, presumably for clothes—but they suggest a butcher shop or a torture chamber—"My mind is all a case of knives," writes George Herbert. This episode is an obligation, as for Odysseus or Aeneas facing the underworld. It represents a crucial turning of mind. It is a flirtation with the nothingness beyond the edges of life, a flirtation necessary in order to let life and strength flow back in.

Helen is conspicuously drunken, in a state of frenzy we might say, a state for realization of what is beyond life. She meets a woman who is suicidal, and she herself says that she may commit suicide, "make a hole in the water"—which is just what she will do, but in the sense of making an impression in the water of imagination. We soon see that water again that is the recurring image in this film for any medium of self-creation. The death in store for Helen is the death, like baptism, of transformation into further life.

What turns Helen around now is the realization that the suicidal woman's problem is money. Helen immediately gives her the $1,500 Ned had repaid at the train stop, repeating Ned's words exactly, with scorn, ironically: "In this envelope are fifteen hundred dollars. It represents my life work. Had I had time to exploit it properly, I could have made a fortune." The words have struck deep in Helen; she has felt the insult of being paid off for giving up Johnny—and we feel her scorn for Ned's life and world as she says certain words with a cutting emphasis: "life work," "exploit," "fortune." Perhaps she scorns herself as well—"life work," "exploit"—feeling guilt at having hurt Ned by having an affair, and guilt at subjecting Johnny to a breakup. Her drunken state perhaps softens the pain she feels, but the drunkenness makes her ironic stance a bit unclear as well, perhaps to her as to us—it is hard irony, but directed where, exactly?

Money is important in this film, and Helen and Ned are shown at various times to be in considerable material need. But money is also to be "thrown around," as the film's final scene puts it; that is, made light of. In Helen's moment of irony as she repeats her husband's words, she realizes, among whatever other things, that she is above this present world of the dead, or is incompatible with it, incommensurable. This is a world of problems that can be defined, and solved—if the solution, which is known, can be made available—money, for example. Are people's problems ever as definable as this? These figures in hell are perhaps not really people, but pictures for Helen, perhaps pictures she makes.

Helen's problems are in a sense worse than ones that are definable and conceivably solvable. But also, Helen has a freedom of imagination and will that definable problems and their solutions can only sully. Life is her mode, even volatile and suffering life. At the death which is materiality and definability, she must turn back, or rise upward. She rises like Orpheus. Like him at the loss of Euridice, Helen is hurt and dismayed, and as with the primal poet, what has happened to her, and the brush with hell itself, will be turned into song.[16] After she walks back through the flophouse room, with the reversed tracking camera, she ascends a wide and steep staircase—clearly "unreal" for the present locale—and there is a long dissolve of this image to that of a broad surface of water.

A speaker in Plato's *Symposium* says that Alcestis is better than Orpheus, because she was actually willing to die for her family, not just visit hell with the hope of returning, and her reward was consequently great, not song but a renewed life with those who mattered to her. Helen is in effect willing to die, to go under forever. She has brought herself to the point of being willing to forgo her family; though that is not her ultimate will. She will achieve song and, beyond that, regain all that was lost—the same but not the same.

Helen's name now flashes in lights in various shapes, and we assume she has made a success and become a great star—unless it is all a delusion or dream—and this question will not be settled entirely. The name we see is "Helen Jones," the stage name suggested by the theatrical agent back in New York. Whether the name has ever before been used by Helen, we do not know, but the repeated flashing of it suggests a desire on her part to be noticed by old acquaintances, recognized, found out. Right away we see Nick/Cary Grant, snapping his head about like a mechanical doll. It is as if Nick is a creature, even a machine, of Helen's, now finding her out as she intended, and to be used as a means for moving her on, which will be to bring her home.

Nick encounters another man in the lobby of a Paris theater and hears of Helen's rise to fame, her use of men, and her coldness—a certain "exploiting" and pursuit of "fortune," we might think. Perhaps Helen's life now is a form of revenge, based on these words that have haunted her, something she has not gotten beyond. If so, this may explain in part her readiness to give this life up. It is something to play out, not to be fixed in.

The performance we, and Nick, now witness is one of Dietrich's most characteristic and memorable, although—and because, who can say?—it represents a far detachment from life, the turning of suffering and feeling into the most polished and above-it-all of words and song and gesture. She appears in white top hat and tails, with a long cigarette holder and cigarette—a bit of a phallic declaration. She meets the exiting chorus line, and fingers the facial veil and cheek of one of the girls. The reality and resonance of this erotic gesture should tell us that the whole stage act to follow, however cool and splendidly artificial, is a transfiguration of real feeling.

Helen goes into her song, "I Couldn't Be Annoyed" (Leo Robin and Richard Whiting), in French, something of a bravura tongue twister, seeming to have too many words to the line, words made light of, as it were, not seeming to carry full weight. Dietrich walks off the stage and out into the theater on a runner as she sings, everything from her first appearance all through the French part of the song being one extended shot, with an elaborate overhead camera movement following her, guiding her, projecting her. The filmic presentation seems to epitomize the artificial, the carefully staged and the showy, a pure indulgence of imagination.

Helen pauses and notices Nick, who touches her hand, just beside her in the audience, and with *this* contact with reality—is it?—that first extended shot is broken by some cutting as the two speak. Then Helen, giving the orchestra a signal, directing, continues the number in English, getting herself back to the stage, again with a moving camera in one unbroken shot, recreating the spell of the first part of the song.

With the English, Helen/Dietrich seems to settle into meaning, singing exactly with the notes of the accompanying music, with a strong beat. But the words suggest the topsy-turviness of surrealism, a free-floating, transitional state:

> If the moon began to waltz
> Or the sun did somersaults
> Do you think I'd care . . .
> Or if bulls gave milk someway . . .
> Or if babies brought the stork . . .

And the words deny feeling in the face of this chaos or lunacy, or rather, they steel the self to feel nothing *if* such chaos and lunacy should come, the next step—would it be?—beyond the sort of thing already going on in life:

> I couldn't be annoyed! . . .
> I'd still eat crackers in my bed
> What have I got to lose? . . .
> I couldn't be annoyed.[17]

The denial serves to remind us who know what Helen has suffered, and who she is, that she in fact has real feelings, but in response to more ordinary things, things not mentioned here. Placed in the course of the whole film, this glittery song and performance declare a need for the earth, even for difficulties, where feelings do come—but without the intense infliction of pain that drives one off the earth.

The song has transformed the real suffering of the past into polished, smiling, seemingly detached art, with game-playing about future possibilities. Something of the attitude here, the poise, might conceivably be carried back into ordinary life where feelings come. Helen/Dietrich's smile, as she does this number, is genuine but something short of warm—not seeming false, but not directly involved in life's dramas. To some extent it is Helen/Dietrich's smile of delight at her own art, her power of mind. It is something like the smile of the decapitated but talking Milena, in her afterlife at the end of *WR*—a smile like that of the Buddha, where distress and what are deeply felt are worked into a complex, perhaps fragile, image or form of gracefulness—gracefulness that can be an active way of approach to what one is faced with, what may come. The image or form may be that of a moment—offered rightly, or looked at rightly, it may be for all time. We, the audience, the contemplators, may take it away with us.

The image of Helen at the end of her song dissolves to her dressing-room mirror, another figure for the screen as it turns out to be, with an inscription in soap or paint, from Kipling—"Down to Gehenna or up to the Throne, / He travels the fastest who travels alone"—and with a drawing of a gallows. The whole picture suggests the readiness for death, and the solitariness, that seem to have driven Helen ever since the giving up of the child. The writing on a mirror suggests impermanence—"writ on water . . ."—as if these words are not the final ones for Helen. And who has written them, the words, and drawn the picture? She herself? A good, or evil, angel? Perhaps the gallows signifies the death, or doing-in, of these words, this message, this attitude. The whole image, showy as it is, seems an extension of the stage act, which was the trying out of an attitude. The note of death here suggests that Helen's present state is a death-in-life, as in the flophouse scene, or the earlier tomb-like apartment with Nick—a death that may be a good death, something to go through.

Helen has a scene with Nick here (with flowers about, as in that earlier apartment/tomb scene); she invited him backstage when they met just then during the act. She called him there "Old Nick"—perhaps he *was* her devil and is no more, or will still be her devil, in what he leads her to next. She will move down to earth; and the Devil, especially in Germany, is associated with the earth, its attractions and materiality—flesh and blood, things as they are. Helen flirts with the Devil as a way to get somewhere beyond the Devil, as did Christ, or perhaps Goethe's Dr. Faust, or Mann's—every step here is in question.

Nick urges Helen to come away with him and see Johnny again in New York, and she insists that she does not want to, and does not care any more about Johnny. But the scene is immediately followed by a view of a newspaper page announcing that Helen is in fact returning to New York with Nick. She was bluffing with him for a moment—or she became fully herself only in private, in a moment we do not see. She certainly has had the means simply to go back to New York alone, if that is her desire. But she needs the attraction of Nick to bring herself to do what she desires. Perhaps she needs him to speak right out to her about Johnny, and it has to sink in. Perhaps Nick provides a cover for her, in her mind, a way of going to New York without admitting to herself fully what it is for.

Helen creates the newspaper report we see now, as people who become newspaper subjects are often said to "create headlines." But Helen creates this report as an artist creates, too. The newspaper here, suddenly filling the screen, is a form of art and self-expression just as much as it is a reporting medium.

The final scene, of Helen's reunion with Ned and Johnny, has very much the quality of being Helen's film, or Helen and Ned and Johnny's together. The newspaper we have just seen turns out to be in Ned and Johnny's hands, and Ned is—though rather bitterly—encouraging Johnny to remember his mother. It is just what Ned said he would work against, when he took Johnny away, and what he will say in a moment to Nick that he has indeed been working against. But now in this little conversation with Johnny over the newspaper Ned appears really to be linked with Helen in the project of reunion.

There is again—it should not be a surprise now—an image of a boat on water. And Helen and Nick arrive on the stair landing outside the original apartment, and it is more broadly the landing for those who travel by this water we have seen, the water of imagination. Helen is dressed strikingly in a skull cap and long slender coat, looking ready to participate in a ritual or strange adventure. Nick goes in to speak to Ned, who puts Johnny away in an inner room and draws sliding doors together, as if readying a film screen, showing his at-oneness with Helen as director.

Ned is caustic with Nick, who offers him money to let Helen see Johnny; Ned says he can "throw money around" too, and that Helen may come in "for nothing," that is, for free. "For nothing" also has an edge of "to no purpose," but Ned seems to know better than that, or to intuit what will happen. We may wonder if the scene that is to occur will be "nothing" in another sense, an unstable scene rather than an ending. Or a nothing that is something, like art, like film itself, just marks or shadows, which can amount to so much. All of life is nothing that is something—nothing if we would insist on ascertaining it, pinning it down, proving exactly what it is. Ned is linked to Helen in the freedom of his gesture, letting her come in for nothing—acting like an artist, willing to create something. The music associated with home begins to play, and Helen comes in.

Johnny emerges as a participant in the direction of this scene. Of course, he may have affected Ned already in determining what to do about Helen. And while Ned and Nick speak about Helen, there is intercutting between Johnny in his room, with his interest rising, and Helen outside on the landing, showing anxiety and directing her attention through the closed door. A bond, almost a sightline through closed doors, is established between the boy and his mother. Now, as Helen enters the apartment, there is a cut that effectively gives the camera to Johnny. First we see him close up in his inner room where Ned has put him, on the floor and playing with his toys. Then there is the cut to a view of the closed sliding doors, the screen of sorts, the view appearing to be Johnny's own. The doors are now pulled open by Helen, who is suddenly there, revealing herself, as it were, entering the film of the door/screen, a film for Johnny, or his own film, made by him, what he wants—or is Helen pulling the screen apart, revealing her actual self as something more immediate than film, or beyond film? (This sequence is amazingly replayed in John Cassavetes's 1974 film *A Woman Under the Influence*. At the end, Mabel/Gena Rowlands, mother, difficult wife, lover of opera, whom her world thinks mad but still wants, is allowed to return home, and in the living room of her house she confronts sliding doors acting like a film screen, before which, up against which, upon which, she must be exposed to old family tensions and must act a role that will be accepted, and going *through* which she enters an intimate world of reunion with her children.)

In *Blonde Venus* there is now a prolonged view of Johnny, seen from above, from Helen's position. Johnny appears *not* to have looked up yet, so that his summoning of his mother with the camera's view up to the doors was—what?—only interior? or what Helen herself imagined or desired him to do? He directs, but only in his mind, or in her mind. But what he directs comes true.

Now Johnny does look up, with astonishment, and his mother Helen kneels beside him and accepts—and returns—the child's long, fierce embrace. The compounding of film imagination with reality and actual contact here seems all but endless. Ned slides the doors shut again, exposing their blank surface to us—we are with him outside now. Ned gives Helen and Johnny their privacy, while enforcing, with these doors, his role as maker of this film/life along with Helen and Johnny. Privacy—film creates and reveals, perhaps even brings life about, but it does not give us all. There is more than film—or any art? or any state of mind?—will encompass.

When Helen has removed her coat and moved about the apartment preparing water to wash Johnny, and Nick has left, it is time for the repeated bedtime story. Johnny requests and directs it, questioning Helen and Ned and telling them what to say and do. We see Johnny in his bed as he orders his parents to walk, and with a cut, Helen enters a shot with Ned. Eventually Helen sings the German lullaby, and starts the carrousel music box. When Johnny goes to sleep, Helen looks up at Ned and sings to him—he is her rose here—seductively, honestly, as if really to win the feeling she wants—or sings gratefully—or perhaps just happily, with her inner thoughts her own—or putting up a front, retaining with her inner thoughts. The whole film—all film, all art—is the putting up a front for thoughts no one outside—nor oneself even?—can see directly—the film's thoughts, not plain but ever interesting.

Ned comes into the frame with Helen now, and the two agree that she will stay with the family—"It's where you belong, Helen." This is Johnny's dream, in a way, as he slumbers—Johnny who is part of Helen, or is her very imagination or will, as well as her fate—and he is part of Ned too. The sense of authorship of this scene keeps shifting, or allowing one figure to be included in another, as the three of them enact this ritual of reunion, which may give shape to their lives from now on. A ritual is a yielding of personal authority, and yet an act of will and desire as well.

Johnny seems to wake up a little, challenging the distinction between the sleeper/dreamer and one who is awake, and his hand reaches up to finger the revolving musical carrousel. He does not cause it to play, but involves himself with it as it plays, his fingers filling the screen in that astonishing close-up—flesh and blood, which is here film, fingering film, as the film's orchestral soundtrack sings out to us, inviting us to dream like Johnny, Helen's child and extension of herself—we who are the film's love, its rose.

Will Helen stay with her family? Can she be imagined with Ned? If she stays, will she work as well? Will they have money, so that their life will be different from what it was?

The film does not declare what will be the case. The film has to do with what is actually happening—not what will be fixed—and with who Helen/Dietrich is, which is not to be fixed.

There is something forced and incongruous, as well as—if you like—emotionally right and conclusive, about the final scene: Helen in her fine, strange clothes, a woman who is featured in the newspapers, coming here; the difficulty of talking with Ned; the image of Helen with her coat off, but in her fine blouse and still in her hat, hurrying across the room with a towel and pan of water to bathe the child. The situation, we see, may fall apart. Or the instability, imaged in incongruousness, may be positive, the poetic instability that a good—or good enough—life is.

The *Bhagavad Gita* teaches, shockingly, that it is the same whether one acts or does not act, whether one wins or loses. This is a paradox to be thought about—thought out a long, long way, like the classic Christian paradox that what becomes of us is determined, and yet we have free will. According to the *Gita*, in order for it to be the same whether we act or do not act, we must become cognizant of the all, and the good of all—not easy concepts. This good is challenging to conceive—like the disrupted good of Nietzsche, or of Helen in this film—"I want to be bad," "I'm no good, except . . ."

The teaching of the *Bhagavad Gita* is not for an opting out—Krishna advises Arjuna, all things considered, to act and to try to win against his enemies (who are his cousins—the problem is domestic), and Arjuna does act and does win. The paradox is that the local and immediate rightness of acting in a certain way, and getting a certain outcome, is not at odds with its being the same whether one acts or does not, wins or loses.

In a sense it is the same whether Helen returns home to her family, or does not. The film declares this by making the return seem arbitrary—playful in a way—while not denying the real needs of Helen's little boy, or the pull he has on her. She plays out the return as her own bit of film imagination—just as she has played out much perhaps of her life before this. The Gita says that to have a vision is actually one with creating, taking action.

It is immediately right for Helen to return, as it is for Dietrich to submit to play the role in this film, because others want it, the world wants it, the film genre wants it—perhaps to show the cost and pain of it. And can we deny that the character Helen, and the actress Dietrich, wants what she does in the film—wants it immediately even if in a larger view she might want that it not be?

In the way Helen makes the return, it is a creative triumph for her, a voicing of herself which her husband and child, and the film audience, can acknowledge and be glad of—for her sake—even though she cannot be fully understood. Creativity links Helen/Dietrich to the imaginative powers that seem to form the film and all of life. This link amounts perhaps to a cognizance of the all, and of the good of all. The creative link is at least a symbol of such cognizance—a symbol for *us* of a cognizance *she* fully has—a way for her and us both to know and take part in what cannot be made clear in terms we have. Film—so much the art of terms we have, the filmable world, and at the same time the art of what we have no terms for, the power that makes the world.

Because of the poetry and triumph, gathered from the course of the whole film, in Helen's taking of action at the end, it is as if she had not done this thing, or had done some other thing. But the melodrama, and our sense of reality, insist, this taking of action is her fate.

On we go.

Short Takes

5

The Path of Art in *Chronicle of a Summer* and *Le joli mai*

> It is something to be able to paint a particular picture, or to carve a statue, and so to make a few objects beautiful; but it is far more glorious to carve and paint the very atmosphere and medium through which we look, which morally we can do. To affect the quality of the day, that is the highest of arts.
>
> —Henry David Thoreau (83)

> What fine chisel
> Could ever yet cut breath?
>
> —*Winter's Tale* V.3

JEAN ROUCH AND EDGAR MORIN's *Chronicle of a Summer* (1960), like Chris Marker and Pierre Lhomme's *Le joli mai* (1963), offers a series of pictures of, and voiced complaints about, hedged-in and frustrated lives. We are in Paris at the beginning of the 1960s. Economic difficulties, political disappointment, race prejudice, memories of the Holocaust, fatigue with the Algerian War, the failure of personal existential experiments: all seem to confine people and make those we meet unhappy—despite flashes of good humor and a general friendliness. Yet near the beginning of *Chronicle* comes an episode that proposes an alternative to what we see elsewhere in the film—proposes, even, an image for the project of the film itself in the face of the many blank walls and closed doors of the world the film documents. This alternative and image is the path of art.

After a series of ineffective brief street interviews, asking people, "Are you happy?"—often getting a "no" or a refusal to talk—and then a visit to a couple who run an auto repair shop and "cook the books" to get by, the film turns to Madi and Henri, two artists and free spirits. The auto mechanic has said that a little extra money made from tax evasion allows him to get together with his friends and "do nothing"—he looks less than inspired, rather resigned, as he says this. On the word "nothing"—*rien*—the film cuts to darkness, perhaps an image of the nothing that is all many can imagine or aspire to. Out of this darkness a door opens into bright light, and *Chronicle*'s subjects/assistants Marceline and Nadine enter Madi and Henri's living space.

Marceline and Nadine appear as silhouettes against the light for a time, and during the visit one or the other, first Nadine, then Marceline, holds a microphone, all underscoring their status as filmmakers, or filmmaking agents, contemplating, not living, the life before them, though, of course, they converse and interact with those they visit here, and they are before us—themselves filmed—not the usual kind of filmmakers. The cameraperson is not seen, but moves behind Marceline and Nadine through the door and turns left to take in the room—a walking and moving, almost, it seems, a breathing presence and participant in the scene.

This first shot reveals an apparent garret room—one wall slanted inward, with an art poster fastened to it—a floor-level bed in the corner left and back, shelves and small tables here and there with books, quirky figurines, and oddments—a bohemian space, made splendid by the large double window/door opening to a small balcony opposite us, letting in all the light. The four introduce themselves, Henri sitting on the bed, Madi in the foreground, wearing a large coral necklace—one thinks, costume, though perhaps it is a treasure—over her white sweater-blouse, offering a plate of cakes. Marceline says the filmmakers have heard this couple is happy—and the film cuts to a close view of the sitting Henri, dressed in black, with a goatee, as he philosophizes a bit on the concept of happiness. We enter an abstract, one might say philosophical, space for a few moments, blank wall behind Henri's head, no décor visible, only Marceline in the left foreground, seen from the side holding her microphone and looking at Henri, overlaying him a bit, visually merged with him. We concentrate on ideas, Henri saying the idea of happiness doesn't concern him, he just tries to pursue a life "in harmony with himself," now along with Madi.

We learn about their life in a series of protracted shots where rich imagery comes back to life. The camera that entered the room so boldly, now seems inventive, finding marvelous ways to look at things—yet, of course, only registering what is there, discovering what is before it.

Madi is framed on the right in profile against the bright window, Henri and the wall to the left, as she talks ebulliently and with a sense of humor about working earlier with friends to make and sell fake antiques, then falling out with the others and being disappointed with business. A second shot, lower angle, as she talks on, gives us more of her face, and the bright light behind her fills the background entirely—the room is gone. Like the auto shop people, she has cheated to get by, but now she has changed her life. The light behind her enhances—in a way even projects—her sense of excitement about life, suggesting expansiveness, adventure, stepping from one life to another. One thinks of Emerson's essay "Circles."

Once again we see the whole room, as the camera follows Madi bending down near the foot of the bed to fetch a plate of fruit from a low table—the camera taking in a vase of flowers, a candelabrum, miniature cars along a shelf—and Madi offers the fruit around, as Henri begins to talk about being a painter in order to learn more. Being an artist broadens into life and the larger understanding. The four settle around the open glass doors to the balcony—we view them straight on, looking toward the opening and light—as the couple go on about time spent in the south, painting, doing odd jobs to get by. Suggestions of sex make Nadine and even the serious-mannered Henri and Marceline laugh and Madi react with slight embarrassment. The grand view off the balcony becomes clear—down onto a large park full of trees with the city and sky in the distance. The view seems to image the couple's spirit and accomplishment of reaching out of themselves over and over, making life worthwhile even out of little. In a new shot, perhaps from the bed, perpendicular to the shot looking out through the balcony, we see Marceline on the left with her microphone, and see part of Henri, both set off and framed behind the open glass door. On the right in a larger space are Madi and Nadine, with two shelves of books behind them, seen with no intervening glass. The image divided by the vertical wood edge of the glass door suggests the golden mean, as in a painting by Piero della Francesca. There is a sense of two worlds, a narrower one on the left, behind glass, and one more directly open on the right—

but filmmakers and subjects are mixed in their placement in these two worlds. Contemplation and the life contemplated are mixed. With a cut, the camera peeks around the door edge to view Marceline and Henri directly, shadowed against the light—then cuts to Madi bathed in light as she speaks of lying in the sun in the south. In the final shot of the whole group from inside the room, looking toward the balcony, Nadine is positioned differently, now sitting on the bed to the left of the window/door. There is a suggestion of fantasy in the use of space, someone out of sight for a moment having moved, or been moved—a further bit of film creativity, as it were in response to the creativity of Madi and Henri, artists and artists of life.

The episode closes with one of the film's most striking gestures. As Madi says that whenever they sell a painting they buy something to make life richer, the camera follows Henri across the room to start up a large music box—a cabinet that displays a large wheel facing the viewer, with many small holes to cue sounds as the wheel turns, and decorated with a sort of allegorical angel-like figure. Eventually we see over her a name made illegible by the punctures on the wheel, and under her the words "*marque de fabrique*," trademark—beauty and commerce, art and commerce, as in the Elizabethan drama, Dickens, film. As the wheel turns and the music plays, the film cuts to closer and still closer views of the wheel, filling the frame and offering to spellbind us.

It is an act of adoration on the camera's part—adoration of the device and, indirectly, of Madi and Henri. And it feels as if the film, cutting in and in, presses to identify itself with the device, perhaps recognizing in the turning wheel that produces music—art—an analogy to the film reel. One point of this whole episode is to open the film to a life alternative to what we see in the rest of the film. Another point, with Marceline and Nadine interacting with the artists, and with the camera becoming conspicuously inventive, is to identify the film itself with creativity. Finally now the camera tilts up past the top of the wheel into darkness, giving a sense of darkness descending down onto the wheel—an image of that black nothing invoked by the auto shop scene, out of which the present episode grew—the nothingness that always presses and has to be overcome.

Chronicle moves on to hear men around a table discuss the drudgery and meager remuneration of work; to observe the factory worker Angelo's hard day dawn to dark; to question the Italian girl Marilou about her depression and spiritual paralysis; to hear about disappointment with political activism and the struggle to keep alive a small part of one's authentic self amid the life society forces one to lead; and so on. Throughout all this we do not forget—are meant not to forget, I think—the alternative life of Madi and Henri. The suggestion is not that everyone should "be an artist" and make much—and enjoy much—out of little. Art and the artist's life do not prescribe—they take a perspective on life, perhaps open a door, perhaps set some new energy at play, and ask us to rethink ourselves, perhaps give us a breath, an impetus, to move on and out.

Emerson's disciple Nietzsche became the subject of Martin Heidegger's four-volume celebratory study. The thinking there seems apt. Says Heidegger: "Art is the basic occurrence of all beings; to the extent that they are, beings are self-creating, created" and "Art, thought in the broadest sense as the creative, constitutes the basic character of beings" (*Nietzsche* 72). Furthermore, "Art is the distinctive counter-movement to nihilism" (73). Quoting Nietzsche, "The will to *semblance*, to illusion, to deception, to Becoming and change is deeper, more 'metaphysical,' than the will to *truth*, to reality" (qtd. in Heidegger 74). "We have *art* in order *not to perish from the truth*," says Nietzsche, calling art "the greatest *stimulans* of life" (qtd. 75). Heidegger comments, "a 'stimulant' is what propels and advances, what lifts a thing beyond itself" (76).

All valid films, documentary and otherwise, take a creative approach to their subjects. It begins with the Lumières and camera placement, and goes far in documentary very early with Flaherty and Vertov and their various creative ways, both of whom interested Jean Rouch so. Films practice art in order to make revelations—we might say, in order to learn, as Henri says of his painting. *Chronicle of a Summer* makes its creativity unusually conspicuous. We hear Rouch's voice at the beginning, inviting us to attend to "an experiment in film truth"—*cinéma-vérité*, rendering in French Vertov's *Kino-Pravda*—where "truth" is not "the truth," captured by film, but *film* truth, a new truth in the realm of art, which enables a new approach to truth, or a rethinking of truth, or a transformation of truth. Right away Rouch and codirector Edgar Morin appear onscreen, talking with their subject and helper Marceline about whether being filmed alters people. William Rothman has written eloquently about the way Morin, again onscreen later, and the camera along with him probe and push Marilou to think and speak about her despair—perhaps her session with Morin starts her path to recovery, which she talks about later. The film introduces people to one another—relationships are begun. It invites a large group to a rooftop lunch and asks them to think about politics, Africa, and race in ways they appear not to have done before. Marceline, perhaps inspired by her meeting with Madi and Henri, contrives with the film to make her own creative breakthrough, performing her monologue of Holocaust memories, walking through the Place de la Concorde and Les Halles. The film at last takes many of its subjects on vacation to the south of France—we see them bathing in the sea, attending a bullfight, rock climbing, singing a campfire song. There is a strong note to all this of escape from life as it is, a strong suggestion that the as-is and as-was can be escaped or overcome. It is not for the film to say how, exactly, or to specify the next realm—just to give the impulse. The communal song continues as the film transitions to a view of a projector beam against the dark—pure light, film at its most abstract, the sheer idea of film, and reminiscent of Madi and Henri's musical wheel set against the dark—and we are in a screening room where *Chronicle*'s participants and others discuss the version of *Chronicle* they have just seen.

Finally Rouch and Morin walk a corridor of the Musée de l'Homme, discussing the film as a registering of life and as a project that affects lives—they are aware of dangers of misrepresentation and of meddling, but they believe in their film. *Chronicle* continually, and very decidedly at the end, declares that it is a film, a creative work, where creativity enables understanding, and achieves what may work as an example and a stimulus. Life, for good or ill, can be film. One can approach and mold one's life—the very "atmosphere," Thoreau says—with something like film creativity.

After *Chronicle*'s Paris in the summer of 1960, Chris Marker and Pierre Lhomme's film *Le joli mai* focuses on Paris in May of 1962, just

at the end of the Algerian War, when all was not settled and violent acts and violent controversy continued. *Chronicle* gets quite close to a small number of people—individuals appear more than once in the film, and we see evolution in their lives. *Le joli mai*, a much longer film, is more panoramic—we meet more people, and more of a diversity, from the desperately poor up through the middling sort to the professional class, a black African, an Arab, a young soldier and his girlfriend. None reappear—no one is seen to change. "Nothing changes" seems to be the running theme of this film, which itself calls out strongly for change. People express discontent, but say they do not like to think, or think about others or about the wider society and politics. Some are good humored and say they are hopeful—vaguely. (Some find distractions: an overworked clothes salesman enjoys movies [but not *Last Year at Marienbad* (1961)]; a taxi driver and tire repairman paints pictures, but his world remains one of shadows and auto parts; a man who "does not like to think" strives for the record in dancing the twist for hours; a reclusive young woman dresses up cats.)

Late in *Joli mai* three intellectuals—economists, perhaps—sit around a table and discuss possibilities for work and leisure, in tediously abstract and circular terms. Cutaways to cat faces, with incongruous spidery harpsichord music, seem to mock the discussion. The film desperately wants to break out. Then, as one man begins to say, "Look . . . see who is working . . . they just add and subtract statistics [i.e., not real work]," the film cuts to a view of Jean Rouch and Edgar Morin sitting at an outdoor café table, then cuts quickly to views of other filmmakers: Jean-Luc Godard driving a little car and pointing his finger at the camera across his passenger, Anna Karina; Jacques Rivette smiling amid people on a city street, tall, majestic, self-assured; and Alain Resnais walking, seen in a closer, tracking shot—like so many of his own—looking serious and determined. These artists and chroniclers of Paris are surely to be taken as doing worthwhile work. Their work may illuminate our lives and the commonweal, may stimulate us to move on and out—just as, the implication is, *Le joli mai* itself may do.

We see *Chronicle of a Summer* affect the lives of its subjects—this can stand as a metaphor for how the film might affect its viewers' lives, or the life of society. We do not see *Joli mai*'s subjects changed or evolving—but the film does ask them questions: Have you thought about *this*? Have you thought about *that*?—perhaps they will begin to think, as we, the film's viewers, may do. With Madi and Henri, *Chronicle* early on gives us an example of creative living, life merged with art—an example with which the film identifies itself in its own way of proceeding. *Chronicle* makes its creative gestures conspicuous as it goes along, declaring its way of understanding and of affecting the world to be art. *Le joli mai* opens with a rich, reflective voiceover commentary on Paris and its history and what has been *thought* there, as we watch cinematographer Pierre Lhomme's breathtakingly fresh images of the city—all in all, a strong creative gambit. Sarah Cooper has remarked, in her study of Marker, that he first fully found himself as an artist with the poetic voiceovers and image construction of *Le joli mai* and the contemporary fiction *La jetée*. *Le joli mai*'s example of an artist, comparable to Madi and Henri, comes late in the film: the theatrical dressmaker who avoids the world, stays home a good deal, and fancifully dresses up her cat. The episode has a note of desperation as well as humor—a sense of its own absurdity, albeit necessary absurdity—that echoes the cutaways to cats and filmmakers during the conversation of the economists a bit earlier. The artistic desperation of the cat lady episode can seem to spark and inspire the film's concluding rich and reflective voiceover meditation, coming soon, on prisons of the mind. The film's panoramic sociology moves it finally to an artistic venture and an artistic call to go beyond ourselves—in Heidegger's words, poetic in the manner of Marker, "reaching out toward what we believe we can but barely overcome, barely survive" (*Nietzsche* 116)

One project of *The Will to Power as Art* is to rethink the concept of beauty from Plato and Kant to Nietzsche and the twentieth century. In a manner akin to Elaine Scarry's book *On Beauty and Being Just*, Heidegger says that beauty sets a standard for life, but one that calls on our own creativity and sense of self-development even to comprehend, much less to live out. Reaching out beyond ourselves to the fearful and saving: Heidegger quotes the First Duino Elegy, "Beauty is the beginning of terror, which we but scarcely endure; and we feel wonder, because it calmly disdains to destroy us" (*Nietzsche* 116). If *Chronicle of a Summer* and *Le joli mai* are beautiful, can we admit their beauty and see a path open for us?

Other lines of Rilke come to mind. In "Archaic Torso of Apollo" the beautifully realized object, distant from us like, if you will, the world of a film screen, is yet bursting with life and challenge: "here there is no place / that does not see you. You must change your life" (61).

6

Fiction and Nonfiction in Chantal Akerman's Films

I GOT TO KNOW CHANTAL AKERMAN some years ago when we coincided as visitors teaching in Harvard's film program. I ran into her one day, early in our acquaintance, as she was rummaging in the projection booth of the main screening room in Harvard's Carpenter Center. She said she was looking to see if a print had come in that she wanted to show to her filmmaking class—Robert Bresson's *Pickpocket* (1959). "They see so much bullshit," she commented. We had no need to say more.

Akerman did talk to me a number of times subsequently about her admiration for Bresson and about his being an inspiration for her, and of course she talked about this publicly. Many things come into play: an aspiration for serious, independent, challenging, indeed radically experimental film art that yet works through the medium of the theatrical feature film; a disposition to pare down, to find a lot in a little, or release a lot from a little; a certain view of life, unblinking—even grim—about people and their motives and what people are up against in this world, yet a view where ecstasy, transcendence, even humor, can come alive. Bresson's *Four Nights of a Dreamer* (1972) is a film full of humor, even "good humor," as is much Akerman from at least *Toute une nuit* (1982) and *Window Shopping* (1985) on. Perhaps Bresson and Akerman are humorous when they want to be utopian, to imagine what people and life *can* be, might be, recognizing that people and life already are this to an extent, as Stanley Cavell argues about classical Hollywood in its characteristic mode of romantic comedy, something he took very seriously—and Akerman's *A Couch in New York* (1996) bears close relation to classical Hollywood romantic comedy.

Akerman remarked to me once how struck she was by Bresson's final film, *L'Argent* (*Money*, 1983), in which a sympathetic young man, an outcast, ultimately goes berserk and kills people. She remarked on how amazingly tense she found the film, each image filled with a tension ready to explode into the next, which goes on moment by moment all the way through the film. Such tension does not sound like Akerman, and yet she has her tension, as does all valid film, as does all poetry, all that is *made*—a tension compounded of extension and intension, an attunement to the physical world as it is, in its extension, and an imbuing of the world with meaning, or a discovery of meaning, intension—so Allen Tate explained long ago in a famous essay, "Tension in Poetry." Akerman's tension is to be *discovered* if not immediately felt. On each viewing of an Akerman film, in my experience, its peculiar tension becomes more and more clear and palpable. Disclosure of the everyday is much of what she is about, and the emergence of a peculiar tension is at the heart of this disclosure.[1] Tension, in the sense of restlessness, or energy moving more than one way, or the physical held in balance with overtones of meaning, is *in* the everyday, something to be revealed that we might ordinarily overlook, something for documentation with an intelligent and probing eye. And tension is in the *presentation*, the abstraction from reality, the very creativity of approach and structure in the film, holding the world up for view in a certain extended form. Here documentation and *fiction*—a making or fashioning—come together or blur.

Go back to *Pickpocket* for a moment, the film Akerman wanted to show to her class as an instruction, and inspiration, a medicine for the sensibility. This film is possessed of a remarkable doubleness. It can look virtually like a documentary, doing its best to give the sense of observing ordinary people going about their lives, traversing the Paris streets, riding the Metro, talking in bars, descending into petty crime. But looked at another way the film is pure choreography, abstraction, all its composition and movement seeming highly controlled, the sound effects of course carefully manipulated, everything coming off as a beautiful, highly artificial shadow play. A crowd swarms placing bets at a racetrack—yet the people flow in a steady rhythm here and there across the screen like ghosts in Dante. A young man stands behind a woman and fingers open her purse and extracts money, as the horses race by offscreen—yet the crescendo and decrescendo of thundering hooves gives us the man's panic and then his excitement over success, like a wave of sexual ecstasy. The messiness of everyday life is as if imbued with direction from the outside, eventually moving, in this particular film, toward transforming change, this man and his world not being subject to the access of grace—coming from the outside, or coming from the inside in a way that is not usually acknowledged—until this film points to it and asserts it.

All film is possessed of a doubleness as between passively observing, registering the world, letting it come forth, and on the other hand actively transfiguring the world, making something out of it. The question is always, Does a film show intelligence about its powers of doubleness? Does the film really do something with this power? Bresson, for one, seems about as far as possible from cliché, from any half-alive formula for making fantasy seem real. And if a film does show intelligence, what are the *specifics* of its way with the real and the created? There are many ways in film of involving the real with the creative, letting the real show itself fully or become itself fully through involvement with the creative, the fictive, the structuring power—while, conversely, letting the special insight or worth of the creative enforce itself through seeming to be newly infused with reality, more possessed of reality than anything yet seen. The French New Wave, with its spontaneity of scripting, performance, shooting, editing, found a way. Pier Paolo Pasolini found a way with his barbs of sexuality and subproletarian behavior woven into a film's larger tapestry of mythic import. And Akerman has found her own way, her own balances and imbalances. Or, as with Bresson or Godard or Agnès Varda or Pasolini, each film of hers finds a way.

Some time after I first got to know Akerman, I wrote an entry on her for Ian Aitken's *Encyclopedia of the Documentary Film*. Akerman was in Cambridge again visiting a friend, and I thought I had better show the piece to her before sending it in. She kindly said that she liked it, saw no problem or gaffe, and especially liked places where I pointed to a strong documentary element in the fiction films. She conceded that it seemed right to have an entry on her in an encyclopedia of documentary, but said, "You know, I don't think, at least with my own work, that there are two kinds of film, fiction and documentary. To me they are all just films. I make them out of my feelings, one after another."

Now we mostly think of there being a difference between nonfiction and fiction, however hard it may be to spell out. We have heard plenty from film theorists about how documentary inevitably changes reality merely by looking at it, and all the more in the full structured account it gives, with editing and explanations. And we have heard, going way back—Samuel Johnson, Aristotle—about how fiction can be realistic. Cesare Zavattini wrote a famous manifesto for realistic fiction film. We hold to there being a distinction between fiction and nonfiction, though we see how much qualification has to be made in using these terms. Perhaps the two terms are necessary to begin thinking about a film, and can be taken away like scaffolding once the work of consideration is done, letting us remain just with the film as it is. We seem to need to think of fate and free will as opposites, but can come to admit the paradox that both are always true of life, that they coincide, that they are terms that can lead us to a third thing, beyond them.

Je tu il elle (*I You He She*, 1974), Akerman's first feature, ends with a long scene where two young women, one of them Akerman, make love passionately on a bed. The scene is filmed in three long takes, each made with a fixed camera. The sound of breathing and of skin moving against bed sheets seems natural and synchronous with what we see. Are these two women acting? What is "acting" as opposed to real action? Where is the line to be drawn? Can deliberate acting be pushed into the realm of erotic abandon, so that it simply becomes that, turns into it? This episode stirs such questions in us. And what is the scene's relation to the rest of the film? In the fiction that comes before, first, the Chantal figure is isolated in her apartment, brooding on existence, moving about, writing, as passages of voiceover give a somewhat inaccurate account of things that we see; and then, in the film's second part, the Chantal figure travels with a male truck driver, ultimately reaching the place where her old girlfriend lives. A number of things might be implied: that the flux of human identity and of a woman's interaction with a man comes to rest in lesbian sexual experience, as the airiness of fiction gives way to fact, the unreal in a sense giving way to the real. Or, that the fact of intense physical bonding and, surely, bonding in feeling, is indeed a relative thing, depending for what it is on its being a contrast to the life that leads up to it and, presumably, goes on after it—a life experienced as if a bit, at least, unreal. How different the love scene in *Je tu il elle* would seem if we did not have to wait for it; if a protracted narrative did not, as it does, explode into this surprising and overwhelming material. And then there is the funny thing that these three long takes of the women in bed—involved in a carnality that appears genuinely felt—can begin to look abstract, a study in shades of white—skin, bed-sheets, wall—or a study of the motion of long dark hair, swishing about like the black hair of Kinuyo Tanaka in the wind in Mizoguchi's *Sansho the Bailiff* (*Sanshô dayû*,

1954), or the hair of Godard's Mary in *Hail Mary* (*Je vous salue, Marie*, 1985) as she thrashes about nude in bed, making love to God perhaps (and I think that *Je tu il elle* got under Godard's skin and influenced the imagery of *Hail Mary*—Akerman told me that Godard wanted to use some of her "nude scene" in *Histoire(s) du Cinéma* [1989], but that she did not like the idea). In short, the women in bed become film, specifically black and white film. They are transfigured. They become something made by an artist—fiction. Even the paucity of cutting seems artistic, it is so deliberate, so out of the ordinary. Reality, it would seem, cannot escape being a representation, even though there is still reality there. Such are some of the peculiar tensions set up in or found by *Je tu il elle*.

With *Jeanne Dielman, 23 quai du commerce, 1080 Bruxelles* (1975) Akerman made one of the crucial films in film history. The film is long, at three hours and twenty minutes, and grand—it has grandeur about it—though it focuses on just forty-eight hours spread over three calendar days in the life of an obscure widow keeping house for herself and her teenaged son, with much routine and repetition, little conversation in their life, and deliberate avoidance of thought, speculation, or any access of new feeling—the compulsion to avoid certainly having something to do with the fact that Jeanne, for all her lower-middle-class respectability, accepts a sexual client each afternoon. The film is crucial just because of its derivation of grandeur from this mundane material, a disclosure of the everyday unlike anything we have seen, and all this before, about halfway through the film, something starts to bubble up in Jeanne, feelings come forth and brooding occurs, things start to go wrong, leading to a violent outburst on Jeanne's part, an act of violence, at the end. A quality in this film of documentation of the mundane, fused with Greek tragedy.

As with the sex in *Je tu il elle*, we want to ask about certain things in *Jeanne Dielman*: Are they not pure documentary—observing a woman in real time mixing up and molding a meat loaf, peeling enough potatoes for dinner, scrubbing the bathtub, and so on? The sense we get is that we need this raw fact and real-time observation to understand where Jeanne's life centers, where she is constrained, and also to understand the pure physicality and repetition that allow, not simply compel, her avoidance of reflection. One notable thing is that this unprecedented documentation of the mundane involves a performance. Delphine Seyrig brings to the molding of a meatloaf or shopping for a button all the dignity and fascination of her walking the hallways in Resnais' *Last Year at Marienbad*. In Jeanne are we dealing, after all, with an extraordinary woman constrained by ordinary life? Perhaps every woman who is constrained by ordinary life is extraordinary. Perhaps we simply see in Delphine Seyrig what we might see if we looked harder elsewhere. Perhaps to see the dignity and fascination of the everyday, it is necessary that it become film—which is, of course, to be filmed in a certain way and screened, but also perhaps to be incarnated in a film being, even a star. Certainly someone who is not an actor can become a compelling film being, or star. Witness the man Flaherty calls Nanook, or Bresson's pickpocket or Mouchette, or even the donkey in *Au hasard Balthazar* (1966).[2] And Seyrig molding a meatloaf or washing the dishes is not exactly acting—acting as opposed to doing. What happens with the raw facts of *Jeanne Dielman* is, as with *Je tu il elle*, a documentation and transfiguration at once, with the suggestion that documentation needs transfiguration, that what is to be documented comes to us only as transfigured, in ordinary experience—so Western philosophy since Kant acknowledges (and Eastern philosophy much earlier)—as well as in film that means to be true to, to be revelatory of, ordinary experience.

Part of the dignity of *Jeanne Dielman* comes from a formal decision, to shoot most everything transpiring in the apartment with a fixed camera at a slightly low angle, cutting only with the end of a whole activity and movement to a new room. Akerman has suggested that the point of view is like that of a fascinated child watching its mother, and has said that her observation of Jeanne she meant to be adoring, patient, sometimes puzzled. The formal pattern gives the film something of the quality of stanzaic verse, or the meter of Sophoclean dialogue. The film turns things into song of a sort, or discovers that things are song.

The point of view like that of a child makes explicit and taps into a power of film that Stanley Cavell says operates in all cases, all films: the interest of a child watching its mother.[3] *Jeanne Dielman* is in part a crucial film because it renders the world into something that is essentially and in very specific ways film, and suggests that such rendering is necessary, that to become itself, the world needs to become film. *Jeanne Dielman* has something important to say about what film is, and part of this is a take on the child's fascination with the mother, a way of making that explicit. Janet Bergstrom has made the interesting suggestion that the child (as it were) in *Jeanne Dielman* wishes not only to observe and also to control the mother, framing her (108). Film would see and create—I would put it—all at the same time.

The camera in *Jeanne Dielman*, the child, does not go into Jeanne's bedroom when she takes a client there, until the third such episode, near the end of the film, when we suddenly get two extraordinary shots: an overhead view down onto Jeanne's face as she lies on her back in bed underneath her client and begins to feel something, pain, pleasure, it is not clear what, but something surprising and unsettling; and then, after the sex, a view into the mirror on Jeanne's dresser, where we see, in reflection, Jeanne get up from buttoning her blouse and go over to the bed and stab the client in the neck with a pair of scissors. Is this melodrama reality? Does it really happen? Is the film wanting to say that such melodrama is as real as the humdrum that has gone before, like a Bressonian access of grace at the end of one of his films? Perhaps the breach into the room and the sex scene are the projection of the child, who is a manifestation of the power of film, which cannot see everything and inevitably brings imagination into play. Perhaps the murder that is presented as an *image*, a reflection in the mirror, is the projection of Jeanne, perhaps herself projected by the child. Perhaps all this action is a try at accounting for, an indirect and metaphorical way of characterizing, the next, and last, thing we see in the film: the eight-minute shot of Jeanne brooding at her dining table in the dark, obscure in her feelings, intense. She looks *as if* she has just exploded and brought her life down in ruins about herself. Perhaps it is wrong to try to deny, or avoid, Jeanne's sexual awakening and her violence. It is there, but approachable only as if a *projection* from the realm of kneading meatloaf and scrubbing the tub. But then that realm came after all as a transfiguration. Circles. Tensions.

    The third film in succession after *Je tu il elle* and *Jeanne Dielman* is *News from Home* (1976). All we see in the film are shots of New York City with seemingly synchronous sound—lonely alleys amid tall buildings, diners at night observed through plate-glass windows, busy streets, the subway, the grid of cross streets viewed from a car moving up one of the avenues, finally lower Manhattan viewed from a departing boat. One becomes absorbed in the look and mood of all the locales, the silence, the loud sound. Yet Akerman's voice comes and goes, reading what appear to be letters from her mother in Brussels, worrying about and missing Chantal, relaying downbeat family news. Akerman spoke to me of making films from her feelings, not considering whether the films are fiction or nonfiction. And one might take the motive or guiding feeling of *News from Home* to be that the filmmaker/adventurer abroad has to be placed against the tug of family back home, unpleasant, touching, something to which she knows she belongs. Perhaps the contrast here, set in this time and place, mirrors the whole of Akerman's position as a connected, dutiful daughter who yet feels drawn away from where she began and into her own life and her work, her art. Perhaps the film mirrors the human condition for many people. Further, the melancholy and emptiness of some of this film's New York material can seem not a contrast to, but an image for, the mood of the letters—then the film seems to plunge into the noisy subway and busy streets to get away from this mood. The New York material and the letters, all fact we might say, serve in various ways to spell out who Akerman is, what she feels.

This spelling out of herself is similar in the later documentary (isn't it one?) *D'Est* (*From the East*, 1993), where Akerman travels through eastern Europe and spends time in and around Moscow, obsessively filming people waiting for transport, standing in groups outdoors at bus stops or filling train stations at night, waiting in their coats and with their possessions in bundles. One feels the force of obsession in the filming and does not really need to be told what Akerman has said, that she had these images already inside of her, part of the history of the Holocaust she had inherited through her family. And yet the images render what is *there*, outside her. *News from Home* and *D'Est* are more than the sum of their parts—their parts are *used* for something, as raw reality is used for something in *Je tu il elle* and *Jeanne Dielman*. And yet the parts are what they are, still the parts.

In "The Paradoxes of Political Art" Jacques Rancière singles out Akerman's documentary *From the Other Side* (*De l'autre côté*, 2002)—along with Pedro Costa's *In Vanda's Room* (2000)—as representative of "a new idea of what 'critical' art could mean today" (149)—art that does not offer political analysis or a direct call to political action, but accepts the gap that exists between art and the rest of life, and focuses itself on the materiality of a situation, or the materiality it can itself achieve, stirring its audience in a general way and leaving interpretation open. *From the Other Side* is shot along the border fence or wall between Mexico and Arizona, where many from Central America risk great danger, and frequently lose their lives, trying to cross surreptitiously into the United States. We hear that people are misled by their guides and die of exposure and thirst, and that many are arrested trying to cross and then returned to Mexico. The film, says Rancière, "turns an economic and geopolitical issue into an aesthetic matter"—this is its power, stirring up conflicting considerations around a focus on "the raw materiality of the fence" (150). Similarly, *In Vanda's Room* foregoes "economic and social 'explanations'" and offers purely its location, the slum dwelling space of its languid drug users and petty entrepreneurs, and the sheer "power and impotence" (151) of the body in this situation. We are left to think on our own.[4]

Fiction and Nonfiction in Chantal Ackerman's Films   185

Earlier in his essay Rancière had invoked the Belvedere *Torso* as written about by Johann Winckelmann, and the *Juno Ludovisi* (a head) as written about by Friedrich Schiller, both works being praised by these critics for their "indifference"—provocative, challenging to our sense of things, but open as to how they might be interpreted, what place they might take in a story we could imagine, how the torso might have us reconceive our sense of our own bodies and their freedom, or the head and face might comment on our lives ("Paradoxes" 137–38).

One thinks of Rilke's poem "Archaic Torso of Apollo," where the beautifully realized object, lacking in meaning in so many ways, is yet bursting with life and challenge: "here there is no place/that does not see you. You must change your life" ("den da ist keine Stelle, / die dich nicht sieht. Du musst dien Leben ändern"—note the intimate form of "you"—du, dich, dein) (60–61).

From the Other Side is not a sculpture, but a succession of images with sounds and words, a flow structured over a certain amount of time. In his collection on various films and filmmakers, *Film Fables*, Rancière talks about the nature of film to open itself to the world, to register and relay what is observed, and film's nature at the same time to form "fables," to develop a linear path under a certain guiding idea or impulse.[5] Midway through "The Paradoxes of Political Art," Rancière speaks of "the labor of fiction" and of "fiction" as "a word that we need to reconceive:

> "Fiction," as re-framed by the aesthetic regime of art, means far more than the constructing of an imaginary world, and even far more than its Aristotelian sense as "arrangement of actions." It is not a term that designates the imaginary as opposed to the real; it involves the re-framing of the "real" . . . Fiction is a way of changing existing modes of sensory presentations and forms of enunciation; of varying frames, scales and rhythms; and of building new relationships between reality and appearance. (141)[6]

For film, either "fictional" or documentary, the labor of fiction consists in a certain framing and presentation of things at any given moment, and in an unfolding through time.

From the Other Side has its guiding impulse, its way of treading the line between the world's extension before it and its intension of significance—has its particular take on how what is there before it relates to creative means for taking that in, taking in and giving out, breathing, thinking, *ātman*, the self (art self, film self) that is the world. This film's guiding impulse is to acknowledge the blank border wall with "its inhuman strangeness" (Rancière, "Paradoxes" 150) as a screen for projection.

From the Other Side opens with some presentation credits—this is meant to be a theatrical film—and then a shot of a young man standing beside a door that opens into a house.

He is near the camera, seen from the waist up, so that we feel an intimacy with him as he gives his name, Francisco Santillán Garcia, and tells, in a friendly but serious manner, the story of his brother who nearly died trying to cross over into the United States. To the right of this young man, the blank white outer wall of the house extends to the edge of the frame. To the left of the open house door the white wall extends the other way. The interior of the house is quite dark, but in the background we see a rectangular window looking out into blank, bright, white sky or terrain. The image before us is very formal—man, wall, window within—and we hear a subdued duo for cellos (identified in the end credits as Monteverdi), giving the episode a ritual quality. There is a suggestion of this young man being placed against a blank screen, of his being seen as a projection, even as his own state of mind and that of those like him are caught up in projections of a future. The window in back of the dark house, a frame within the frame of the door, which is a frame within the frame of the film, suggests an opening out, suggests hope—and along with the cello duo we hear children's voices offscreen,

suggesting hope and energy. But the man has his back to a wall. What we see and hear compounds projection, hope, and frustration—even the blank frustration of death. The formality and metaphoric power of the image is countered by the warmth of this man genuinely telling his story, with Akerman's voice (recognizable from her other films) intervening occasionally, in Spanish, with a question.

The interview between Akerman and the man is succeeded by the film's title, *De l'autre côté*—white letters against black—indicating all the more, by positioning, that what we have just seen is meant as a kernel for the film, as, in a sense, containing the whole film within it, like musical material near the start of a symphony.

There will be many such interviews over the course of the film, eventually giving the side of Americans to the north of the wall, who feel overrun and violated by the nightly stream of immigrants and drug couriers. And there will be much play (Rancière cites Schiller's "free play" of art) with frames within frames and blank expanses.

There ensue three such blank expanses. First there is a shot of a wide, unpaved, dusty street or crossing or town square, the blank earth extending from the camera out and around through much of the frame, low buildings settled about, occasional walkers or cars slowly moving through the space. We hear the soft appropriate sounds of a poor border town—low motors, tires on earth, a barking dog, a song likely from a café or bar. The shot is held for a long time—there is a

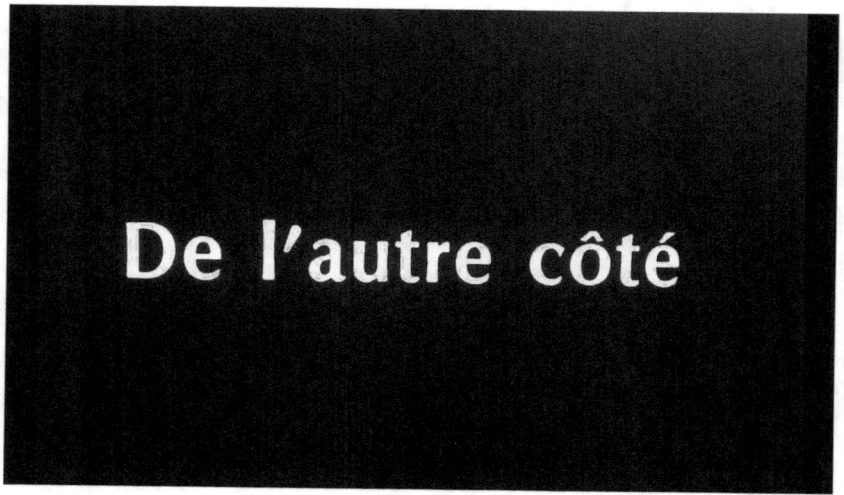

feeling of immersion in reality, of *living* here for a time. And yet the late afternoon light, softly yellow, beautiful as it gets into the dusk, makes a contemplatable artistic object of all this, like a painting come to life. Akerman says that it was very hard for her to tell how long to let this and similar long-take views go on, that she could judge and edit only in the projection room, taking in the large screened image and its sounds as an experience, not just an idea or marker—comprehending the ongoing image, we might say, as a musical passage. (Bresson always edited in the projection room.) The open space, picking up on, opening out from, the blank walls and frames of the beginning interview with the young man, suggests the empty canvas, the nullity, from which human hopes proceed, a ground for creating life as if creating art. The next shot gives us another long-held view of a broad earthen street, mostly in shadow as evening progresses, low modest houses spread across the back, now with three children throwing and batting a ball and running to bases, playing a sort of reduced baseball game. The children seem as if projected on the screen of this earthen space, full of their own energy and hopes, and the hopes of their families and community. The third shot of this series presents a road on the left, broad and empty, in shadow, and on the right our first view of the border fence, bright white as it catches the late sun, incongruous and surreal in its intrusion into the setting—though there are reasons for it—looking like the screen of a drive-in cinema, facing south as we view it, whence many would cross it, breaching the screen and pushing into the world of the film beyond, which may be a delusion.

The series of three shots, opening from screen to screen, comes back to another interview, more extended than the first, with an elderly woman with a rich history, who has lost a son trying to cross over.

She sits facing us, her back to a wall, on her right a table of support encased in plastic, presenting a blank rectangular surface to our view, and resting on the support, next to the woman's head, a television set, facing us with a turned-off screen which yet reflects the filmmakers moving about—behind us, so to speak—with behind them a bright rectangle, presumably a window looking out. Eventually this claustrophobic situation, with its constricted frames within frames, will expand, or explode, into more views outdoors of expanses and broad roads.

It is hard to keep in mind the exact sequence of images and episodes in *From the Other Side*—so that in a way it does become something like a sculpture, as if everything happens at once, coruscating about that repeated view of the fence, or view of it in different lights and from different perspectives. The pattern continues of moving from interviews with frames within frames to views of broad expanses. The frames show variety—a barber shop's broad mirror at the back of the room, a sheriff's office window with an outdoor view that looks oddly two-dimensional and may be a landscape poster; projections vary in their feel and in what drives them. The broad expanses show variety, too. In America, famous for its projections and wanting to make dreams come true, the

expanses look possessed and settled—a field of wheat, a pasture with cattle grazing.

Before getting to America, and in a difference way once we are there, there is a feeling of sameness but difference as images and episodes succeed each other. There is an energy at play, as human beings and the film itself try one thing after another, meet frustration, seem to go in a circle. The Americans, too, are frustrated.

About a quarter of the way into the film, the camera begins to move, and there are a couple of protracted sequences—with no cuts—where the camera moves slowly along the fence apparently in a motor vehicle, contemplates the fence's blank screen, and turns back toward the Mexican border town and moves on along, looking at houses and shops and the whole human settlement. This moving camera has partly the feel of wanting to participate in the general drive to move on, to break through, to find a hole in the fence or to breach it, and go north into another world. Turning back into the town feels like defeat, the defeat so often suffered by people here. But we know that Akerman and her crew can go where they please, so the whole process of moving and turning seems more purely observational, a push to try something new in coming to terms with this world.

The moving-camera views of the fence and the town, especially in evening light, have the feel of being on another planet, a feel of fascinating but disturbing strangeness, of the surreal. It is all reminiscent of the extended episode in *Les rendez-vous d'Anna* (*The Meetings of Anna*, 1978) where Akerman's protagonist, a young Jewish female filmmaker from Brussels—a self-projection of Akerman—travels across Europe at night by train, looks out the window, and observes the strange world of towns, stations, subdued human activity, and night lights and colors that passes by. How can this be here? How can this *be*? both films seem to wonder. The films' questions cut deep, like Heidegger's about Being, drawing on the pre-Socratics. How is it that we are here? How is it that we *are*? Stanley Cavell writes about Robert Gardner's sense of the "bizarre" and "surreal" in *Forest of Bliss* (1986), his observational film about Benares, India, with no spoken or written commentary. Cavell links the sensibility here to Wittgenstein's alertness to the bizarre and surreal and his notion that the beginning of philosophy is "not to accept what we say or do as familiar but as strange, acknowledging our strangeness to ourselves" (Cavell, "Introduction" 12).

The camera of *From the Other Side* comes to move in various ways—with a border guard walking with his flashlight through the brush at night; with a jeep or truck noisily moving down a dirt road at night; with a night-vision machine with sighting lines as for a weapon, scanning around from a high point (possibly a tower, possibly a helicopter, though we don't hear the sound of one)—where masses of immigrants hiking along in dark clothes appear white, like ghosts, as they are apparently herded into a prison compound. Akerman, overall so sympathetic to the immigrants, gives her film over at moments to the hunters. The camera hunts with them—but in order to observe them, acknowledge them, let them be—to hunt *them* in a sense.

In the film's surprising final sequence, we travel fast in a car on what appears to be—from the expensive construction, signs, and lights—an American interstate- or expressway-style highway, as a woman's voiceover in French, recognizable as Akerman, gives us the story of an immigrant woman who worked as a house cleaner in southern California, moved about, and seems now to have disappeared. Akerman starts speaking about the woman in the third person, but switches to the first person, singular and plural, for statements from her family and a woman who employed her. These switches are like the giving over of the camera to different points of view throughout the film. We have not seen anything like this in the film so far—rushing through what seems an endless dark void—the extension of the wall becoming that of the long road we speed along over, the film's intension becoming bottomless and mysterious in a new way. The desire to move on, or to probe and understand, is pushed into hyperspeed—yet it feels like being caught in unstoppable fate, or falling through space. We have heard many testimonies in the film, but nothing like this warm voice in French, the speaker unseen. No reason to think that in this strong personal intervention Akerman is making the story up—a fiction. But the facts have been transformed into this episode of arresting new visual experience and a storyteller's rehearsal, identifying herself with her characters—nonfiction fiction.

The immigrant woman, disappeared, is finally called a mirage—in French *hallucination*—the last word of the film. Film figures are mirages, however mysteriously connected to the real—a "human *something*" Cavell calls them in *The World Viewed* (26). The French voiceover of the unseen woman is a mirage in a special sense. She/it is the film itself, pressing more than ever to come close to her subject, acknowledging that film is identified, if not a perfect fit, with human beings in their reality, film figures with their projections and uncertain status, legal and indeed ontological—mirages. Will we allow them, this film, this place with its many places, as Rilke would have it, to see us?

7

Surprise and Pain, Writing and Film

On Ross McElwee's *Time Indefinite*

In looking forward to writing this essay and in giving it, first, its title, I wanted to set myself up to give thought to what it is that appeals to me in Ross McElwee's films—to the very particular and acute sense of anticipation I feel when a new film of his comes along and I am about to see it, and to the qualities of his films that, so far, always bear out this sense of anticipation. I do think of McElwee as a writer, though someone who is a thoroughgoing filmmaker and whom I cannot really imagine as doing his work and coming across purely in the medium of writing.

In using the word *surprise* in this chapter's title, I want to point to a quality I think of as peculiar to writing, especially to such work as the essays of Montaigne—a linear movement forward and along where each idea or expression or registration of feeling seems to give birth to the next without knowing what that next might be. Or to put it differently: one thing is there, and a new thing seems simply to happen to the first, to come to it out of the blue, like an access of grace, and to make a connection, so that the making of connection is itself interesting. The "Apology for Raimond Sebond" begins with some thoughts on the limitations of knowledge, then after a few sentences moves into reminiscence about Montaigne's father and his entertaining of learned men at his house. Soon the essay is caught up in reflection on Martin Luther's effect upon the unlearned populace, where we sense admiration as much as alarm. Then Montaigne comes back to his now deceased father's not-to-be-denied request that Montaigne translate into French Sebond's *Natural Theology*, a book Montaigne has reservations about. He briefly evokes his role as intellectual advisor to ladies who read Sebond. Then the essay is off on its hundred pages and more of speculation on the human condition, with memories and pictures from life and personal reflection, and odd bits of knowledge coming in from many sources, each as if remembered suddenly due to some thought that has just been written down, the whole adding up to what has often been taken as the intellectual inspiration for Shakespeare's *Hamlet* (Montaigne 368–70).

The reader taking up such work knows that what is in store is a journey, a movement forward where feelings are stirred and the mind is illuminated, again and again, and one does not know precisely where things will go, though there will be moments of looking back and recouping, circling and drawing an emphasis. It is not a series of random events: the making of connections keeps a thread spun, a golden or silver thread, from starting out until stopping. Whatever such work has to give, whatever it adds up to, must come through this linear, experiential process.

By pain I mean seriousness, weight, the coming up against fact. In reading Montaigne or, for me, viewing a McElwee film, one is not entering an escape world, opening oneself to a sequence of purely delightful surprises. One comes, again and again, to recognitions of life in its imperfection, even messiness, and to hard ideas, ideas that are struggled for and that offer to recast life, to cope with it better through understanding, but that admit they cannot fully get a hold on life, comprehend it and settle it. Going to a McElwee film, I look forward to humor and to marvelous images, to discovery of intriguing people, and of course each time to more of Ross, as he presents himself, and in all this I know there will be a periodic coming to earth, life taking hold. I will be sobered. Near the center of *Time Indefinite* (1993) Ross and Marilyn, newly married, now expecting a child, shop for a baby's crib and linens and an electric breast pump. The camera stares at these strange-seeming objects, and takes in the friendly saleswoman and her recital of mounting costs, as Ross and Marilyn undergo a Walker Percy–like humorous/anxious encounter with the consumer world and suburban values, feeling pressed to accept it all.

Ross seems especially put upon, unseen, only his muted voice coming from behind the camera, addressing Marilyn, "I find it difficult to breathe. . . ." Without resolution to this, there comes news of Ross's grandmother's death, with older film footage of her singing outdoors in autumnal light—and this seems to usher in Marilyn's miscarriage on New Year's Eve, upon which Ross looks to his physician father for a rational consolation that is not forthcoming. Then suddenly there is news of the father's altogether unexpected death, and the film is cast into a mode of serious reflection it could not have expected and which is never overcome, despite the continuing discovery of marvels in life.

I do not want to spend time on qualification. Of course, there is surprise in a good deal of film, in painting, in music. And there is formulaic and predictable writing, some of it powerful and valid (Homer, in a sense). Important to what I am thinking about here is linearity, movement, one surprising thing happening after another, the surprise overturning the work and casting it in a new direction. And surprise in music and in most film—even documentary—more of this in a moment—comes within a structure important to grasp. McElwee films suggest structures, even comparison to established genres, such as romantic comedy.

I am not trying to draw lines between categories. The categories blur. I am just trying to develop an idea of something, as I see it, real and essential to a Ross McElwee film, that it moves as does certain writing, unpredictably, thinking on its feet, going forward without being sure where, and not spinning out its own fancy but allowing itself to be brought up short by life, even by thought about life, as it were from the outside. This particular conjunction of film and writing in McElwee might help to think about a larger question, or, as I see it, what is in our time a triple question, where the categories may be separable but not the questions: What is writing? What is film? And indeed, what is philosophy?

Stanley Cavell asks at the end of his magnum opus *The Claim of Reason*, "Can philosophy become literature and still know itself?" The knowing itself, the unstoppable reflection that will not be co-opted by anyone's agenda, the radicality, seems crucial here. If literature comes to life with this reflectiveness, where are we as between literature and philosophy? Earlier, Cavell argued in *The World Viewed* that film was born in a crisis of skepticism, and that it exists as a way of reflecting on the sense of loss of contact with the world and as a means of trying to reconnect and to learn what connection can be that is not the possession that would satisfy a skeptic. Where are we as between philosophy and film? (496).

Let us narrow in on McElwee's procedure and see how it illuminates these questions. The unpredictable quality in his work, the surprise, which I take to be like that of writing, is not altogether due to the films' being nonfiction, taking the world as it comes and reflecting on it stage by stage. Many documentaries feel planned and logical and all too well possessed of shape. One of McElwee's teachers, Richard Leacock (who appears in *Time Indefinite*), wrote a famous brief manifesto, "For an Uncontrolled Cinema," and Leacock's own films, or I would prefer to say his shooting, his filming, has a wonderful quality of surprise, attending to the world as it changes. Leacock's filming seems to answer to Pier Paolo Pasolini's ideal, expressed in his theoretical essays, of a world that flows on unceasingly and registers itself on film in its totality.[1] Leacock has the eye for this. Toward the end of *Happy Mother's Day* (1963), at the official luncheon for Mrs. Fischer (mother of quintuplets) and then at the town's celebratory parade, Leacock's camera moves or zooms to find children playing, showing off, delightfully countering the overall staid and formal atmosphere of the proceedings. Marching in the parade, children, adolescents, even adults find their ways of anarchic self-expression within the parameters of formal activity—a drum majorette has more than usual bounce to her step, a middle-aged man waves his arms wildly as he plays the drum. The feeling of the film is of life continually calling the camera's attention to itself.

But I do not take Leacock to be a writer in the sense I am talking about. I miss reflection—not what Cavell attributes to the very medium of film, its meditating on our closeness to and distance from the world—Leacock has that in plenty. But I miss the saying of something, the quality of speaking. Of course, Leacock avoids spoken commentary, something crucial to McElwee's films, something he has developed in a most distinctive way and made an art of. But the saying something, the speaking, in film is even more a matter of structuring, of deciding what to include and what to omit, of deciding what to put next to what other thing, what transitions to make, how to build or to let an extended argument take its way. One has the impression that McElwee shoots a good deal of film over time, whether in pursuit of a general idea like tobacco culture or stories behind the evening news, or not in pursuit of anything, just keeping up with life as it happens, as with the material for *Time Indefinite*, and that he then works long and hard sorting and arranging, juxtaposing and structuring, all the time developing his voiceover commentary and carefully timing it with the images. The succession of experiences for the viewer, the encounters, the ideas, one opening unpredictably into the next, is something *achieved*. And this is not a hoax. Ross's films are honest. One feels that he writes—shooting, editing, developing a commentary—from a take on the world and from an active mind. One's feeling is not that he constructs a simulacrum of writing.

    I think of Jean-Luc Godard as a writer. And Godard said long ago that for him his written essays and his filmmaking were two versions of the same activity (171). Godard works mostly—there are some striking exceptions—within the realm of the scripted film, with actors and made-up stories and characters, without voiceover commentary. The quality of surprise, movement with surprise, saying something, reflection, admission of pain, is due to structuring. No one could predict that Nana/Anna Karina in the middle of *Vivre Sa Vie* (1962) would dance out by herself a whole loud jukebox number, while her pimp talks to an associate instead of taking her to the movies. It is a gesture of protest against her life, and at the same time a gesture of taking delight in herself. With the long dance Godard bends the expected and usual pace of narrative to his own voice, and to Karina's. Of course, in a Godard fiction there is an important element of nonfictional observation of the world, the surprising world—those are the real Paris streets in *Vivre Sa Vie*, that is Karina almost more than a created character. Perhaps any writing will have such an element of nonfictional observation, of pure appreciation of the world as found. (D. H. Lawrence objected to philosophy after Plato, saying that it was not writing, meeting life at every turn, as do Plato's Dialogues [*Phoenix* 520].) Godard's film writing, like McElwee's, is a matter of a certain kind of writing mind making a conjuncture with film, through shooting, editing, forming. And it is not the mind of Godard the person or McElwee the person at issue. I am more inclined to the idea that the film—in the case of these two filmmakers the conjuncture of a writing mind with the medium of film—*is* mind, that the film has a mind of its own.

    One more comparison will help to narrow in on McElwee. Consider Chris Marker, another master of the voiceover commentary, certainly a writer, perhaps a philosopher. In *Le joli mai* (1963) and *Sans soleil* (1983) Marker has his beautiful, reflective commentary spoken by someone other than himself, in these cases a woman, and someone who never appears onscreen, and the effect is to cast the words onto a level of pure ideas, consistent, we might say ontologically, and final, for all their complexity and admitted self-contradiction and even ephemerality—Simone Signoret's voice at the end of *Le joli mai* reflecting on freedom as we get views of a prison and of the Paris streets; Alexandra Stewart's less familiar voice in *Sans soleil* reflecting on the bitterness of history, after a presentation, with archival footage, of the political career of Amilcar Cabral in the Cape Verde islands.

McElwee's commentary, by contrast, does not so much give us a person as, through the personal, open a variety of levels of engagement with the viewer. We do not get the whole Ross, and sometimes see and hear a Ross onscreen in counterpoint with rather another Ross speaking in voiceover. The sense of a person, which is not the sense of a whole and delimited person, makes us feel that the words mean more than we can see, that someone, someone other, is affected by what is being talked about, that the words may go in more than one direction, that we are being given ideas and something below or beyond the level of ideas, which cannot wholly be made out, but which we are invited to respond to. I am reminded of the first time I heard Stanley Cavell lecture, many years ago, when with the force of a salutary nail driven into the head he looked me in the eye, as it seemed, and reiterated that for Wittgenstein reflecting on what J. L. Austin, in the title of a famous essay, termed the problem of "other minds," the crucial consideration was the mystery of another's pain.

Time Indefinite, like Bergman's *The Seventh Seal* (*Det sjunde inseglet*, 1957), begins at the shore, here the land and a long row of dwellings on the left, set against the vast sea and an enormous sky, suggesting human life confronting what is beyond human life or comprehension, or what is bigger or stronger than life—perhaps death, or a wonderful transcendence. The beautiful colors, not like Bergman, draw us into the depths of the shot, though across the foreground falls the shadow of the fishing pier from which the shot is taken.

⁓

Ross, filming the world, is a fisherman, a hunter, like Nanook, or, in William Rothman's account, Flaherty himself filming Nanook, hunting him, or like Peter and Andrew, called to be fishers of men, to save them (*Documentary Film* 14–15; see as well Gospel of Matthew 4:18–20). Ross is ambivalent, to say the least, about fishing, as he explains when the film returns to this pier and its activities in ten minutes or so. And as he explains almost immediately, he has misgivings about filming, something he feels called, compellingly, to do, and yet something that seems to set him apart from life. We will see film of various kinds and qualities, made by various people, in the course of *Time Indefinite*, and it will become a pressing issue, what it is that film does with life, or does for life. The impossibility of disentangling film from life, or film imagination from life, is a great concern of *Bright Leaves* (2003), as it is of Godard's 2004 film *Our Music* (*Notre musique*), where "our music" is film and is at the same time the dialogue necessary between persons, actually separate persons, in order for life to be lived.

The vista of beach, most unlike Bergman's, becomes quickly recognizable as a comfortable American resort, not too far north, so that it is in a way no surprise, with a cut, to be thrust into the midst of a McElwee family party on a beach cottage porch, where Ross and his friend Marilyn will announce their engagement—a party dominated by Ross's father, who does not like all the filming going on and yet at one point asks to wield the camera. Ross calls his father "the one who keeps these reunions going." Read: "these montages," these films, this film. *Time Indefinite* is, among other things, a film about paternity, the seed of life, the seed of film.

But in a way the family party is indeed a surprise, because this footage comes to have a certain double aspect: it is a home movie, where we are intent on the people and a certain real time and place. But with the handheld camera very steadily panning left and right, a sort of fresco or mural is created where amiably chattering people become pure film figures, animated shadows, a little ghostly, the effect compounded by Ross's voiceover putting things at a distance. There is a frisson of reminder that these real people, so full of life's joys, so unabashed in their southernness, are living up against the beyondness suggested in the film's opening.

⁌

Flashes of black indicate a camera battery failure and give us the opportunity to see film of various kinds in short order: the present scene in failing light and with a camera wildly turned about as the photographer grapples with his problem; a wholly black stretch with sound; substitute video footage taken by Ross's stepmother. We are given opportunity to think about what becomes of people—mortal people—on film, and about whether any film is the right film, or whether more than one kind of film is better. The interruption allows Ross to explain himself a bit as a filmmaker, with his compulsion to film daily life, and allows, as I would like to put it, the film itself to remember, to wash over us in a series of passages that seem to come from a more-than-human, stronger-than-human, somehow other-than-human center or source: footage of Ross's brother and father at an earlier time, Ross's sister talking in a canoe, Ross with his older friend Charleen and her arranged date for him in Charleston—moments we may recognize from *Backyard* (1984) and *Sherman's March* (1985), life become film, become film yet again—and then Ross on vacation with Marilyn, film, he tells us, as a mode of love.

Did the camera battery failure really happen? It is so opportune for dealing with what Ross introduces as his father's contra-filmic "Freudian force field," as well as for opening the episode of various passages of film. If it did not happen, it would make the film seem airier, more aesthetic, less open to admit fact. I think one has something more than the two alternatives of thinking either that the battery failure happened or that Ross manufactured it for the sake of making his film. Wise literary criticism has maintained long since that writing can be sincere even though we are not sure about the writer (see Leavis, "Reality"). *Time Indefinite*, all things considered, has us accept the battery failure as an assertion of reality, and this is not the same as the suspension of disbelief whereby we take in fiction. To be suspicious of the battery failure and to turn this against the film would be a destructive act, uncalled for. Writing, and film, will give us plenty of signals when it is good to be suspicious. There are no rules for this. And we can never get it wholly right.

The film returns after its memories to the family reunion—hush puppies are frying—and the film is drawn—Ross is drawn—to the pier, first down below where we see it stretch out to the horizon like the Golden Gate Bridge in Hitchcock's *Vertigo* (1958), another film about romantic love, images, loss, intimations of what lies beyond life—though there are no babies.

⁓

We go up onto the pier and witness fishing, and launch into Ross's wonderful monologue encompassing his childhood questions to his father: "Does a fish have a soul? . . . Does God take all the dead fish into heaven? . . . If it's an aquarium, who cleans it? Do angels clean it? . . . Why does anyone or anything have to die? What's the matter with staying right here?" These questions stick, and align themselves with the whole inquiry of the filmmaker, of the film, first to last, and with film's "impulse to preserve," as filmmaker Robert Gardner calls it, taking the phrase from Philip Larkin ("Impulse" 169).[2] Film is given something of Emerson's open-eyed authority of boys (Emerson 261), and Thoreau's sunlight that is morning and mourning (Thoreau 587).[3]

On the words, "What's the matter with staying right here?" a man throws the waste part of a cleaned fish off the pier, and the camera follows his gesture, looking out to the shoreline and surf and eventually turning down to stare at just the churning sea—the Beyond, heaven, the void, annihilation that perhaps gives new life. The sea with its reflecting surface and constant motion, its unseen depths that we posit or believe in, suggests the screen and the very medium of film.

⁓

In *Time Indefinite*'s central monologue, back at the pier after the shocking sudden death of Ross's father, Ross tells of his anger at death's periodic visits to his immediate family over the years, and speculates on this as the source of his compulsion to film life. Life goes to annihilation. Perhaps this can be the death and rebirth of life on film, life in film's "time indefinite," as Ross puts it later, picking up on the apocalyptic phrase from the Bible, which we hear and see read to Ross at the front door, the threshold, of his father's house by a Jehovah's Witness.

After the view down into the sea, a cut gives us the lovely image of hands shucking ears of corn, a parallel to the fish cleaning, an image of vegetable life like that of animal life undergoing preparation for the transfiguration of giving nourishment, of being feasted upon—and with

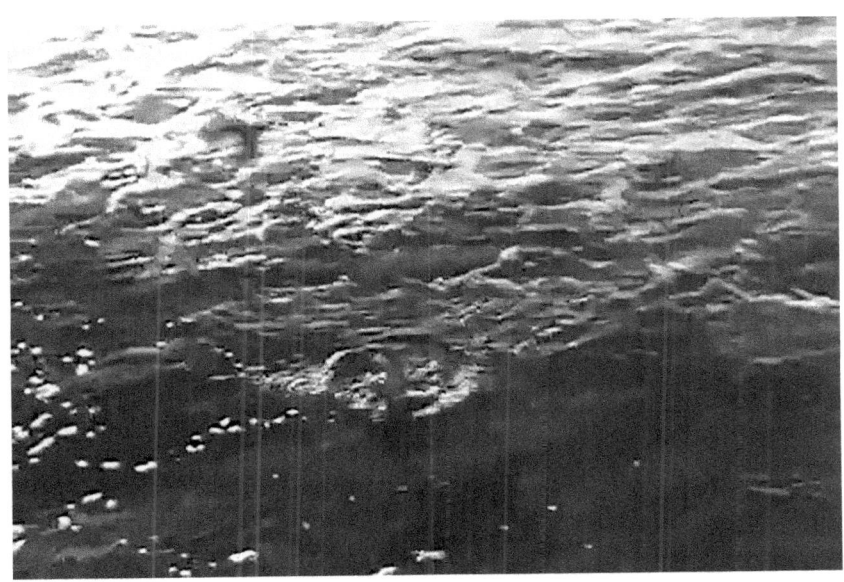

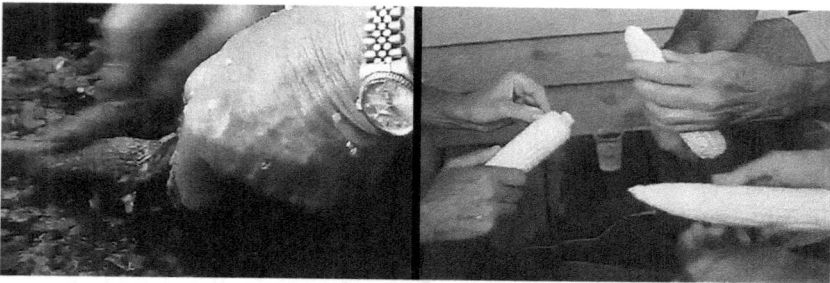

a glare at the camera on the part of Ross's father, the film is once again washed over by old footage, this time the ghostly images taken by Uncle Fred or Uncle Nate, now appearing in otherworldly partial color, of Ross's parents long ago and of Ross as a child.

Ross's father's painful glare seems to produce these images as a flight away, an alternative. At first it is the day of Ross's baptism, his infant subjection to the ritual of death by water, and rebirth. The camera's look off the pier and down into the ocean a few minutes ago, its beginning of a plunge down, seems now carried out in this occasion of baptism. The new life here—the young mother, now dead, the youthful father and

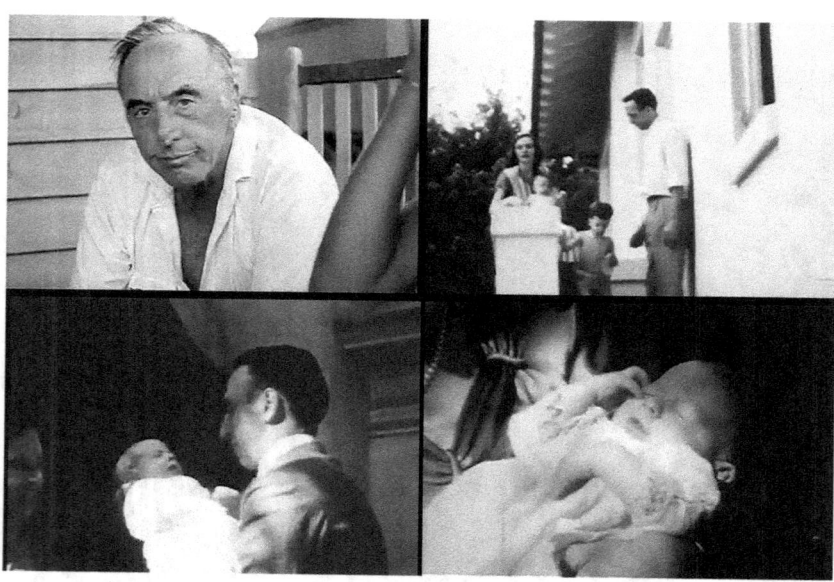

the infant, in shimmering light, for a moment in slowed motion—is a life of film. Then there is the toddler Ross receiving his first kiss, from a toddler girl, and going back for more, twice. If anger at death drives filmmaking—anger as the push for life, or toward life—then so does eros drive filmmaking. Or rather, anger at death, or desire for death and its transfiguration, desire for death's life, *is* eros. Such entanglement of eros and death is the ultimate "Freudian force field." Over all these images Ross speaks of his having been bred to filming through so much early exposure to film. The images, more than the words, tell us what film and exposure to film are.

The flight of fancy, into the past, into strange images, into a lost reality, comes to earth in Cambridge, Massachusetts, and preparations for Ross and Marilyn's marriage, and the film takes its way through things that happen—marriage, fatherhood, deaths, birth, reunions. One wants to go on with the film, moment after moment. What is writing for? To be read.

8

Two Women in *L'Avventura*

MICHELANGELO ANTONIONI's *L'Avventura* (1960) came to film lovers at a time major French New Wave films were appearing one after another, also the early films of Ingmar Bergman and Federico Fellini, with Tarkovsky just around the corner, and new cinema of Germany and Latin America, the Apu trilogy, the later work of Luis Buñuel, and more. It seemed a time of contemporary cinema or a rich and challenging art, fruitful of works to be attended to and thought about.

To me and, I think, to many, Antonioni's work seemed a breakthrough in film history. There was the very adult take on people and human relations, including sexuality. And formally, the films seemed to extend or stretch time, or convert time into space, which could be approached and dealt with visually.

My first Antonioni had been *Blow-Up* (1966), which with its unresolved murder plot and enigmatic final image of the protagonist blurred out on a field of green grass, prepared me to regard Antonioni films as puzzles to be addressed.

L'Avventura presents the story of two young women friends, Anna (Lea Massari) and Claudia (Monica Vitti) who go on a private boat cruise with other friends, including Anna's lover Sandro (Gabriele Ferzetti), off the southwest coast of Italy (Tyrrhenian Sea), eventually visiting Sicily. The party stop at a volcanic island (Lisca Bianca), climb the rocks to the top, and walk around looking out to sea and down from the cliffs.[1]

When it is time to leave, Anna can't be found, despite much searching around and calling out. Sandro and Claudia continue on a journey of their own in the region, looking for Anna or clues of her, becoming lovers along the way. The film ends very ambiguously at a posh resort hotel in Sicily.

From the first and throughout, the film suggests a blurring of identity between the two women, Anna and Claudia, to the extent, even, that Anna seems to create Claudia and what will be her story, the rest of the film after the island disappearance.

In addition, there is much suggestion in the film of an identification of the sea with the screen, or mind screen, death, and creation.

There is a connection to Vittorio De Sica's film *Two Women* (*La Ciociara, The Woman from Ciociara*, 1960), in which a woman (Sophia Loren) and her young daughter journey on foot through war-torn southwest Italy, facing many trials, including gang rape. But they survive, and come through. There is also relation in the blurring of identity, or exchange of identities, to Bergman's *Persona* (1966), *The Silence* (1963), and *Cries and Whispers* (1972), and to Robert Altman's *Three Women* (1977), where the murals of a woman painter (Janice Rule) seem to generate the film. The creative woman in these films, going back to *Nashville*, imagines or reimagines a world, a film world, where identities are not fixed.

In *L'Avventura*'s first shot, famously beautiful Lea Massari walks toward us through a curved arch, like the statue of a goddess stepping down and out from her niche.

She radiates, for me, a sense of powers yet to be revealed. Massari will play the mother who sleeps with her son in Louis Malle's *Murmur of the Heart* (*Le souffle au coeur*, 1971). In Chantal Akerman's *The Meetings*

of Anna (*Les rendez-vous d'Anna*, 1978), Massari is Anne or Anna's mother, who takes her daughter (Aurore Clément) to bed, both of them nude, where Anne relates her very positive lesbian experience with a woman in Italy. The last thing we see in the film is Anne's answering machine playing a message in which a woman's voice asks, "Anna, where are you? (*Dove sei?*). In Michael Haneke's film *The Piano Teacher* (*La pianiste*, 2001) Massari is the mother of the pianist (Isabelle Huppert), whom the pianist seems to sexually assault in bed. So Massari carries an overtone of sexual license, even perversities.

Back in *L'Avventura*, first Claudia from the side, then Anna's father, from the back, appear suddenly in the frame with her, like ghosts summoned up, her familiars, part of herself. The two women are soon in a car, being driven, presumably, to the boat for their outing. They view the road and the world about them through the frame of the car's front windshield, like a movie running before them, perhaps projected by them, or by Anna, whose family car this is.

Soon, with some ellipses—conspicuous film techniques—the car arrives in old downtown Rome, and parks at what turns out to be Sandro's building. On the ground floor is an art gallery, with pretentious Americans wandering about.

With a series of point-of-view and reverse shots, Claudia waiting in the car seems to envision or imagine the scene between Anna and Sandro upstairs—fairly high up, as if in a little lovers' paradise, as shots out the window and back up toward it indicate. There follows a typical Antonioni love scene, with tender gestures of fingers in the hair and suggestive but not graphic nudity. There will be a similar scene between Claudia and Sandro in a meadow later in the film. The most intense such scene is probably that between Monica Vitti and Richard Harris (Giuliana and Corrado in *Red Desert* [*Il deserto rosso*, 1964]) where, pretty clearly, intercourse is meant to be taking place. In *L'Avventura* the iron bedstead plays a role, with views of the lovers through its lacework, suggesting the aestheticization of the whole business, either in characters' minds or in a flash of filmic self-reflection, passion becoming film—film putting us into contact with passion.

In *Red Desert*'s love scene, where the wall changes color, the iron bedstead also plays a role. There it is not lacy but a straight metal rod, suggesting erection, and also perhaps Corrado's aggressiveness, which is considerable in this scene. Claudia seems to imagine herself in Anna's role in the love scene—there are quick alterations between the two—forecasting Claudia's later role with Sandro.

Soon we are on the boat, where the hosts seem to be Patrizia and her admirer Raimondo. Sandro, stretched out on a chaise longue, brushes

away a small dog—"filthy beast"—a whippet or perhaps dachshund of some kind—perhaps an emblem of sexuality. There are views of the extensive dark sea, suggestive at once of death and of the screen, and talk of going for a swim. Soon Anna is walking determinedly toward us, seeming to sweep us along with her as she climbs up onto the boat's rail, and dives into the dark water. She wants us to enter her death, her film.

Soon she is crying "shark!" (*Pisce cane!*). Others go into the water to help her—at her bidding, we might say. The boat motors toward Lisca Bianca and Anna, and we contemplate the huge layered rock formations that buttress the island. Anna remarks that she finds it frightening. A man appears from below decks wearing his swimming trunks and carrying spearfishing equipment. He looks like a sea-god with trident. Soon she is entering Claudia's cabin—maybe they share it—for what is, I think, a crucial scene.

The camera looks up at the two women descending the steps toward us into the cabin—like Anna's descent and approach to us—to the world of the film—at the beginning. Anna replays that entry, this time with Claudia. Soon the two are undressing, viewing each other, clearly, in the nude from the waist up. Anna gives Claudia one of her tops and says to wear it, it looks better on her. The top identifies the wearer as Anna, and will shock her father when he arrives on the island next morning, seeing the top on Claudia, knowing Anna is missing.

There is a sexual overtone to the dressing scene, as there is to the moment of physical intimacy between the two women (Bibi Andersson and Liv Ullmann) in Bergman's *Persona* (1966). The bodies at times appear merged in the frame. Here Anna creates Claudia, giving birth to Claudia as her recreated self.

Soon everyone is on top of the cliffs, walking around the island. There are repeated views out to sea—the metaphysical surround, destiny, Anna's screen, the place of her projection of everyone's lives, of life itself. There are views up to the sky, where clouds gather and darken. We hear the rumbling of thunder, especially when tension flares between couples as conversation proceeds, and continuously we hear the surf washing onto the rocks. There are views down into crevasses. In one case we see a big stone crash down (onto the rocks), and think of Anna and what might happen to her. Later, when she is discovered missing, people walk around and peer down into these crevasses, calling out for her. Maybe she is there already.

In one large descent we see a dark cave mouth and large pool of water surface in front of it, the water surface clearly reflecting the surround. In a smaller descent, we see a small version of the same setup, little cave mouth and reflecting pool or puddle. Again and again, signs of a creative cave where something or someone, let us say Anna, projects her film onto her screen, which is our screen.

Some of the party—Claudia, Sandro, and others—decide to stay the night on the island. A rainstorm breaks, drenching people, as we see in repeated shots—a further embrace of Anna's cosmos. People take refuge in what turns out to be a shepherd's cottage. The shepherd comes in and explains the array of photos in the cottage, his family distant in Australia or deceased. The collection of images reminds us that we are in a world of spirits, ghosts even. And the images suggest film, here sequenced and animated by the man's voice, his words, as in Alain Resnais' *Night and Fog* (*Nuit et brouillard*, 1956) and so many other films. Only *Night and Fog*'s images (by novelist and camp survivor Jean Cayrol) can bring us into the camps. *L'Avventura*'s or Anna's images and words bring us into the world and adventure of this film.

There is a close facial shot of Claudia prone in bed, stirring a bit, suggesting she is dreaming or Anna is dreaming through her, what is happening, or has happened in the film, and what will ensue. There is the image of a man's bare back. Sexual feelings never go away here, as in Antonioni generally. Here Anna is Antonioni.

Inside, Claudia handles Anna's clothes. We look at stormy waters. We see Sandro outside in the high wind. The camera pans slowly across the ground, looking out to sea. A foghorn sounds periodically, as in *Persona*, notably on the rainy night when the two women become tenderly, physically intimate, with strong sexual overtones. Here, I think, the mysterious foghorn points more to the mystery of the two women's identity as one.

Soon we see the sunrise on a distant horizon over the seas in beautiful black and white. The world transfigures itself—or Anna transfigures it—becoming film, say her film. The sunrise announces a new beginning for things, or part two of the film.

Sandro, and everybody, looks down at a cave entrance, where an architectural dig seems to be in progress. A large ancient ceramic vase is discovered, but soon dropped by one of the group and smashed on the rocks.

The creative cave brings back, produces ancient Rome, which the modern bourgeoisie destroys. This takes us back to the film's beginning, where Anna's father berates modern developers for encroaching upon and destroying what is old. Sandro has sold out his creative architectural career to become a commercial cost estimator for builders. The smashing of the ceramic also makes me think of Antonioni's fondness for citing, in interviews and elsewhere, Lucretius to the effect that there is a secret violence deep in the heart of nature that flares out or erupts unaccountably at times. This principle comes back later when Sandro spills black ink and ruins a young man's beautiful architectural drawing, almost starting a fistfight. The film ends with a view of Mount Etna in the distance, always capable of exploding or overflowing. Perhaps the secret violence produces the shark, or Anna's fabrication of it. Perhaps the violence sparks Anna in the first place to fashion her film, and thus swallow up everyone, including the viewer, by that "water inescapable," in Wallace Stevens's words. Being brutalized, as it were, to make a film has its positive side, just as an approach to Etna and one's own death can move to transcendence, as seen in Hölderlin's drama *Empedocles on Etna*, beautifully rendered on film by Jean-Marie Straub and Danièle Huillet, those artists two as one, or, as here, one as two.

Sandro and Claudia journey around the islands, looking for Anna or clues or signs of her. At a police station they hear about smugglers operating at night in the area. The possibility is raised that Anna has been kidnapped, perhaps sold into slavery. Perhaps the film, or Anna, or Antonioni here acknowledges that its two women have been, in a sense, smuggled into the film and enslaved to play out its purposes.

Shortly before the couple's departure Anna's father has arrived, and is relieved to find that there is a Bible in Anna's luggage, thinking it indicates she was not contemplating suicide. In her bag is also a copy of Scott Fitzgerald's novel *Tender Is the Night*. Perhaps Anna has identified with the possibly mad and suicidal Nicole Diver (diver!), the female protagonist of the book. Keats's poem *Ode to a Nightingale*, from which the phrase "tender is the night" is taken, is certainly suicidal. As for the Bible, it is full of stories of people deceiving and misunderstanding one another. Perhaps Anna saw there a reflection of her world, as many have done. And the Bible ends with apocalypse.

People thought that eruptions of Etna and, closer to Rome, Vesuvius signaled the end of the world. Besides the volcanoes, *L'Avventura* invokes apocalypse, as I read it, with the film's frequent allusions to Bergman's film *The Seventh Seal* (*Det sjunde inseglet*, 1957). I am thinking of the shots from atop the island, of a figure or line of figures framed against the sky and seen on the edge of the land.

In *Stromboli* (Roberto Rossellini, 1950) Karin (Ingrid Bergman) walks across the top of the island's volcano, struggling to enter a new life. In *Viaggio in Italia* (*Voyage to Italy*, Rossellini, 1954) Katherine (Ingrid Bergman) visits Mount Vesuvius and the site of destroyed Pompei, also on her way to a new life. My friend Professor Giuliana Bruno insists the title of the film should be translated as "journey *in* Italy" (rather than *to*).

Attunedness to apocalypse haunts Antonioni films: the atom bomb in *Eclipse* (*L'eclisse*, 1962) and *Blow-Up*; ruin of the environment by industrial pollution in *Red Desert*; and most telling, I think, the preoccupation with desert in *The Passenger* (*Professione: Reporter*, 1975), as a bit earlier in *Zabriskie Point* (1970). The desert is the last stage of earth's development, everything ground to sand. It is also a place for taking thought, for our renewal, and the start of new creation. Witness the Desert Fathers—their writings and their founding of monastic cultures and traditions. Christ meditated in the desert for forty days and nights before beginning his mission and calling the Disciples—all beautifully and dramatically rendered on film in Pasolini's *Gospel according to Matthew* (*Il vangelo secondo Matteo*, 1964). The ancient Jews wandered in the Sinai for forty years preparing to enter the Promised Land and start their civilization. Forty, that number again, as if the film, or god, is making an incantation in order to work some magic.

In *Zabriskie Point* the desert is where the film's protagonist Mark (Mark Frechette) paints and decorates his airplane (stolen) hippie-style. It is the scene of a sexually suggestive dance performance by Joseph Chaikin's Open Theater, and where Mark and coprotagonist Daria (Daria Halprin) make love. All this to music on the soundtrack by Pink Floyd, the Rolling Stones, the Grateful Dead, and other 1960s bands.

At the beginning of the film we see a seemingly real student political meeting.

Many at the time felt that the counterculture and radical student politics would ruin or bring down civilization—something Wilhelm Reich approved of and promoted. Even the desert is threatened here. A developer, Daria's employer, wants to create a suburbia here, houses with lawns, and a golf course. We see mind's-eye images and a mock-up—all reminiscent of the beginning of David Lynch's film *Blue Velvet* (1986), where order and a slick surface cover, as it turns out, evil and nastiness.

The last thing we see in *Zabriskie Point*, still in this desert, is Daria's vision of repeatedly blowing up her boss's Frank Lloyd Wright–style house. It makes for some exciting cinema. The rerun itself seems to explode out toward us, like a horizontal picture window or wall of the house. Furniture and furnishings, clothes from the closet, food from the kitchen, even a refrigerator, drift slowly and beautifully down in front of us.

The film, Daria, and Antonioni vent rage against the house and all it stands for. But the film finds a way to aestheticize the violence and thus, perhaps, create a distance for thought, as Schiller in the *Aesthetic Letters* says should happen with a work of art. The repeated sound and imagery of the explosion give the film a propulsion as in Eisenstein (say *Strike* [1925] or *October* [1927]) so that we are moved not only mentally.

In *L'Avventura* Claudia and Sandro stop on their journey around the islands to talk to a country pharmacist who is rumored to have encountered a girl traveling alone. This man and his wife, who bicker generally and seem unhappy, dispute whether the girl who passed through was blonde or brunette. At their friends' beautiful Sicilian villa Claudia (the blonde Vitti) puts on a short black wig, thus looking more like Anna all in all. The blurring of identity is underscored, not least between the actress and who/what she becomes in character and on film. This blurring occurs even between Claudia and Sandro, in their tender love scene in a field (much caressing with fingers in hair). Claudia clutches Sandro to her and cries, "My love! Mine! Mine! (*mio mio*)," reminiscent of the woman in *WR* who cries out in ecstasy, "Give it to me! It's MINE!" It is as if Claudia, or Anna behind her, wants to merge with Sandro, become one. The setting of this love scene is a meadow sloping down to a railroad track, with the sea in the distance, reminding us that all is embraced in Anna's film. The setting here, except for the sea, recalls the field in Satyajit Ray's *Pather Panchali* (1955) where the boy Apu and his sister Durga (precisely, the goddess of destruction/creation) go for the adventure of seeing a train go by.

Two Women in *L'Avventura*   213

The love scene began with a sudden cut from the deserted town the couple had driven into. The couple stop in this town and walk around and shout out, to no avail. The empty square has the look of a De Chirico painting—empty and ominous. I also think back to news items a few years ago about development of a nuclear device that would kill people but leave buildings intact. At one point we view the couple and their car in long shot down an alley.

In a Hitchcock-like gesture the camera starts moving slowly forward as if walking with us or pulling us along. Nowhere else in the film are we so made aware of the presence of the camera, with the sense of a higher power observing and perhaps controlling everything.

This disturbingly empty town is the emptiness, or the nothingness, at the heart of this film—the emptiness in human relations, of the blank canvas of the desert relations, or the nothingness we meet in attempting to fathom the film's mysteries, or in all failed endeavors at achieving precise knowledge, failures of knowledge that Roland Barthes was happy to see in this film and others of Antonioni.

Claudia and Sandro's adventure periodically transitions back to the town and the little hotel where they are staying. We see Claudia in bed, looking, again, as if she may be dreaming. We see the arrival of the famously expensive prostitute Gloria Perkins, and she is mobbed in the street by a pressing crowd of men, in a scene recalling the gang rape of Sophia Loren and her daughter in De Sica's *Two Women*. Claudia

herself, out for a walk, undergoes a similar mobbing. She takes refuge in a hardware store and asks to buy a can of paint. "Blue," she says in English, revealing an antic side. We cannot know Claudia fully, any more than Anna. Claudia and Sandro travel on, reaching a luxury seaside hotel, where the others from the boating group welcome them in. A decadent party is in progress throughout the hotel.

Early in the morning Claudia misses Sandro and goes searching for him and asking about him. She finds him stretched out on a couch downstairs with Gloria Perkins, and sees him pay her off.

Sandro exits the hotel and walks across the open square in front—another empty space—to a bench looking out to sea. He looks quite dejected. Claudia walks up and puts her hand on him, in that famous ambiguous gesture.

Here is much to see and hear, but you cannot know.

9

The Unknown Piano Teacher

My own experience viewing Michael Haneke's films, going back to an early stage, has been one of constantly being reminded of films other than his, other filmmakers, other film projects. Perhaps Haneke means to announce that he is ringing changes on concerns already in place, or that he means to disrupt such concerns. Perhaps the allusions, or some of them, are not deliberate, something in film just taking over, the author diving not so much into his own work as into the very medium of the fictional feature film, which has its ways over time of wanting to go, its own drives to recurrence and transformation. In any case, the invocations of other films in Haneke seem to help see more precisely what the Haneke films are doing.

In *The Seventh Continent* (*Der siebente Kontinent*, 1989), with the sense of fragmentariness, the numerous brief shots of parts of actions, parts of human beings in action, objects without their context, a physical world seemingly more present than any human consciousness within it, one thinks of Resnais, of such a passage, say, as the brilliant opening of *Muriel, or the Time of Return* (*Muriel ou le temps d'un retour*, 1963), where the assault of images, the quick cuts, makes it hard to decipher the human encounter between Hélène (Delphine Seyrig) and her customer, in Hélène's apartment where everything is an antique for sale—objects marked by the past, by various pasts, and mixed together dressed up for new consumption—in all respects like the characters in the film. For Haneke, does Resnais' old project need to be revived in the 1990s? Is there a difference? Fragmentariness in Resnais suggests the difficulty of perceiving anything whole, perhaps because nothing is in fact whole, for the characters in the film or for us, if we will think about it, getting rid of our illusions. There does emerge in *Muriel* a sense of people with rich, if confused, human concerns. Perhaps people's blankness in *The Seventh Continent* shows Haneke's sense that times have worsened, that Resnais' world, where things and appearances—or habits of the work world, as in *My American Uncle* (*Mon oncle d'Amérique*, 1980)—overwhelm human consciousness, has degenerated to a condition of complete dehumanization. The only desire is for death, annihilation, figured as the longing for a beautiful utopia, Australia, the seventh continent, seen as a poster image. (I do not think so much of Bresson's fragmentariness, though clearly Haneke loves Bresson, and he alludes to him, or quotes him, often. The fragments in Bresson seem weighted with a meaning we cannot quite discern, like the weighted images of a dream. There is a sense that Bresson knows, or that his film knows, a whole, a greater entity than we see, of which we can have only intimations.)

The prominent car wash in *The Seventh Continent*, where the physical and its maddening sounds press on the characters and on the viewer, recalls Godard's *Two or Three Things I Know About Her* (*2 ou 3 choses que je sais d'elle*, 1967), a film about the sub-bourgeoisie, rather than the struggling middle class, as in *The Seventh Continent*. The car wash in these films is both the condensed provocation of the world as it is, and a baptism into new possibilities. Robin Wood has said that Haneke's use of the Alban Berg Violin Concerto in *The Seventh Continent*, when the father and child go to sell the family car, represents the director's wish to find the most sublime and liberated alternative to the condition of this world (Wood, "Michael Haneke"). The same might be said of Godard's use of the late Beethoven string quartet, the F Major, opus 135, into which *Two or Three Things* explodes upon Juliette's car's emergence from the wash and its drive down a leafy Paris street. Godard manages to suggest a possible strong creative dimension even to acceptance of one's fate, the wife/mother/prostitute Juliette's fate in *Two or Three Things*, like the prostitute Nana's fate in *Vivre sa vie* (1962) or Ferdinand's fate in *Pierrot le Fou* (1965) or the Virgin's fate in *Hail Mary* (*Je vous salue, Marie*, 1985). Godard is more a romantic than Resnais or Haneke. But perhaps *The Seventh Continent* suggests a beauty and a good to its family's rite of self-annihilation, preceded by the drawn-out ritual of destruction of worldly goods, the cutting up of money and flushing it down the toilet, and so on. The fragment of Berg's Violin Concerto, this premier Austrian modernist's variation on a Bach chorale, itself derived from an older source than Bach, is not just an alternative to this family's world but an epitome of their impulse to destroy and escape this world. The Berg, the beauty and orderliness of Haneke's shooting and editing (like Resnais'), the final actions of the family all come together as a form of knowing and reacting that moves the viewer to a new perspective, washing over the viewer like those waves that come to life in the poster image of the Australian shore.

Haneke's dialogue with other films and filmmakers goes on, for me, all but unendingly. His acknowledgment of lively human feeling in the child in *The Seventh Continent*, as when she cries out at the destruction of the fish tank, looks forward to a hope he seems to place in children and the young later—in Benny at the end of *Benny's Video* (1992), when he seems, unlike his parents, to regret all that has happened in violence and covering it up; in the boy who would sacrifice himself near the end of *Time of the Wolf* (*Le temps du loup*, 2003); in the youths at the end of *Caché* (2005), who seem possibly the so-far unidentified accusers and punishers of the adult world's suppressed historical guilt—and all this links Haneke to his contemporary in Iran, Abbas Kiarostami, who suggests repeatedly that children can come to life morally in ways impossible for their blinkered, wounded, sometimes authoritarian elders (and when Kiarostami leaves the world of children for that purely of adults, in *Taste of Cherry* (*Ta'm e guilass*, 1997), his theme is, of course, a disposition for suicide). The deaf children struggling to learn to communicate who appear in *Code inconnu: Récit incomplet de divers voyages* (*Code Unknown*, 2000) at the beginning and the end, recall the stuttering boy and his therapy session at the start of Tarkovsky's *Mirror* (*Zerkalo*, 1975). If *Mirror* suggests that the past and reality of the Soviet Union can be spoken after all, *Code Unknown* answers with a bleaker picture of incomprehension in contemporary, prosperous, multiethnic western Europe, though Haneke does acknowledge, most pointedly in the children, positive desire and struggle. Berg's Violin Concerto is offered as a tribute to a young woman who died of polio (Manon, the daughter of Walter Gropius and Alma, widow of Gustav Mahler, who wrote the *Kindertotenlieder*), and Haneke's use of the Berg in *The Seventh Continent* may be taken as a tribute to the little girl's feeling and possibilities in that film. This little girl, pretending at school to be blind, crying out there in a certain way, recalls the little boy pretending to be paralyzed in Antonioni's *Red Desert* (*Il deserto rosso*, 1964), another film about dehumanizing materiality. But *Red Desert* ends on a note of survival, the mother telling her child, who is now walking, of birds who learn to cope with poisonous gas and get around it. Perhaps Haneke's films are more aimed at survival than is usually acknowledged. Allow yourself to be provoked in the right way, come into film as knowledge—a very Tarkovskian concept—and you may be saved.

Resnais' fragmentariness comes to mind again with the narrative style of *71 Fragments of a Chronology of Chance* (*71 fragmente einer Chronologie des Zufalls*, 1994) and *Code Unknown*. More pertinent perhaps is the American Robert Altman, who with films such as *Nashville* (1975) and *Short Cuts* (1993) began giving the picture of the complex life of a city, with many characters, many separate little worlds, the film moving from one to another and back and around seemingly at random. All is characterized by miscomprehension, and frustrated desires that issue in violence, as film itself seems to struggle to see, to comprehend, to keep up. Altman touches as deep a social and political despair as does Haneke. Yet there are differences. Altman takes a more mystical, fixated interest in death. And his films touch specifically American forms of ecstasy not available to Haneke's world. Altman, taking hours, lingering over his material, is an elegist. Haneke, more ordered, moving things along, is a teacher—this quality in him gives a nice resonance to the English-language title of *The Piano Teacher* (*La pianiste*, 2001).

Altman's interest in the death wish has been linked by his more astute critics to Hitchcock's nihilism. And Hitchcock figures very strongly in the Haneke mix. The cutting up of a dead body and cleaning away of a violent crime, from *Rear Window* (1954) and *Psycho* (1960), recur in *Benny's Video*, and *Psycho*'s subjection of everyday, familiar people to the annihilating wrath of Norman Bates, rising up in their midst, recurs in *Funny Games* (1997; 2007). Robin Wood thinks of *The Birds* (1963) in regard to *Funny Games*. Benny, overhearing his parents' discussion of the cutting up and cleaning up that they plan, is put in the position of *Rear Window*'s photographer Jeffries (James Stewart), aware of Thorwald's actions at a distance, speculating, reacting. This link of Benny to Jeffries would go with Haneke's theme of the young coming to life morally. Benny has killed a young woman, suddenly and spontaneously, taunted by her. But Jeffries, too, something of an overgrown boy, is implicated in the crime he wants to expose; he has projected his own violent impulses and resentment of a woman onto the screen, and thus behind the screen, onto that window across the courtyard—so it feels in the film. Moral awakening goes with implication. Benny comes back in a sense—the same actor—to torment and destroy a well-off family in *Funny Games*. This is a more claustrophobic film than *Psycho* or *The Birds*. Norman Bates and the birds are other to, represent an alternative to, the everyday people and everyday world that they assault. Hitchcock suggests that the universe holds strange recesses beyond us that we might venture into, or be forced to venture into, meeting dissolution. The tormenting and murderous duo in *Funny Games* seem part of the family in a way, well-bred young men who have run amok, something the world of the family has bred up radically to go against itself.

When I first saw *The Piano Teacher*, two scenes struck me as uncanny replayings of scenes from other films. When Erika Kohut (Isabelle Huppert) cuts her genitals with a razor blade, it seems a recurrence of the unnerving episode in Ingmar Bergman's *Cries & Whispers* (*Viskningar och rop*, 1972) when Karin (Ingrid Thulin) cuts herself with the shard of broken wineglass, and moments later, sitting in bed, with a mad look on her face, reaches from her crotch to smear her face with blood, to the astonishment of her stuffy, difficult husband across the room. I believe that *The Piano Teacher* is a character film, an attempt to get at, to evoke, a remarkable individual, and to get at, to evoke, new realms of human possibility. Isabelle Huppert brings her own resonance to the film. But part of the resonance of Erika Kohut here is Ingrid Thulin. Karin/Thulin's act with the broken glass in *Cries & Whispers* is the rebellion of a narrow and unhappy character there, but the act connects to the Thulin presence over a range of films, perhaps to the perverse mother in Visconti's *The Damned* (*La caduta degli dei* [*Götterdämmerung*], 1969), who, naked, takes her grown son (Helmut Berger) to bed; certainly to the character of Ester in Bergman's *The Silence* (*Tystnaden*, 1963)—the genital cutting in *Cries & Whispers* seems to counter Ester's masturbation scene in *The Silence*. Ingrid Thulin as Ester, this intellectual woman bigger than her world, ill in the superior way a Dostoyevsky or Thomas Mann character is ill, able to relate to others only through gestures of overbearing dominance or embarrassing abjection, seems particularly relevant to Erika Kohut in Haneke's film. Ester/Thulin, able to come to the self-wounding act of Karin/Thulin, tells us something of who Erika Kohut is.

The other scene in *The Piano Teacher* that seems (to me) to replay another film is later, when Erika gets into bed with her mother and appears to assault her sexually, saying in a childlike way at the end of it all, when everything has calmed down, that she has glimpsed some of her mother's pubic hair. What this brings to mind is Chantal Akerman's *The Meetings of Anna* (*Les rendez-vous d'Anna*, 1978), where the lead character (played by Aurore Clément) gets into bed, nude, with her mother for what turns out to be a warm, calm conversation, ultimately turning to the topic of sexual relations between women. The mothers in both Akerman's and Haneke's films are played by women who made a big impression in key roles in Italian film around 1960, and whom Akerman and Haneke seem to bring back from a certain obscurity, older, trailing clouds of an earlier identity with implications in that for who their daughters are. The mother in *Les rendez-vous d'Anna* is Lea Massari, the girl (named Anna) who disappeared on the island in *L'Avventura* (1960), an alienated society beauty who has to give way, in narrative importance, to the Monica Vitti character (Claudia), a mature, charitable outsider to the film's social world, who becomes a traveler. Akerman's protagonist, Anne (she is called Anna only by her female Italian lover of one night, in a message on the telephone voice recorder at the end of the film), is a version of the Vitti character, like her a contradictory, if loving, daughter to what Massari represents—in *L'Avventura* the girl everybody wants, later in *Les rendez-vous d'Anna* the dutiful wife. In *The Piano Teacher* the mother is Annie Girardot, who was Nadia the ill-fated prostitute and lover of two brothers in Visconti's *Rocco and His Brothers* (*Rocco e i suoi fratelli*, 1960). Haneke's Erika Kohut is born of turbulence, even violence, a world of the displaced and the upward striving. Nadia was a victim caught in the counterforces of her world. Erika is more comparable to the brothers, figures of transformation, in their case leaving behind the world of the peasantry of southern Italy and seeking a better life and admiration in the avenue of prizefighting, their form of art. And what links Akerman's character Anne and Haneke's Erika, is that both are artists, Anne a filmmaker and Erika a pianist. The films use these occupations to underscore both women's practice as artists of life, fashioners of their own lives. Anne is a listener, except when baring herself to her mother. She is one who reacts and remains polite. But she keeps moving, walking train corridors all through the night, traversing Europe, turning away from many forms of life, thinking, searching. Erika Kohut is more active, proceeding by fits and starts. Surely Anne as filmmaker is a figure for Akerman herself, making a creative act out of the observational, working with what is there. The art of a pianist and piano teacher is similar, bringing to new creative life the scores of Bach and Schubert, and forming the new generation of those who come to her for study. Perhaps Erika is a figure for Haneke, creating anew out of the stuff of film culture, focusing himself specifically as teacher, like Hitchcock not sparing the rod.

Women who are artists of their lives, standing apart from others, battered by experience with others, at times seeming mad, to others and to themselves; a crucial and formative mother-daughter dynamic; alignment of the filmmaker and of the very medium and technique of film with the central woman, with her imagination; the film revealing, in what seems like self-revelation, more and more facets of the woman as it goes along, making clear that we will never get everything—all this puts us in the world of the films Stanley Cavell has described and named as "melodramas of the unknown woman" (*Contesting Tears* xv), taking the name, of course, from Max Ophüls's 1948 Hollywood film *Letter from an Unknown Woman*, starring Joan Fontaine—as it happens, a film like *The Piano Teacher* in being about Vienna, though not made in the German language; a film about the world of music and musicians, where music aligns itself with the imagination of the heroine, her imagination of her life; a film whose central woman's character is formed on an axis of masochism and sadism, where we are asked radically to rethink these dispositions. Lisa (Joan Fontaine with overtones of her uncertain roles in Hitchcock's *Rebecca* [1940] and *Suspicion* [1941]) brings harm on herself and others, chiefly upon her lover Stefan (Louis Jourdan) through her paralyzing letter, which gives us the film—the letter, her art, fully aligned with Ophüls's dark images, the film's all but palpable sound effects and music, the elaborate crane and tracking shots. Or does Ophüls, does the film, stand at any distance and judge Lisa? Hard to say, we are so caught up in her poetic self-revelation, which can never fully come clear.

Cavell discusses *Letter from an Unknown Woman* and other melodramas—the Sternberg/Dietrich *Blonde Venus* (1932); *Stella Dallas* (1937), with Barbara Stanwyck; *Now, Voyager* (1942), with Bette Davis; *Gaslight* (1944), with Ingrid Bergman, and still other films, as part of American film culture of the 1930s and 1940s, and American culture more broadly, and in specific relation, as opposite, to a line of romantic comedies he designates "comedies of remarriage," films that center on conversational breakthroughs, and women and men finding their equals. But Cavell acknowledges that the interests of the melodramas go back to European figures, such as Greta Garbo in films of the 1920s and 1930s, and of course Dietrich. And it is easy to see the interest of the unknown woman extending into more modern American films such as those of Altman (*Nashville* with its mad women singing of their desires that are never fulfilled) or films of John Cassavetes (*A Woman Under the Influence* [1974], *Opening Night* [1977]), or films of Mizoguchi and Rossellini in the 1950s, Ingmar Bergman, Antonioni, Akerman, and beyond. If the inspiration of the American melodramas and comedies is, as Cavell argues, Emersonian, the inspiration in European film for the sense of the evolving and fragmented self, and the challenge it poses to the status quo, is Nietzschean—and the Nietzschean inspiration derives, Cavell likes to point out, from the Emersonian. What is important about the melodramas of the unknown woman in connection with Haneke is that these films represent something that film wants to do: put the right actress together with certain material and let the woman emerge; direct and embellish and photograph and shape it as this potent situation demands. Josef von Sternberg and Marlene Dietrich, who had established their own way of doing things, found themselves, with *Blonde Venus*, overtaken by something in a sense bigger than they: the genre, Cavell calls it, defining the term carefully, of the melodrama of the unknown woman. Haneke wades into these waters, into this realm with its strong vibrations, taking up the story of Erika Kohut and casting the star Isabelle Huppert, with her distinctive air of innocence, seriousness, and thoughtfulness, her intensity, her believability as a person of depth. One comes away from this film with memories mainly of Huppert's face, of wonderful passages of music, and of physically or emotionally violent sex acts. All these go together to make, or to begin to suggest, this woman. (One might say that Haneke prepared for *The Piano Teacher* developing the Juliette Binoche character, Anne, in *Code Unknown*. It is possible to come away from that film feeling that it centers on the soul in development of this woman artist—she is a professional actress. Everything can seem to come back to her, as she makes her way through the film, taking in its various worlds as her path crosses those of others, as she tries out roles—in life, on the stage, in films—the three blurring. Binoche's screen presence, with her distinctive air of psychological and moral uncertainty—so different from Huppert's determinedness—rather takes over *Code Unknown*.)

After announcing the players, but before the title and full credits, *The Piano Teacher* gives us a protracted domestic scene, as Erika comes home at night to her mother, and the two fight physically over a dress Erika has bought, eventually reconciling and retiring for the night, together. Toward the end of the episode the camera dwells on Annie Girardot's face, hurt, regretful seemingly of a lifetime's painful experiences, human, even warm. This mother is not the simple, pushing tyrant of Elfriede Jelinek's novel, on which the film is based. This opening can seem the matrix from which all the rest of the film is derived, projected as the daughter's fantasy or film or dream out of the dark and close interior spaces of this domestic world, just as the course of events in *Blonde Venus* or *Letter from an Unknown Woman* can seem the fantasy of the woman character at the center of it. As Erika and her mother settle into bed, turn off the light, become quiet, and, presumably, begin to dream, the screen announces the title, *La pianiste*. Erika draws something from her mother, her capacity for feeling, her violence, and also needs to form herself in opposition, to liberate herself, to get out of this house, to spin something out of it. Erika will never let her face become as open as Annie Girardot's. She insists to her mother in the pillow conversation here that music and musical judgment is her own field, that her mother should stay out of these concerns. This drawing from and opposition to the mother on the part of the central woman is characteristic, Cavell says, of the unknown woman story—this dynamic is played out most elaborately perhaps in *Now, Voyager*.

Cavell also says that a child or child substitute will be present, at once a burden and a field for creativity and self-realization. It is easy to think of Erika's piano students as her children in a sense, perhaps even Walter, her lover. But the crucial opening with her mother comes to focus on one student in particular, Anna Schober, who Erika says has a talent for Schubert, and whom we come to see working on the accompaniment for Schubert's song cycle *Die Winterreise*. Erika is hard on this girl in lessons, as she is on everybody, but she is also encouraging at important junctures: when Anna is upset in the street, fearing she will not be good enough to play in the student concert, Erika tells her she may well be able to play, that she should keep working and try the piece with the singer; and when Anna is ill in the bathroom before the concert rehearsal and the (male) singer is harsh to her, Erika tells her not to take it all so seriously, they won't eat her, it's just a rehearsal. Of course, in one of the film's most disturbing acts, Erika puts broken glass into Anna's coat pocket during the rehearsal, causing her to injure her right hand badly. This is perhaps done out of jealousy, when Erika sees Walter giving Anna kind attention. But there is something perversely mentoring about it. Erika causes the girl, with her talent for Schubert as Erika has acknowledged it, to bleed, just as she has caused herself to bleed with that razor blade. In an interview with Anna's mother, Erika sends Anna the message to take this opportunity to work hard on her left hand playing, which is needed and important. In the film's first episode after the credits, the musicale in a private apartment, Erika does her most extended bit of playing and establishes her musical identity, in the final movement fugue of Bach's C-Major Concerto for two keyboards, where we see Erika play a passage for left hand. In a strange way, at some level, Erika would lead her child, the talented nervous Anna, into the world of blood and the left hand, the hand of deviance, a deviance embraced in the sane insanity of music, of Bach.

After the opening domestic scene, while the credits come, intercut shots give us moments from Erika's piano instruction. Several times, the camera looks straight down onto the keyboard and playing hands—the point of view of the person playing, or of the teacher, and at one point Erika takes over and plays for the student, Anna Schober, as it happens. Haneke in effect gives his camera to Erika, suggesting that the film is her projection, that she is its director, or that he is she—try thinking of every shot as Erika's, her point of view away from herself, or her self-regard; it is possible. (Sternberg said, "I am Miss Dietrich. Miss Dietrich is me," and by "Miss Dietrich" he meant the woman in the films.) We hear, and see played, striking passages by various composers. Erika makes some comments on playing technique, but here and throughout the film her comments mostly go to the meaning and feeling of the music. Unlike the character in Jelinek's novel, the film's Erika is deeply interested in music. She identifies herself through it. The film is interested in music. Haneke is interested in music. Music is a presence in the film—like Huppert herself—as it is not in Jelinek's novel, which could just as well be about some other career (and music can be a presence in prose fiction, as it is in Mann's *Doctor Faustus* or *The Magic Mountain*). The views down onto the keyboard ultimately give way to wider views, first of Erika working with Anna under a portrait of Bach, the composer through whom Erika will principally announce herself; then a shot taking in much of the studio with Erika standing at a window, looking out, a portrait of Robert Schumann on the wall to her left. Erika faces the large rectangle of the window and the bright world beyond as if giving her attention to a film screen, imagining her life, about to project it. We do not hear Schumann's music during the film, but Erika says that he, along with Schubert, is her favorite composer, and she mentions Adorno's remark that Schumann's C-Major Fantasy for piano represents the mind that holds sane while knowing that it is on the border of insanity. We do not hear Schumann's music, but the film *is* in a sense Erika's C-Major Fantasy. Arnold Schönberg—dedicated atonalist and Berg's teacher—some of whose music we hear in the film, famously remarked that there is still much good music to be written in C Major. And so we begin Erika's film, with the elaborate musicale scene where she, as it were, summons up her appreciator and lover, Walter Klemmer, and presents herself in the Bach C-Major Concerto.

It is possible to take the story that follows in more than one way, which adds to its interest. Robin Wood has written that he identifies with, and sympathizes with, Erika entirely as someone whose desires cannot be fulfilled, someone whom upbringing, culture, the world as it is, and her tempestuous nature drive to a life of frustration, neurosis, loneliness, and self-destructive acts. Taking the film this way would see the complex unknown woman, larger than her world, as giving signs about herself with her every act, musical or sexual, crying out, declaring herself, never being fully read or rightly responded to.

But one can also see the relationship of Erika and Walter as the playing out of a dynamic that is just what Erika wants. Walter is rather a fantasy figure, striking in looks, multitalented, immediately in love with Erika as a result of her Bach performance. The affair begins on the occasion of the rehearsal at the conservatory for the student concert. At first we hear a good deal of the same Brahms Serenade for strings that Louis Malle uses obsessively in *The Lovers* (*Les amants*, 1958), finally having it spark off and accompany Jeanne Moreau's night of abandoned love with the Walter Klemmer–like young man she has brought home off the highway. In the bathroom sex scene at the concert rehearsal in *The Piano Teacher*, Erika is all the master, Walter humiliated. In Erika's room at home, having Walter read her letter of instructions for abusing her, the tables begin to be turned, with Walter disgusted and self-righteous, or pretending to be, and Erika beginning to quail. Erika seeks Walter out at his ice hockey rink, and in the storeroom sex scene there he is all angry master and she submissive. Their declarations of love through all this seem genuine, though everything else can seem play-acting of a kind they desire, or something that blurs the border between play-acting and rough human interaction that is not exactly what is desired. In any case, perhaps the desirable is fully gone when Walter invades Erika's apartment near the end of the film, bloodies her face, and rapes her, and we watch her face in a very protracted shot while the rape goes on, she seeming only stoically to endure it, still, quietly asking him to stop. Can she have wanted it to come to this? I think it is impossible to say. All that is left of the film is, next day, Erika's taking of the kitchen knife and going off with her mother to the concert, meeting Walter briefly in the lobby, then, left alone, stabbing herself and walking away into the night (Jelinek's novel makes it clear that the wound is slight; in the film it is not clear). Perhaps this is one more melodramatic move in the game, the affair that began at a rehearsal and now comes to the concert for which the rehearsal was held. Perhaps there will be more.

The abundance of music in the first part of the film gives way to the playing out of the love affair in the second part. After the rehearsal, the only music we get is in Walter's lesson with Erika where she is trying to show him that a Schubert sonata represents a wide scale of strong feeling and comes of a core experience of suffering such as Walter cannot know, with his charm, lack of depth, and fatedness to succeed in the world's terms. Erika seems to admit that Walter can never be her equal. The falling away of music as Erika gets more and more involved with Walter can seem both a turning away from music on Erika's part, which is a mistake for her, or a playing out of something implicit in the music. The music of this film—Bach, Schubert, and so on—is larger than all the world; it contains everything. Part of the teacher Haneke/Erika's lesson for us, something he/she wants to get us to think about, is that all the intense and subversive human drama we might imagine is there in Bach and Schubert, just as it is there in the culture of film, where, in some needful way, different in the case of every piece of music, every film, life is coped with and made livable, even if this means we must go from the music or film and be changed.

At last Erika walks off into the night, like Stella Dallas. But the camera does not track back before her, looking at her face, admiring her, wondering who she is now, as the camera does with Stella. Rather, Erika disappears from the frame as the camera holds on the façade of the conservatory, the great mother (and Erika's mother is now inside, no doubt wondering where Erika is). Repeatedly Erika has been associated, has associated herself, with the journeyer in *Die Winterreise*, wounded, wandering, apart from and unlike all others, on the edge of madness. She ends here in motion, still going, walking alone, like Mann's Hans Castorp wandering in the snow, obsessed with a *Winterreise* song other than the three we hear in *The Piano Teacher*, namely "Der Lindenbaum":

> By the well, before the gate,
> Stands a linden tree;
> In its shade I dreamt
> Many a sweet dream . . .

Substitute music conservatory for linden tree. The tree, and the snow, of course, hold the lure of death for Hans Castorp, but he goes on. Death and rebirth, imagination, dreams, new life, film all come together in Haneke's Erika, who is Haneke, who takes over Haneke, with her human depth and her boundless desire.

10

Three Immersions

Jean-Pierre and Luc Dardenne's *Rosetta*

ROSETTA IS BEST UNDERSTOOD IN terms of a lineage it draws from Robert Bresson's *Mouchette* (1967) and Agnès Varda's *Vagabond* (*Sans toit ni loi*, 1985). Three young women stalking and tramping their way through life, deprived, meeting frustration on many fronts, yet persisting, moving on. It is a striking image—this battered but persistent girl—recurring and haunting the later decades of the twentieth century. Perhaps she is still to be seen.

It's plausible to read social critique in these films—thinking about Mouchette's dire circumstances of rural poverty, Mona's sarcasm in *Vagabond* about her former bosses and the respectable world she shuns, Rosetta's difficulties with employment. The Dardenne film, focused on the suffering of a girl desperate to find work, seems even to have sparked reform legislation in Belgium—like *Oliver Twist* in Dickens's England (Mai 81–82). But the film experience in these cases does not go far in the way of social and systemic analysis—that is for some other medium. And the films do something much more remarkable—much stronger—than make us feel for the young woman subject to social abuse.

Rosetta (1999) gives us an incarnation—or whatever film is, whatever a person on film is—of pure rage and busyness. Employment difficulties seem not so much the cause of this girl's rage and energy as a pretext for them, an artistic means (with proper social consciousness) to allow her rage and persistence, her constant motion, to emerge. At the film's opening we see Rosetta (Émilie Dequenne) charging about the confines and hallways of some kind of food factory, slamming doors, tramping heavily, breathing hard and angrily, struggling with various people, shouting. The hand-held camera stays close to her, unsteady, desperate-seeming in its bid to follow, letting the image blur in quick panning movements. In the Dardennes' previous film, *The Promise* (*La promesse*, 1996), their characteristic hand-held camera seemed to embody the pressures working upon the young protagonist, tearing him between family loyalty and sympathy with, and a promise made to, black immigrant outsiders. In *Rosetta* the camera seems to emanate from the heroine, to answer to and suit the energies boiling within her, to be the means she needs to stage herself. In the course of the opening scene, we learn that Rosetta has been fired from her job because her term of employment has run out and there is nothing permanent for her. But this cannot account for what we see and hear, even if we suppose it has happened many times before, exasperating her. What we see is a pure woman-in-chaotic-motion, a screen figure of pure motion, a goddess of motion. We see her carried away by security personnel, struggling, the camera still close and unsteady. And there is a cut to a close view of her later, outside in the streets with the background soft about her, meditative in profile as if thinking over her recent performance, or seeing it in her mind's eye (did it happen?), intermittently eating a waffle and drinking water from a bottle—she has appetite—now still as the camera is still.

We are given an icon of the woman at her source, the woman who has acted and will act. Next she sits riding in a bus, and the camera faces her, but her eyes are cast down. The camera moves in extremely close, but cannot penetrate her character. Soon she is plunging into woods and muddy underbrush, a home domain for her it transpires—the world of Mouchette and of Mona in *Vagabond*.

Mouchette opens, after the credits sequence (more on that in a moment), with close views of underbrush—an immersion in underbrush—where in a series of shots we see a gamekeeper walking behind bushes and settling into place, watching a poacher set a snare, then freeing a bird, taking the snare, and emerging onto a road to walk home. In town he meets a line of schoolgirls, who turn into the yard of their school. One girl (Nadine Nortier) walks toward us, up to the camera, and stops as another girl, offscreen, calls to this one, "Mouchette!" The film then attends to the gamekeeper, who goes home to his wife. In what we have seen, Mouchette, wearing a poor drab shift and clogs, has stilled herself for a moment, exchanging looks with the gamekeeper, becoming pensive,

showing her extraordinary under-a-bushel beauty. Her moment of thought, like Rosetta's out in the street, seems to contain that episode in the woods as part of herself, as Rosetta's moment of thought seemed to contain her chase through the factory. Mouchette contains more than the woods, though. Before the credits, we saw a woman in a church saying, "What will become of them without me?" She exits, and we watch her empty chair as the credits are superimposed. This woman will turn out to be Mouchette's ill and moribund mother. Her words in the church setting give to what follows a quality of ritual or of being blessed. Mouchette, and the film, will fill that chair. During the credits we hear sweet string music and a chorus—Monteverdi's setting of "*Deposuit potentes de sede et exaltavit humiles*"—"He has put down the mighty from their seat and exalted the humble." The film will exalt the humble. It proceeds now without background music until part of the same Monteverdi returns in the final scene, when Mouchette, wearing a shroud intended for her mother, rolls herself downhill into a pond—the consummation of what the mother invoked.

Mouchette lives in town, but the woods define her, generating her feral nature, a force of life and resistance—and generating also her destiny, her fate. The long middle section of the film is played out at night in the woods, where Mouchette sings, confronts epilepsy, suffers—and embraces—sexual assault, becomes embroiled in the plots of poacher and gamekeeper. It is raining and Mouchette gets soaked—a preliminary immersion to that in the pond at the end. This film proceeds by setting up environments that enclose and oppress Mouchette, soliciting her reactions—the woods with the gamekeeper and poacher who know her and will draw her into their game; the school; the family hovel with the dying mother, needy baby, and tyrannical, petty-criminal father; the small town with its contempt for her. Jacques Rancière has written about the film that it presents us with a body that perpetually says no—with its posture, its gestures, its muddy feet on somebody's carpet, the look of the face, the tone of voice ("*Mouchette*"). This is right. But Mouchette also perpetually says yes. There is a sense of adventure about her existence. Her capacity for this is signaled strongly by her ecstasy driving the bumper car at the fair, and the night in the woods unfolds as desirable adventure as much as suffered fate. Mouchette suffers and says yes, radiating her paradoxical beauty, right up to saying yes to the pond and the transcendence of an access to Monteverdi's music. Mouchette is an icon of the paradox of suffering the world, saying no, saying yes, and rising to the heights of adventure, all at once.

An icon of a state of passivity and activity, and, specifically, a *film* icon, a goddess of a certain sort. We do not know what film is, this mysterious power. Critics who are philosophically minded, theorists, filmmakers, and indeed films themselves have thought about it—yes, art thinks, it is not merely that someone thinks through or by means of art. Thinking about film does not reach full understanding—it seems unlikely that it ever will. Such thinking deepens what understanding we have, points us more directly toward film, opens us more to film's presence. William Rothman, citing Stanley Cavell, remarks that photographs and film seem to us not so much to *represent* things as to *give* us the thing, strangely transfigured as the thing is in photographic or filmic form ("Face to Face" 154). Bresson's film gives us Nadine Nortier enabled through the character Mouchette to amaze us with passivity and active adventurousness at once, these qualities as if purified to an abstract plane, fit for contemplation—the contemplation that enlarges us and changes us, if only by deepening our understanding of what we already are, what our life is.

As the essays in this book have repeatedly observed, film often finds an image for itself—a way of thinking about itself—in water. Water is a source of creativity and of renewal. It provides a reflecting surface, like the film screen—in both cases the world is there, but transfigured—there and, in a sense, not there. Death and rebirth to a new life come about, as in baptism—the same, but different. Water has depths, and the screen induces us to think of what—psychological, physical, spiritual, narrative—lies behind the little we see. Water flows and ripples, like film—part of its transformative power.

Mouchette's move from suffering to adventurousness is signaled by her getting wet in the storm at night. At the end of the film, she rolls into the pond. We look down on her spinning vertiginously along the ground, and hear a great splash, but do not see her. We have had views of the pond, clear water with stones at the bottom along the edge, trees and bushes—the shore world—reflected on the surface. Now we look down on the pond and see the violent ripples Mouchette has made, the water deeply stirred like a creative cauldron. We do not see her. Has she sunk into the depths? Floated up and pulled herself out somewhere? Swum away? She has entered some life-or-death realm as if entering a film, perhaps her own film, her projection. Her fictional death or new stage of life, the shedding of an existence, is in turn shed by her entering into the immortality of a film icon. Is film concrete enough to be immortal, like sculpture or lines of poetry? Perhaps it is enabled all the more by its very ghostliness, wherein it *gives* us the world—here, specifically, Nadine Nortier inflected by her role as Mouchette—rather than *representing* something.

⸻

Mona in *Vagabond* (Sandrine Bonnaire) is indirectly a creature of the woods. For the most part she is "on the road," as she says and others say of her. We see her in open spaces—along roads, in fields and villages. It is hard to remember the precise series of events in the film, and this serves the artistic purpose. We are given a state of wandering. There is a certain amount of circularity, as places and people reappear—Mona re-encounters them, or people come back to talk to the camera about earlier encounters with Mona, which we have seen. We do see her camping in the woods several times—briefly, as if we do not need to see more, this being her home ground, from where she starts. Deep into the film, more than halfway, in a more extended scene, Mona is assaulted and raped, camping in the woods. Here there is much obscuring imagery of brambles and tree branches, reaching from bottom to top of the frame. The woods are fearful. But altogether Mona is living at risk. She courts trauma and suffering as well as pleasure. The opening shot of the film gives us a broad field under cultivation, but with a few trees in the foreground and background, as if to remind us that all was woods before clearing to make fields, farms, villages, towns. Mona represents a certain wildness that wanders about in and flirts with the cultivated world, but in essence rejects it, says no to it. Several times people speak of envying her freedom and independence.

The film's opening, with cultivated land, leads to a worker's discovery of Mona's dead body, dead in a ditch from exposure to cold, strangely covered with red stains. "They threw her in a wine vat," a man explains to the police. The rest of the film emerges as a retrospect, and at the end we do see Mona chased and frightened and doused with wine during some kind of primitive festival to celebrate the harvest and winemaking. Mona is menaced by large men in monstrous costume, adorned with tree branches and leaves—the woods, a reflection of her own wildness perhaps, come to assault her again. She wanders away and collapses in the ditch. She is a version of the Frazerian god, of whom Christ is one avatar, sacrificed—killed and planted—to rise again, all for the good of the community. Her good, her challenge for us, is her wildness and independence. Her resurrection is as a film figure.

Just after the discovery of the body, a woman's voiceover begins the story, speaking of talking to people and trying to reconstruct Mona's last winter, leading up to her death. A vista of white sand fills the screen, perhaps a desert, a place for purification and new beginning—a blank canvas upon which to create—a figure for the film screen itself, for film. A legend of Mona is to be developed. The woman's voice, never identified, perhaps stands in for the film's writer and director already credited, Agnès Varda, here figuring herself as a depersonalized priestess and keeper of the flame. The voice does not return, though the people we see addressing the camera throughout the film can be thought of as giving testimony to this woman whose voice we have heard.[2]

The sand turns out to be that of the seashore, and as the voiceover says of Mona, "I think she came from the sea," we get a very distant shot of Mona, entirely nude, emerging from the sea and walking onto the shore. This signal immersion, the vagabond taking a bath in the sea, with, as it turns out, two motorcycle boys watching, is presented as an emergence. We are given the coming into being of a goddess such as Aphrodite/Venus. The image of the expanse of blue sea and the white sandy foreground is like nothing else we see in the film. And Mona never again appears nude. We are given a transcendent identity marker for this woman and her powers, to set against the world she wanders in—perhaps to set against the woods that house her but do her harm. But wildwood and sea are not at odds. The sea image is framed in the foreground by huge brambles left and right growing on a dune—echoed in Mona's pubic hair (the hair of her head, wet and clinging, overlit in the sun, is hardly visible). The sea origin sets Mona on her path of destiny, to wander in the world's woods, to enjoy herself, to submit to harm and die into legend, die into film—as she emerged from film, if you will, film figured as the blank screen of sand and as the sea.

Mona does not appear nude again, nor do we see her bathe—it is remarked later how bad she smells (she has given herself to the earth—she is already dead in a sense—the god undergoing a journey of the dead to challenge the dead in their habits). But nearly midway through the film, just after we see Mona wandering at night through town, facing a barking dog and looking into people's windows, the camera discovers a nude woman sitting in a bath, her breasts in view. She is maybe early 30s, looks chic, and seems sophisticated as she talks on the phone while sitting there, speaking of having given a ride to the vagabond, introducing, it turns out, a flashback about her interaction with Mona, one of the most protracted in the film. She is a professor and scientist, doing research on plane tree disease—woods, disease. She is very taken with Mona and wants to incorporate her into her life—but will only go so far. Later her young male assistant finds her at her bathroom sink being electrocuted by the lights she is touching—a very strange and striking scene, suggesting at once illumination and punishment, perhaps the pain of rebirth. The woman, recovered, goes on to talk of seeing her life flash before her eyes, and then of feeling bad about leaving Mona to enter and camp in the woods (where she will be assaulted). A second, younger woman is found nude, her breasts in view, this time emerging wet from a shower bath. She is the wife of the professor's assistant, who tells her about meeting Mona, with her "witch's hair." This young woman will not come close to Mona; she is hard, concerned with money, grasping, unhappy. These two women, nude and vulnerable, echo Mona's self-exposure at the beginning of the film. Their subsidiary immersions—to Mona's in the sea—represent chances for rebirth as Mona's kin. Only Varda, figured by the voiceover at the beginning, takes up the challenge of Mona, at once acknowledging and creating her—acknowledging her in the form of film, creating her as film.

⁌

We left Rosetta entering her woods, near the beginning of the film. She exchanges her city shoes for boots she keeps hidden—we see this several times over the course of the film, giving it a ritual quality, marking off the two domains of her existence. She walks off through the woods at a distance from us—a distance we rarely see in the film. She is defined by her setting here. Finally we see a large pond or portion of a river out beyond Rosetta.

Her immersion in this water is not to come for a time, but there are subsidiary and preparatory immersions. She lives with her alcoholic mother in a house-trailer camp within the woods, and she soon appears there fresh from a bath or at least from washing her hair—we see it wet about her head. She empties a large plastic tub and then rinses it out. It turns out the trailer has no indoor running water, so there is much to-and-fro fetching it from the general camp spigot, pouring and sloshing it about the house. Rosetta drinks a lot of water—as if calming, or feeding, her nature—constantly filling her portable water bottle, at home or about town, constantly drinking. At a new job making waffle batter in large quantities, there is pouring and stirring of milk and water, flour and eggs, in a huge vat. Here, as at home, sloshing sounds and images of flowing impress themselves on the viewer, characterizing Rosetta's world.

There are some intense physical struggles. Rosetta wrestles with her mother in the trailer over some food the mother has been given which Rosetta does not want to accept. A bit later she is enraged when a boy she has met where he works in a chain waffle stand, Riquet (Fabrizio Rongione), arrives at the camp on his motorbike to find her—she jumps on him and they struggle fiercely rolling around on the ground, often in what looks like sexual postures. It turns out he has come to tell her of a job opening in the waffle kitchen. In these instances of struggle the very close hand-held camera creates a blur, seemingly infected by the rage at hand, or created by and serving that rage, as in the opening chase through the factory. These moments can be rationalized, or moralized. Rosetta does not want her mother and herself to be thought beggars (she says this)—her mother tends to trade sex for alcohol and food and other favors. Then Rosetta is ashamed to be found in the camp by the boy—she does not want to be intruded on. But the explanations do not account for the fury we see. There is pure unaccountable rage against the mother, against their life, against life itself. With the boy it is almost as if she intuited his being a messenger from the business world, and rages against the idea of having a job—though she insists so often that she wants that. In the end she will renounce her newest job and opt for suicide. Rosetta is primarily, for us, a film being, and the nature of her film is the relentless close hand-held camera working through long takes, rendering her activity, engendered by her activity. The blurs of the physical struggles epitomize her film existence. Rosetta is immersed in this film style, *is* this film style, as are we as we attend.

Rosetta goes into the pond a little beyond a third of the way into the film, after we have seen her using her hidden trap to poach fish here, seen her selling used clothes mended by her mother, soothing abdominal cramps with a hair dryer, and working at her new job of making waffle batter—in short, a summary of her life, which seems, really, just to go in circles throughout the film. Now Rosetta fights with her mother over the issue of going into rehab and plods after her into the woods, where she is knocked into the pond. We hear a big splash, and quick pans back and forth link the girl in the water and the fleeing mother. Finally we just contemplate Rosetta—again at an unusual distance—splashing in the wide water around her which fills the screen—becomes the screen—crying desperately "Mother!" over and over. The water is greenish and murky, a creative cauldron, suggestive of amniotic fluid. The tough Rosetta is reduced to being a helpless child, struggling for life, or struggling to be born. Indeed, she manages to pull herself out of the water, as it were giving birth to herself. If we keep in mind water as creative realm, water as film, we can see how Rosetta, at a point where her life has been summed up, is seen to be born out of and into film. Rosetta's immersion and recovery register as trauma. It is trauma to be born into film, as it is trauma to be born at all, trauma to die. Rosetta herself is trauma. She is born into a style of film that answers to her nature.

Rosetta's attack of abdominal cramps, which happens a couple of more times in the film, is likely menstrual—her mother seems to think so—but is possibly due to anxiety or to some chronic illness. Perhaps more than one factor comes into play. In any case, the attack and the close view of her exposed belly with the phallic-shaped hair dryer passing over it, suggests the potential for motherhood in Rosetta. She is in a way her mother's mother in this story, looking after her, supervising her, correcting her. And immersed in the pond, Rosetta becomes her own mother, giving birth to herself—most immediately into a new phase of life, going to Riquet's lodgings and making friends with him. She is born into her film.

In that first scene with cramps, Rosetta, lying in bed, rises up a bit and begins stuffing tissue along the base of the window next to her, presumably to keep out the draft. It is a foretaste of the attempted suicide at the end of the film, where she seals up the crack under the trailer's door and turns on the gas. There is a death drive about Rosetta and her faculty for conception. When she rises up from her cramps and seals the window, the camera—her camera, if you will—allows the window with its glass curtain nearly to fill the frame. Beautiful bright white light suffuses the film—specifically, the space toward which Rosetta looks, which she summons up or half creates—a look toward death in an image as transcendent as any in Bresson.

The bright glass-curtained window is, of course, suggestive of the film screen, where Rosetta projects herself. The murky pond is more than ever suggestive of the screen at the time of a second immersion, Riquet's. He comes looking for Rosetta at a time when she has lost her new job. She would like him to disappear so she can take his job at the waffle stand. We get a view of the pond now reflecting trees and the world of the shore, as is typical of water surface images that films find as images for themselves, for film. Riquet falls in and struggles, nearly drowning, as did Rosetta. He calls to her desperately, as she did to her mother. She wants to let him drown, but changes her mind in time and helps him out. Getting rid of him is her projection, her scenario, which she changes while it is in progress.

Riquet's interest in Rosetta, and hers in him, never becomes quite clear—as is often the case with people's interest in each other. Sexual attraction, pity on Riquet's part, the desire for a friend, the tendency of people this age easily to connect, just to see what happens—all come into play. After her own trauma in the pond, she comes to his place, eats, drinks, converses, listens to music, dances—all very awkwardly, the dance ending in a cramp. She stays the night in the next room, which might become her new quarters, and speaks to herself: "You found a job. I found a job. You made a friend. I made a friend. You have a normal life. I have a normal life." All this can seem a first step toward what is clearly desired. But one senses much resistance in Rosetta's interaction with Riquet, even as she goes forward. And her litany with herself seems an experiment—with an air of "can you believe this?" as much as "this has happened" or "this is what I surely want." She lies on her side in the dark, with closed eyes—there is the feel of a dream. Rosetta is an experimenter, like Mouchette and the vagabond Mona, for all her fierce determination. Soon she is fired again, nearly lets Riquet drown, then betrays him to his, and her sometime, boss for cheating, and takes over his job. Is the betrayal just for the sake of a job? There seems something vengeful about it, as if perhaps to get back at him for taking an interest in her, even though this helps her. Something in her says no to everything. He shows his displeasure, hanging about her booth with an angry look, following and harassing her on his noisy, ugly-sounding motorbike, scuffling with her, reminding her perplexedly that she saved his life. Her act of betrayal almost seems calculated to bring punishment on herself. "Go on, hit me," she screams at him.

Toward the end of the film we see Rosetta working at the waffle stand, doing all the petty tasks—can this be what she wants?—and she finishes the day, locks up, and goes home to play out her final scene. She enters her woods, changing her shoes once more, and walks into sight of the pond. There is a sudden cut to a close view of her looking thoughtful, giving herself time, as she spies something. We move forward and discover Rosetta's mother passed out on the ground, presumably drunk. A nasty surprise for Rosetta, if not unusual. But with the view of the pond, with its suggestions of death and creation, and then the quick cut and image of Rosetta thinking, it is almost as if she conjures her mother to precipitate the finale. She struggles to raise the woman up and half carry her into the trailer, as she will soon struggle with the heavy gas canister. She slows herself down, her bustling and determined walk becomes a labor. Something about her craves to be inanimate, as Freud says of the death drive that we all share.

Inside, Rosetta puts her mother to bed and starts to boil an egg. She then goes outside to the pay telephone and calls her boss to say she will not be returning to work. Perhaps she has decided she cannot continue to profit from betraying Riquet. Perhaps she has decided she doesn't really want the work she is able to get. Has she already decided to end her and her mother's lives?

Back inside, Rosetta and the camera give a lot of attention to the process of removing and cooling the egg, peeling it, and starting to eat it, closing the window and blocking the bottom of the door along the way. She takes the egg to bed and continues to eat, as we hear the gas hiss—death in the air. Perhaps she is just hungry—though it seems odd, in contemplation of death. Perhaps she wants a final pleasure. The egg suggests fertility—her fertility, her egg, her conception, her creation of death. Death and life are mixed up in these gestures—turning on the gas, eating—taking nourishment, fostering life, looking forward.

The hissing stops—the gas has given out—so Rosetta gets up and struggles to carry the canister across to the superintendent, and struggles more to carry the heavier full canister back home, falling three times along the way, like Christ with the Cross. The camera—her camera—backs steadily before her, in tribute. After the first fall, the ugly buzzing of a motorbike is heard and Riquet appears, still looking angry, circling her and tormenting her as she walks. On the third fall Rosetta stays down, clutching the canister as we look down onto her back—moving about as if giving birth to, or wanting to incorporate, the big object, as she did earlier with her employer's large sacks of flour, first while making waffle batter, later in desperation and not wanting to leave this job she has quit. Now, collapsed on the canister, she falls into desperate choking weeping. We see Riquet's back and arm as he lifts her up—but he backs out of the frame—we never see the face he shows her, only her face fairly close as she looks toward him, a plea for connection and help in her eyes—still breathing heavily, but calming. The hand-held camera never becomes quite still—it *is* her agitation, which never ceases. And on an intake of Rosetta's breath, the film cuts to black.

It is very moving. One feels great tenderness toward Rosetta, and the film ends with a gesture toward human connection, after all. Rosetta directs her look slightly askew from the camera—she keeps her cover in regard to us, her obscurity, to an extent. Yet Riquet is literally—visually—not there.

Rosetta's look and her appeal, though a bit askew, are for the film viewer. And we viewers cannot cross the barrier of the screen. Rosetta's story is over. She is finished, except for a replay of the film. Rosetta is a film being—rage, motion, a blur, persistence, negativity. The cut to black is the death she invokes—she *as* film—death reaching for rebirth, which can only be the state of the film viewer stirred by encounter with her.

The issue of the social system, laws, and "other," real-life Rosettas is not irrelevant, but stands to the side of the real event of this film. There is only one Rosetta, if kin to Mouchette and the vagabond. Here is life bestirring itself, pained, saying no, striving—life realized as film—realized as Rosetta.

Postscript

The Integrity of Film

When I first read Victor Perkins's seminal book *Film as Film*, published a year after Stanley Cavell's *The World Viewed*, I was struck, and am all the more struck on rereadings, and reading of Victor's subsequent writing on film, by two things above all: (1) the close reading of and close engagement with the details and particularities of individual films, something I was and am glad to be encouraged to pursue in my own way, as I have aspired to do in writing the essays in this book; and (2) the proposal of film and of individual films as having a strong integrity, being work that is not to be co-opted by considerations from outside. The work stands on its own, within its own realm, however much it may listen to or reflect, and speak to, the world about it, past, present, or future. This, too, is a principle I have aspired to embrace, in my own way, in these essays.

All of this echoes for me in the thinking and writing of the American New Critics—John Crowe Ransom, Allen Tate, Robert Penn Warren, and others—and kindred English critics such as G. Wilson Knight, William Empson, and the Leavises. The New Criticism finds, and avers, that the work of art, looked at with openness, will always surprise one. An understanding of history, of psychology, of the ways of working of cultural assumptions, may help one to understand art. But understanding brought from the outside will never go far enough, and may distort what is there. The work needs to be followed out, paid attention to in detail, submitted to, sometimes talked back to, as I have done in these essays. Like great poems and novels and Shakespeare plays, the films I have addressed in this book have more to say than any set of ideas that might be used to frame them. The works have a way of going on talking, as from an endless depth, and ought to be allowed to talk themselves out, with their twists and rebuttals and qualifications. "The work belongs within the realm that is opened up by itself," says Heidegger in his large, powerful essay "The Origin of the Work of Art" (41).

Kindred principles and procedures to the New Criticism of literature and of film inform some discussion of the other arts, such as T. J. Clark's book on two Poussin paintings, *The Sight of Death*, and Joseph Kerman's earlier *Opera as Drama*. My friend, the experimental poet, critic, and historian Susan Howe, phoned me some time back, extolling Clark's book, saying that it's like good current film analysis, reading image by image, moment by moment, mood by mood, as one takes the work in. Years earlier, another friend, who had taken a degree at Cambridge, supervised by Mrs. Leavis, extolled Kerman's book on opera to me, saying it's like great modern literary criticism, but focused on sounds, harmonies, and musical changes instead of the poetic power of words as embodying the drama that is the work's concern.

For me, Heidegger's essay, which I have invoked more than once in the preceding chapters, provides the philosophical probing and rationale for all the criticism I most admire. Heidegger's essay and *Film as Film*—I hope the same can be said of *Writ on Water*—reinforce and deepen one another, read in alteration. All together they seem to testify to a modern eagerness for a new engagement with art, coincident with the eagerness to receive a new form of art: film. Maybe it all started with Coleridge.

Pointing out some echoes of Victor's writing with kindred thinkers, I would hope to place a new charge on his writing, or to liberate something in it that can make it all the more affecting for readers now and to come.

Near the beginning of *Film as Film*, Victor examines the jeep scene early in *Carmen Jones* (1954), where the framing and cutting embody the tension between Carmen's disposition for movement and freedom and her guardian Joe's disposition for control and possession.

Engagement with salient detail leads the critic back into the heart of the film: "Throughout *Carmen Jones*, the contrasts between open and closed images, static and mobile action, are worked out" (82).

Victor begins his essay on Hitchcock's *I Confess* (1953) by commenting on the obscurity of the opening shot, across the Saint Lawrence River toward the Château Frontenac in the city of Québec, where the straight lines of the building, suggesting political and social order, are blurred by the giving of attention to "the indeterminate, drifting form of a silvery cloudscape" (Perkins, "*I Confess*" 33) above and water below, in the foreground. Soon we make out what seems a woman's voice singing urgently and expressively, but with no words clearly audible. "Acoustic fog," Victor calls it (33), with an indication—the song—that the film is essentially a woman's melodrama—Ruth Grandfort's (Anne Baxter), as it turns out, who wants to confess a passion or a love affair, but does not. Victor's engagement with, and thought about, the image and sound here, again sends him to the heart of a film, in this case an experience of obscurity, with the sense of something struggling up or out into clarity.

Near *Film as Film*'s early pages, analyzing the jeep scene in *Carmen Jones*, Victor begins speaking about a film's "world," a concept he will approach in various ways in *Film as Film*, and in his impressive later article "Where Is the World? The Horizon of Events in Movie Fiction." Early on *Film as Film* acknowledges that we think of a sonnet or a sonata as creating a world, a poetic world or a musical world, the suggestion being that a film creates a filmic world, to which we must attune ourselves on its own terms.

Contrasts between images of stasis and motion, confinement and freedom in *Carmen Jones*? Or between surface and urgent depth in *I Confess*? Over and over in *Film as Film* Victor speaks of "tensions" in film. A valid film "absorbs its tensions" (Perkins 131). It is an "embodiment of tensions," and as such is a "vision" (151). Elements of a valid film relate to each other seemingly without effort. Relationships, synthesis—this is what "makes a film a *film*" (184). Film as film—there is an entity—impersonal in a sense—that embodies tensions and puts them into relationship.

Another now departed friend, the extraordinary filmmaker—that is, writer-director—Chantal Akerman, reminisced to me years ago about seeing Bresson's film *Money* (*L'Argent*, 1983) at its premiere at Cannes. She said she was mainly impressed, to the point of being almost overwhelmed, by the tension of the film, meaning not plot but the quality of each image being filled with a tension ready to explode into the next, which it would do, in a succession of unsettling juxtaposed moods. *L'Argent* for Chantal, and we may surely say for us, is an embodiment of tensions.

It is common in the literary New Criticism of the twentieth century to speak of poems, plays, novels as each a set of tensions. See, for example, René Wellek and Austin Warren's *Theory of Literature* (1942), or Cleanth Brooks's book on lyric poems, *The Well Wrought Urn* (1947), or his study of Faulkner, *Toward Yoknapatawpha Country and Beyond* (1963). Ransom in *The New Criticism* states that the relation of parts or aspects of a work constitutes its "intention" and gives us a poetic experience (224). Ransom is at pains throughout his book, as are the critics he takes up—Richards, Eliot, Winters—to insist on the uniqueness of poetic experience and poetic or literary interest. Allen Tate's essay "Tension in Poetry" proposes extension, a survey of material, as by a moving camera or a series of cuts, we might say, as against intension (with an "s"), the probing for, or the emergence of, a deeper principle that orders or gives meaning to the work's parts or aspects. Ransom's "intention" (with a "t") or Victor's synthesis or relation, I would say.

Here we are close to Schiller's idea in the *Aesthetic Letters*, that form in a work gives shape and meaning to content—form being a subtle and organic force emerging from within content as we take it in—as Perkins says will be the case with what he calls a film's "significance" (*Film* 119). Schiller says that form gives the reader or auditor the experience and understanding of freedom, because of the consciousness of choice being deployed over and over. Victor in *Film as Film* has much to say, of course, about the choices deployed in film, urging us to be attuned to them.

Victor notes that intellectual detachment may hinder understanding of what is in fact an "experience." The film vision, the film as film, is an experience. Victor says at one point, "Significance provides the path by which we approach and seek to make manageable the intricacies of structure" (*Film* 120)—relations of tensions, we may say. Years ago, speaking at a film conference in London, I caused Victor to collapse in laughter, bringing up T. S. Eliot's remark that meaning in a poem is like the piece of meat the burglar throws to quiet the house dog, so his accomplice can sneak in the back and take out the goods. We want something to occur below, as well as at, the conscious level.

Film as Film's chapter "The Participant Observer" proposes for the viewer an experience of merging with new points of view—the points of view of characters, the point of view of a film, right down to its framings and cuts and gestures of the camera, not to mention subtleties of the actors—and thus for us a broadening of humanity. This echoes for me F. R. Leavis's essay "Tragedy and the 'Medium,'" proposing for poetic drama a merging of the reader or auditor with the words themselves and their uses. Leavis quotes D. H. Lawrence on the need for a breaking down of the "established ego" (257), letting it flow out and merge with what is beyond it—in Leavis's instance, the stimulus and power of words, of poetry, and thereby "tragic experience" (253). Leavis also quotes W. B. Yeats, taken with Japanese Noh drama and speaking of "a drowning, a breaking of the dykes" (257) in confrontation with this drama's formality and conventions, virtually on the level of ritual, and within this, wild poetry and music. "You are the music while the music lasts," T. S. Eliot has it in his *Four Quartets* (39). Ozu's film *Late Spring* (*Banshun*,

1949), a great favorite of Victor's, draws, as I read it, an analogy between Noh drama and film.

Consciously graspable meaning did matter to Victor. The short answer to his interrogative article title "Must We Say What They Mean?" I take to be "yes." Victor's article is a rebuke to David Bordwell's book *Making Meaning*, in which perception of meaning in film and the penchant for interpretation is taken to be an illusory disease of the mind. Victor avers that seeing meaning in things is inherent to perception, as John Crowe Ransom also avers in *The New Criticism*. Ransom was very big on what he called "texture" (55), the flooding in of particulars and specific embodiments to qualify and enrich, and in a salutary way roughen and soil a poem's central discernible motive, its logic or skeleton or "significance," we might say. One wants not to lose a sense of the reality of, in Walt Whitman's phrase, "the soiled world" (250)—a phrase Susan Howe takes from Whitman and uses in her discussion of films of Tarkovsky, Chris Marker, and Vertov (395). At one point, Ransom calls the poem a "texture of meaning" (219)—a term I hope Victor would have accepted for film—a texture of experiences, certainly, experiences to some extent below consciousness and earthy, but experiences as provocations to think.

Victor plays with titles. "Must We Say What They Mean?" plays upon the title of Stanley Cavell's influential essay (did it not remake American philosophy?) and first book *Must We Mean What We Say?* The short answer to Cavell's interrogative, as with Victor's, I take to be "yes." Our words and what we say do mean. The question is whether we take responsibility for them, just as the question with our perception of meaning in film is whether we reflect and test our understanding, taking responsibility for it.

The title *Film as Film* plays, of course, upon Rudolf Arnheim's book title *Film as Art* (1933), in which art is understood to be a conspicuous and self-proclaiming abstraction from life, something clearly apart and different. Film for Victor has integrity, let us say aesthetic integrity, and Victor certainly thought of film as an art. But there is not a dramatic withdrawal from life about it. There is more of Bazin in Victor than Arnheim. The Hitchcock of *I Confess*, mirrored in his character Ruth Grandfort, divided, Victor says, "between the desire for recognition and the terror of being known," "was one of us, after all" (Perkins, "*I Confess*" 39).

Film as Film's final chapter, "The Limits of Criticism," says that the critic looks for patterns of relationship, but that there is no *proving* what is discerned. I have offered here to discern some—mutually reinforcing, as I see it—relations among ideas and procedures, Victor's and others. I hope Victor's forgiving remark about proof will spare me in your thoughts.

Notes

Chapter 1

1. V. F. Perkins gives a rich extended discussion in *Film as Film* of the issue of what we believe in a film. The book is also very shrewd on the question of relations among elements of a film.

2. In *Pursuits of Happiness*, Stanley Cavell discusses the 1938 film *Bringing Up Baby* (Howard Hawks, with Cary Grant and Katharine Hepburn) as making us start to think of our own lives as having the nature of film in them, and as suggesting that all film if considered closely, not just this one, would make us so start to think. In *Bringing Up Baby*, the story of a romance, we begin to feel that our relation to a lover in life, and perhaps to any other person, may be like the viewer's relation to the leading, seductive, perplexing film director, or to the film itself—call it what you like.

Chapter 2

1. David Sterritt writing on *Hail, Mary* in his book on Godard, sees in the film's donkey an allusion to Bresson's *Au hasard Balthazar* (1966). Sharon Cameron's book *The Bond of the Furthest Apart* offers a rich discussion of *Balthazar* and its maintenance of a nonhuman point of view.

2. Sandra Laugier writes in "The Holy Family," drawing on Françoise Dolto, about the analogy of ordinary childbirth to the divine story.

3. Boris Pasternak's *Doctor Zhivago* offers perhaps the most comprehensive and powerful modern representation of this take on things. And, of course, there are films of Bresson and Tarkovsky.

4. Stanley Cavell in his foreword to the book Maryel Locke and I edited on the film, links this C-Major Prelude to the idea of openness and virginity.

5. Here the basic rhythm, the time signature, continually changes—a challenge for conductors and performers, as well as for listeners.

6. This issue is explored fully in Caruana and Cauchi's collection *Immanent Frames*, drawing on the philosophy of Charles Taylor.

7. Filmmaker Ross McElwee, an admirer of *Hail Mary*, called my attention to the danger of staging and filming the scene with the infant in the water. The risk taken here epitomizes, I think, the philosophical risk taken by the film as a whole.

Chapter 3

1. Stanley Cavell gives testimony to this in "On Makavejev on Bergman," describing an appearance of Makavejev's at Harvard in the 1970s, where he screened wordless sequences that he had edited together from Ingmar Bergman films, and resorted to various theatrical means to start conversation and provoke thought. See Rothman, *Cavell on Film* (SUNY Press, 2005).

2. The book contains an interview with Makavejev conducted by Phillip Lopate and Bill Zavatsky.

3. Apparently, Makavejev intended to make a Serbo-Croatian version of the entire film (but never did), where the Milena character, played by Milena Dravic, would in fact read the early narration. I thank Vlada Petric for this information.

4. According to Raymond Durgnat, the footage of the couple comes from the 1969 Woodstock Rock Festival. Durgnat's book is a good, lively discussion of the film's political implications and of its connections to other films and to books and ideas of its time. Durgnat and I are saying very different things about *WR*, but I believe our two discussions are complementary.

5. Stanley Cavell explores this feeling in "The World as a Whole: Color" in *The World Viewed*.

6. In the years after Christian Metz's *The Imaginary Signifier* one heard much to the effect that film is normally to be entirely identified with.

7. The explosion in Serbia, Croatia, Bosnia, and Kosovo may seem anticipated in a film such as *WR*, with its harsh juxtapositions, its tearing in so many different directions. But *WR* is a bomb for the mind, for the sake of freeing us from bad historical habits—not a bomb in the body of the world, set off by historic hatreds.

8. André Bazin discusses this material very incisively in "The Myth of Stalin in Soviet Cinema," in *Bazin at Work*.

9. The script identifies only *The Vow*—one of the films Bazin discusses.

Chapter 4

1. My companions on this occasion were Marian Keane and William Rothman. We were all three involved at the time, as TAs, in Stanley Cavell's large Harvard lecture course on film and philosophy. Cavell asked me to lecture

to the class on *Blonde Venus*, and said afterward, "You should write that up." Thus began the present essay.

2. E. Ann Kaplan suggests in her highly negative account of *Blonde Venus*, in *Women and Film*, that Dietrich's shifting eye movements and her whole distanced or ironic manner of playing in this film, are gestures of resistance against the narrative and the prevailing interests and approach of the film. Does Kaplan imagine that Sternberg did not notice Dietrich's eye movements and behavior? That he did not approve of and encourage, in short direct, her manner of playing? This is impossible. Dietrich, and the director, Dietrich and the authorial spirit of the film, are at one here. Henry Adams is relevant here: Who made Chartres Cathedral?

> The Chartres apse . . . overrides the architect. You may, if you really have no imagination whatever, reject the idea that the Virgin herself made the plan; the feebleness of our fancy is now congenital . . . we shrink like sensitive plants from the touch of a vision or spirit. . . .
>
> You had better stop here, once for all, unless you are willing to feel that Chartres was made what it is, not by the artist, but by the Virgin. . . . Any one should feel it that wishes; any one who does not wish to feel it can let it alone. No artist would have ventured to put up, before the eyes of Mary in Majesty, above the windows so dear to her, any object that she had not herself commanded. Whether a miracle was necessary, or whether genius was enough, is a point of casuistry which you can settle . . . and which you will understand as little when settled as before; but for us, beyond the futilities of unnecessary doubt, the Virgin designed this rose. (127–28, 143)

3. *Blonde Venus* has the reputation of getting its reconciliation ending imposed by the censors. This is not true. The production story is well laid out by Peter Baxter in *Just Watch! Sternberg, Paramount, and America*, drawing in part on earlier research published by Lea Jacobs. Sternberg and Dietrich submitted an original story with the reconciliation ending roughly as we have it in the film. In the course of writing and rewriting scripts, as various Hollywood factions came into play, a harsher ending was proposed and then rejected. Ultimately Sternberg had his way with the film, backed by New York executives against other Hollywood figures. In any case, I am concerned here with what we have in the film now, with what it simply is.

4. William Rothman's *Documentary Film Classics*, picking up on Jean Rouch's idea of film truth, cinéma vérité (drawn from Dziga Vertov's *kino-pravda*), looks closely at major nonfiction films, pondering the measure of art at work, in people's presentation of themselves and in the making of the films, arguing that art is not at odds with integrity or revelation.

5. Hermione, referred to by Homer as "a girl like the pale-gold goddess Aphrodite" (*Odyssey*, IV), is shown in Euripides's *Andromache* to have fallen to the lot of a series of men.

6. I take the notion of criticism as treading a line between sympathy and judgment, from Yvor Winters's essay on Melville, in *Maule's Curse*.

7. To "see through" the film is to abstract a "social reality" from all the unusual offers the film makes toward intimating a sense of creation. The social reality will be seen according to an idea already possessed of what social reality is. In effect, the film will not be listened to. This looking through the film, and ignoring much of it, I find to be the case with E. Ann Kaplan's piece already mentioned, and also with the chapter on *Blonde Venus* in Bill Nichols's *Ideology and the Image*, which Kaplan cites as a crucial text for her. And I find the same temper at work in Robin Wood's *defense* of the Sternberg/Dietrich films against political criticism, in his article "Venus de Marlene." For Nichols and Kaplan *Blonde Venus* serves capitalism and the patriarchy. For Wood the film is intelligent and critical about the established order: Helen looks unfortunate, and is meant to look so, at home in motherhood, in her musical performances, and in her adventures—she is the pawn of the culture, the film wants to tell us. Well, yes, but Dietrich and the film tell us much more than this.

8. Peter Baxter in *Just Watch!* notes the prevalence of water in Sternberg's films, and associates this with journeys, relevant to Sternberg's, and much of his audience's, immigrant experience. Baxter also relates water to film as an imaginative medium. But here he limits himself subscribing to the Marxist theoretical understanding of Hollywood film as just a corporate-controlled delusional fantasy.

9. I have in mind *Cahiers du Cinéma* of the 1950s, Sarris's *American Cinema* and *Films of Josef von Sternberg*, and Wood's *Hitchcock's Films*.

10. In a discussion published in *New German Critique* Julia Lesage comments that Dietrich in Sternberg's films is a subcultural icon, a lesbian figure to identify with, a defier of patriarchy; Lesage says, specifically, that the white tails scene in *Blonde Venus* gives her as a viewer a definite sexual feeling. Judith Mayne says that many lesbians see this as a parody of lesbianism, a male projection. Michelle Citron says it can work both ways. Andrea Weiss confirms that Dietrich was an icon for lesbians in the 1930s (see Citron et al.).

11. Parker Tyler in *Screening the Sexes* has a wonderful discussion of free-flowing sexuality between male and female identities—among film characters and between film characters and audience. I prefer Tyler's discussion to Christian Metz's influential discourse on the role of desire in film viewing, in *The Imaginary Signifier*. Metz insists on an absolute barrier between film and audience, as he does on a barrier in life between desire and its object. For me, films mingle imagination and life. In life, desire can meet its object, however much reforming this may mean for desire and its first intentions.

12. Besides Sternberg's autobiography, *Fun in a Chinese Laundry*, there are quite a few articles. See the bibliography in Herman G. Weinberg's *Josef von Sternberg*.

13. "Hot Voodoo" (unpublished song; words and music by Ralph Rainger and Sam Coslow).

14. See F. R. Leavis, "Tragedy and the 'Medium.'" See also George Toles's discussion of dissolution and unity in the face of film sentiment in "Thinking about Movie Sentiment: Toward a Reading of *Random Harvest*."

15. See William Rothman's remarkable chapter on *Psycho* in *Hitchcock: The Murderous Gaze*.

16. I take the image of Helen as Orpheus from Andrew Sarris, *The Films of Josef von Sternberg*.

17. Unpublished song with lyrics and music by Richard A. Whiting and Leo Robin.

Chapter 6

1. Andrew Klevan draws the title of his book *Disclosure of the Everyday* from the discourses of ordinary-language philosophers, especially Stanley Cavell in his connection of this tradition back to Emerson, who found such depth in "the meal in the firkin; the milk in the pan; the ballad in the street . . . the glance of the eye; the form and gait of the body" (Cavell, *Pursuits* 14–15).

2. Robert Flaherty, *Nanook of the North* (1922). Robert Bresson, *Pickpocket* (1959); *Mouchette* (1967); *Au hasard Balthazar* (1966).

3. Cavell develops this notion in his essays on *Stella Dallas* (1937) in *Contesting Tears* and *Cities of Words*.

4. In *The Intervals of Cinema* Rancière elaborates on Costa's films and their uses of pure surface and materiality to challenge thought, devoting a full chapter to them, "Pedro Costa's Politics."

5. Throughout *The Intervals of Cinema*, Rancière dwells on film's tendency to do two things at once, or pull in two directions.

6. The author elaborates a more specifically political significance to the labor of fiction. "Re-framing of the 'real'" is "the framing of a dissensus," a political refusal of the usual frame. And for Rancière "the aesthetic regime of art," which disrupts and leaves us free to think, is contrasted to other regimes of art with political valences, where either we are told what to think, or it is assumed that we know what to think and therefore need not be told.

Chapter 7

1. Pasolini, "The 'Cinema of Poetry'" and "The Written Language of Reality."

2. Gardner elaborates on the idea in his book *The Impulse to Preserve*.

3. Thoreau's concern with acknowledgment of loss that is at the same time an opening to a new dawn, a concern which builds to the book's concluding sentence, is a major theme of Stanley Cavell in *The Senses of Walden*.

Chapter 8

1. Geoffrey Nowell-Smith's excellent British Film Institute monograph on the film contains a map of the boating group's whole journey.

Chapter 10

1. I talk more about film and water in "Self-Reflection in American Silent Film." Bresson writes, "*On two deaths and three births*. My movie is born first in my head, dies on paper; is resuscitated by the living persons and real objects I use, which are killed on film but, placed in a certain order and projected onto a screen, come to life again like flowers in water" (13).

2. The voiceover is not credited. It does not seem to be the voice of the woman academic who takes an interest in Mona later in the film, nor does it sound to me like Varda's own voice. The point is to be impersonal.

Works Cited

Adams, Henry. *Mont-Saint-Michel and Chartres*. Princeton UP, 1981.
Arnheim, Rudolf. *Film as Art*. U of California P, 1957.
Baxter, Peter. *Just Watch! Sternberg, Paramount and America*. British Film Institute, 1993.
Bazin, André. *Bazin at Work: Major Essays and Reviews from the Forties and Fifties*. Translated by Alain Piette and Bert Cardullo, London, Psychology Press, 1997.
Bergstrom, Janet. "Invented Memories." *Identity and Memory: The Films of Chantal Akerman*, edited by Gwendolyn Audrey Foster, Southern Illinois UP, 2003, pp. 94–116.
Blackmur, R. P. "*The Idiot*: A Rage of Goodness." *Eleven Essays in the European Novel*. Harcourt, Brace and World, 1964, pp. 141–63.
———. "T. S. Eliot: From *Ash Wednesday* to *Murder in the Cathedral*." *The Double Agent: Essays in Craft and Elucidation*. London, Arrow Editions, 1935, pp. 184–218.
Bordwell, David. *Making Meaning: Inference and Rhetoric in the Interpretation of Cinema*. Harvard UP, 1989.
Bowra, Maurice. *The Odes of Pindar*. Penguin, 1969.
Bresson, Robert. *Notes on the Cinematographer*. Translated by Jonathan Griffin, London, Quartet Books, 1986.
Brooks, Cleanth. *The Well Wrought Urn: Studies in the Structure of Poetry*. Harcourt, Brace, 1975.
———. *William Faulkner: Toward Yoknapatawpha and Beyond*. Yale UP, 1978.
Cameron, Sharon. *The Bond of the Furthest Apart: Essays on Tolstoy, Dostoevsky, Bresson, and Kafka*. U of Chicago P, 2017.
Cantor, Jay. "Death and the Image." *Beyond Document: Essays on Nonfiction Film*, edited by Charles Warren, Wesleyan UP, 1996, pp. 23–50.
Caruana, John, and Mark Cauchi, editors. *Immanent Frames: Postsecular Cinema between Malick and von Trier*. SUNY Press, 2018.
Cavell, Stanley. *Cities of Words: Pedagogical Letters on a Register of the Moral Life*. Harvard UP, 2004.

———. *The Claim of Reason: Wittgenstein, Skepticism, Morality, and Tragedy*. Oxford UP, 1979.

———. *Contesting Tears: The Hollywood Melodrama of the Unknown Woman*. U of Chicago P, 1996.

———. Foreword. *Jean-Luc Godard's Hail Mary: Women and the Sacred in Film*, edited by Maryel Locke and Charles Warren, Southern Illinois UP, 1993, pp. xvii–xxiii.

———. Introduction. *Making* Forest of Bliss: *Intention, Circumstance, and Chance in Nonfiction Film: A Conversation between Robert Gardner and Ákos Östör*. Harvard Film Archive, 2001, pp. 9–14.

———. *Must We Mean What We Say?* Cambridge UP, 1969.

———. *Pursuits of Happiness: The Hollywood Comedy of Remarriage*. Harvard UP, 1981.

———. *The Senses of Walden*. North Point Press, 1981.

———. *The World Viewed: Reflections on the Ontology of Film*. Harvard UP, 1979.

Citron, Michelle, et al. "Women and Film: A Discussion of Feminist Aesthetics." *New German Critique*, no. 13, 1978, pp. 83–107.

Clark, T. J. *The Sight of Death: An Experiment in Art Writing*. Yale UP, 2006.

Cooper, Sarah. *Chris Marker*. Manchester UP, 2008.

De Lauretis, Teresa, and Stephen Heath, editors. *The Cinematic Apparatus*. St. Martin's Press, 1980.

Deren, Maya. *Divine Horsemen: The Living Gods of Haiti*. McPherson, 1983.

Donne, John. *The Collected Poems of John Donne*, edited by Roy Booth, Wordsworth, 1994.

Durgnat, Raymond. *WR: Mysteries of the Organism*. British Film Institute, 1999.

Eliot, T. S. "Andrew Marvell." *Selected Essays*. Harcourt, Brace and World, 1950, pp. 251–63.

———. *Collected Poems 1909–1962*. Harcourt, Brace, 1991.

———. *Four Quartets*. Harcourt, Brace, 1943.

———. *The Sacred Wood: Essays on Poetry and Criticism*. Methuen, 1928.

Emerson, Ralph Waldo. "Self-Reliance." *Emerson: Essays and Lectures*, edited by Joel Porte, Library of America, 1983, pp. 257–82.

Euripides. *Euripides IV: Helen, The Phoenician Women, Orestes*, translated by Richmond Lattimore, U of Chicago P, 2013.

Fitzgerald, F. Scott. *The Last Tycoon*. London: Alma Classics, 2013.

Gardner, Robert. "The Impulse to Preserve." *Beyond Document: Essays on Nonfiction Film*, edited by Charles Warren, Wesleyan UP, 1996, pp. 169–80.

———. *The Impulse to Preserve: Reflections of a Filmmaker*. Other Press, 2006.

Gilbert, Sandra M., and Susan Gubar. *The Madwoman in the Attic: The Woman Writer and the Nineteenth-Century Literary Imagination*. Yale UP, 1979.

Godard, Jean-Luc. *Godard on Godard*. Edited and translated by Tom Milne, Da Capo Press, 1986.

Haskell, Molly. *From Reverence to Rape: The Treatment of Women in the Movies*. U of Chicago P, 1974.

Hearne, Vicki. *Adam's Task: Calling Animals by Name*. Alfred A. Knopf, 1986.

Heidegger, Martin. *Being and Time*. State University of New York Press, 2010.
———. *Nietzsche*. Vols. 1–2, translated by David Farrell Krell, HarperCollins, 1991.
———. "The Origin of the Work of Art." *Poetry, Language, Thought*, translated and edited by Albert Hofstadter, Harper and Row, 1971, pp. 15–87.
Homer. *The Odyssey*. Farrar, Straus and Giroux, 1998.
Hopkins, Tom. "Love, Death, and the Mirror." *Film International*, no. 6, 2003, pp. 24–33.
Howe, Susan. "Sorting Facts; or, Nineteen Ways of Looking at Marker." *Framework: The Journal of Cinema and Media*, vol. 53, no. 2, fall 2012, pp. 380–428.
Joyce, James. *Ulysses*. Paris, Shakespeare and Company, 1922.
Kaplan, E. Ann. "Fetishism and the Repression of Motherhood in Von Sternberg's *Blonde Venus* (1932)." *Women and Film: Both Sides of the Camera*, Psychology Press, 1988, pp. 49–59.
Kerman, Joseph. *Opera as Drama*. U of California P, 1988.
Kierkegaard, Søren. *Diary of a Seducer*. Translated by Gerd Gillhoff, London, A and C Black, 2006.
———. *Fear and Trembling*. Translated by Sylvia Walsh, Cambridge UP, 2006.
Klevan, Andrew. *Disclosure of the Everyday: Undramatic Achievement in Narrative Film*. Flicks Books, 2000.
Knight, George Wilson. *The Wheel of Fire: An Interpretation of Shakespeare's Tragedy*. Meridian Books, 1964.
Laugier, Sandra. "The Holy Family." *Jean-Luc Godard's Hail Mary: Women and the Sacred in Film*, edited by Maryel Locke and Charles Warren, Southern Illinois UP, 1993, pp. 27–38.
Lawrence, D. H. *Last Poems*. Edited by Richard Aldington and Giuseppe Orioli, Scholarly Press, 1971.
———. *Phoenix: The Posthumous Papers of D. H. Lawrence*. Viking Press, 1972.
———. *Psychoanalysis and the Unconscious and Fantasia of the Unconscious*. Edited by Bruce Steele, Cambridge UP, 2004.
———. *Studies in Classic American Literature*. Edited by Ezra Greenspan et al., Cambridge UP, 2003.
Leacock, Richard. "For an Uncontrolled Cinema." *Film Culture Reader*, edited by P. Adams Sitney, Cooper Square Press, 2000, pp. 76–78.
Leavis, F. R. *English Literature in Our Time and the University*. Cambridge UP, 1979.
———. "The Irony of Swift." *Scrutiny*, vol. 2, no. 4, 1934, pp. 364–78.
———. "Reality and Sincerity." *A Selection from Scrutiny*. Cambridge UP, 1968, pp. 248–57.
———. "Tragedy and the 'Medium': A Note on Mr. Santayana's 'Tragic Philosophy.'" *Scrutiny*, vol. 12, no. 4, 1944, pp. 249–60.
Lowell, Robert. *Collected Prose*. Edited by Robert Giroux, Farrar, Straus and Giroux, 1987.
Mai, Joseph. *Jean-Pierre and Luc Dardenne*. U of Illinois P, 2010.
Makavejev, Dušan. *WR: Mysteries of the Organism: A Cinematic Testament to the Life and Teachings of Wilhelm Reich*. Avon Books, 1972.

Metz, Christian. *The Imaginary Signifier: Psychoanalysis and the Cinema*. Translated by Celia Britton et al., Indiana UP, 1982.

Montaigne, Michel de. *The Essays of Montaigne*. Translated by E. J. Trechmann, Modern Library, 1946.

Nichols, Bill. *Ideology and the Image: Social Representation in the Cinema and Other Media*. Indiana UP, 1981.

Nowell-Smith, Geoffrey. *L'Avventura*. British Film Institute, 1997.

Pasolini, Pier Paolo. "The 'Cinema of Poetry.'" *Heretical Empiricism*, edited by Louise K. Barnett, translated by Ben Lawton and Barnett, Indiana UP, 1988, pp. 167–86.

———. "The Written Language of Reality." *Heretical Empiricism*, edited by Louise K. Barnett, translated by Ben Lawton and Barnett, Indiana UP, 1988, pp. 197–222.

Pasternak, Boris. *Doctor Zhivago*. Translated by Manya Harari and Max Hayward, Pantheon Books, 1991.

Perkins, V. F. *Film as Film: Understanding and Judging Movies*. Penguin, 1972.

———. "*I Confess*: Photographs of People Talking." *Cineaction*, no. 52, 2000, pp. 28–39.

———. "Must We Say What They Mean? Film Criticism and Interpretation." *Movie*, no. 34, 1990, pp. 1–6.

———. "Where Is the World? The Horizon of Events in Movie Fiction." *Style and Meaning: Studies in the Detailed Analysis of Film*, edited by John Gibbs and Douglas Pye, Manchester UP, 2005, pp. 16–41.

Pound, Ezra. *ABC of Reading*. Faber and Faber, 1961.

Rancière, Jacques. *Film Fables*. Translated by Emiliano Battista, Berg, 2006.

———. "*Mouchette* and the Paradoxes of the Language of Images." *The Intervals of Cinema*, translated by John Howe, Verso, 2014, pp. 41–67.

———. "The Paradoxes of Political Art." *Dissensus: On Politics and Aesthetics*, edited and translated by Steven Corcoran, Continuum, 2010, pp. 134–51.

———. "Pedro Costa's Politics." *The Intervals of Cinema*, translated by John Howe, Verso, 2014, pp. 127–42.

Ransom, John Crowe. *The New Criticism*. New Directions, 1941.

Reich, Wilhelm. *Character Analysis*. Third enlarged ed., translated by Vincent R. Carfagno, Farrar, Straus and Giroux, 1980.

Rilke, Rainer Maria. *The Selected Poetry of Rainer Maria Rilke*. Edited and translated by Stephen Mitchell, Vintage, 1989.

Rothman, William, editor. *Cavell on Film*. SUNY Press, 2005.

———. *Documentary Film Classics*. Cambridge UP, 1997.

———. "Face to Face with Chantal Akerman." *Immanent Frames: Postsecular Cinema between Malick and von Trier*, edited by John Caruana and Mark Cauchi, SUNY Press, 2018, pp. 151–67.

———. *Hitchcock: The Murderous Gaze*. Harvard UP, 1982.

Sarris, Andrew. *The American Cinema: Directors and Directions, 1929–1968*. E. P. Dutton, 1968.

———. *The Films of Josef von Sternberg*. Museum of Modern Art, 1966.
Scarry, Elaine. *On Beauty and Being Just*. Princeton UP, 1999.
Schiller, Friedrich von. *Letters upon the Aesthetic Education of Man*. Translated by Reginald Snell, Dover, 2004.
"The Second Shepherds' Play." *Renaissance Drama: An Anthology of Plays and Entertainments*, edited by Arthur F. Kinney, Wiley, 2005, pp. 69–88.
Sharaf, Myron. *Fury on Earth: The Life of Wilhelm Reich*. St. Martin's Press, 1983.
Sterritt, David. *The Films of Jean-Luc Godard: Seeing the Invisible*. Cambridge UP, 1999.
Stokes, Richard, editor and translator. *The Book of Lieder*. Faber and Faber, 2005.
Tate, Allen. "Tension in Poetry." *Essays of Four Decades*. William Morrow, 1970, pp. 56–71.
Thoreau, Henry David. *Walden*. Oxford UP, 1997.
Toles, George. "Thinking about Movie Sentiment: Toward a Reading of *Random Harvest*." *Arizona Quarterly: A Journal of American Literature, Culture, and Theory*, vol. 49, no. 2, summer 1993, pp. 75–111.
Tyler, Parker. *Screening the Sexes*. De Capo Press, 1993.
Von Sternberg, Josef. *Fun in a Chinese Laundry*. Macmillan, 1965.
Warren, Charles. "Chantal Akerman." *Encyclopedia of the Documentary Film*, edited by Ian Aitken, Routledge, 2006, pp. 20–23.
———. "Self-Reflection in American Silent Film." *The Wiley-Blackwell History of American Film, Volume I: Origins to 1928*, edited by Roy Grundmann et al., Wiley-Blackwell, 2012, pp. 489–92.
Weinberg, Herman G. *Josef von Sternberg: A Critical Study*. E. P. Dutton, 1967.
Wellek, René, and Austin Warren. *Theory of Literature*. Harcourt, Brace and World, 1956.
Whitman, Walt. *Leaves of Grass*. Oxford UP, 1990.
Winters, Yvor. "Herman Melville and the Problems of Moral Navigation." *Maule's Curse: Seven Studies in the History of American Obscurantism*, New Directions, 1938, pp. 53–89.
Wood, Robin. *Hitchcock's Films*. Paperback Library, 1969.
———. "Michael Haneke: Beyond Compromise." *Cineaction*, vol. 73, no. 4, 2007, pp. 44–55.
———. "Venus de Marlene." *Film Comment*, vol. 14, no. 2, 1978, pp. 58–64.
Woolf, Virginia. "On Not Knowing Greek." *The Common Reader: Volume 1*, edited by Andrew McNeillie, Vintage, 2003, pp. 23–38.
Zavattini, Cesare. "Some Ideas on the Cinema." *Film: A Montage of Theories*, edited by Richard Dyer McCann, E. P. Dutton, 1966, pp. 216–28.

Index

ABC of Reading (Ezra Pound book, 1961), 4
Accatone (1961), 55
Acuff, Roy, 11
Adam's Task (Vicki Hearne book, 1986), 22
Adams, Henry, 249n2
Aeschylus, 24
Aitken, Ian, 179
Akerman, Chantal, 4, 177–192, 206, 219–221, 243
Alighieri, Dante, 130, 148, 178
Altman, Robert, 4, 11–31, 54, 206, 218, 221
American Cinema, The (Andrew Sarris book, 1968), 250n9
Andersson, Bibi, 208
Andromache (Euripides play, 425BC), 249n5
Anger, Kenneth, 2
Antonioni, Michelangelo, 4, 205–214, 217, 221
Aquinas, Thomas, 45
Aristotle, 180
Arnheim, Rudolf, 245
At Land (1944), 140
Au hasard Balthazar (1966), 182, 247n1, 251n2
Augustine of Hippo, 34
Austen, Jane, 50
Austin, J.L., 198

Awful Truth, The (1937), 94, 131

Bach, Johann Sebastian, 34, 36, 39, 40, 41, 42, 47, 216–217, 220, 223, 226
Backyard (1984), 200
Bad Day at Black Rock (1955), 2
Barthes, Roland, 213
Baxter, Anne, 243
Baxter, Peter, 249n3, 250n8
Bazin, André, 2, 245, 248n8
Beatty, Ned, 19, 24
Being and Time (Martin Heidegger book, 2010), 81
Benny's Video (1992), 217–218
Berger, Helmut, 219
Bergman, Ingmar, 21, 41, 198, 199, 205, 206, 209, 211, 219, 221, 248n1
Bergman, Ingrid, 82, 95, 100–101, 211, 221
Bergstrom, Janet, 182
Berlioz, Hector, 40
Binoche, Juliette, 42, 222
Birds, The (1963), 1, 218
Birth of a Nation, The (1915), 124
Black, Karen, 18, 23, 28
Blackmur, R.P., 3, 4, 41, 141
Blakley, Ronee, 17, 30
Blonde Venus (1932), 4, 13, 27, 29, 35, 36, 40, 50, 91–163, 221–222, 249n1–249n2, 250n7

Blow-Up (1966), 205, 211
Blue Angel, The (*Der blaue Engel*, 1930), 57, 106, 109, 119
Blue Velvet (1986), 212
Bond of the Furthest Apart, The (Sharon Cameron book, 2017), 247n1
Bonnaire, Sandrine, 231
Bordwell, David, 245
Bowra, Maurice, 114
Brahms, Johannes, 225
Breathless (1960), 51
Bresson, Robert, 154, 177–179, 182, 188, 216, 227, 243, 247n1, 251n2, 253n1
Bright Leaves (2003), 199
Bringing Up Baby (1938), 247n2
Brontë, Charlotte, 141
Brook, Clive, 109
Brooks, Cleanth, 243
Brown, Norman O., 58
Bruno, Giuliana, 211
Buñuel, Luis, 135, 205

Cabral, Amilcar, 198
Caché (2005), 217
Calderón de la Barca, Pedro, 2
Cameron, Sharon, 247n1
Camille (1936), 95
Capra, Frank, 14
Carmen Jones (1954), 242–243
Carradine, Keith, 21
Caruana, John, 248n6
Cassavetes, John, 160, 221
Cather, Willa, 11
Cauchi, Mark, 248n6
Cavell, Stanley, 2, 12, 27, 83, 94, 95, 114, 177, 182, 191–192, 195–196, 221–223, 230, 241, 245, 247n2, 248n1, 251n1
Chaplin, Charlie, 14, 103, 106, 114, 115, 152
Chaplin, Geraldine, 12, 14
Character Analysis (Wilhelm Reich book, 1933), 59

Chesnutt, Charles, 1
Christie, Julie, 21
Chronicle of a Summer (1960), 4, 167–175
Cities of Words: Pedagogical Letters on a Register of the Moral Life (Stanley Cavell book, 2004), 251m3
City Lights (1931), 103
Claim of Reason: Wittgenstein, Skepticism, Morality, and Tragedy, The (Stanley Cavell book, 1979), 195
Clark, T.J., 242
Clément, Aurore, 207, 219
Cocteau, Jean, 138
Code inconnu, Récit incomplet de divers voyages (*Code Unknown* [2000]), 217–218, 222
Coleridge, Samuel Taylor, 242
Come Back to the Five and Dime, Jimmy Dean, Jimmy Dean (1982), 25, 28
Contesting Tears: The Hollywood Melodrama of the Unknown Woman (Stanley Cavell book, 1996), 27, 95, 221, 251n3
Cooper, Gary, 83, 87
Cooper, Sarah, 174
Costa, Pedro, 184, 251n4
Couch in New York, A (1996), 178
Cries and Whispers (1972), 206, 219
Cunningham, Cecil, 127
Curtis, Jackie, 58, 81–84, 87

D'Est (*From the East*, 1993), 184
Damned, The (*La caduta degli dei* [*Götterdämmerung*], 1969), 219
Dardenne, Jean-Pierre, 5, 227–228
Dardenne, Luc, 5, 227–228
Davis, Bette, 95, 100–101, 151, 152, 221
De Chirico, Giorgio, 213
De Lauretis, Teresa, 67
De Mille, Cecille, 106
De Montaigne, Michel, 193–194

De Sica, Vittorio, 206, 213
Dequenne, Émilie, 228
Deren, Maya, 137–140
Diary of a Seducer (Søren Kierkegaard book, 1843), 140
Dickens, Charles, 2, 133, 170, 227
Die Meistersinger von Nürnberg (Richard Wagner opera, 1868), 46
Dietrich, Marlene, 4, 29, 91–163, 221–222, 224, 249n2, 250n7
Disclosure of the Everyday: Undramatic Achievement in Narrative Film (Andrew Klevan book, 2000), 251n1
Dishonored (1931), 109
Divine Comedy, The (Dante Alighieri poem, 1472), 90
Divine Horsemen: The Living Gods of Haiti (Maya Deren book, 1983), 137
Doctor Faustus (Thomas Mann novel, 1947), 128, 224
Doctor Zhivago (Boris Pasternak book, 1957), 247n3
Documentary Film Classics (William Rothman book, 1997), 249n4
Dodson, Betty, 74–77
Dolto, Françoise, 247n2
Donne, John, 30–31, 111
Doolittle, Hilda, 98–99
Dostoyevsky, Fyodor, 141, 219
Dovzhenko, Alexander, 38
Duino Elegies (Collection of poems by Rainer Maria Rilke, 1923), 57, 131
Durgnat, Raymond, 248n4
Duvall, Shelley, 22
Dvořák, Antonín, 36, 42, 47, 49

Eisenhower, Dwight D., 64
Eisenstein, Sergei, 2, 106, 212
Eliot, T.S., 12, 35, 41, 42, 50, 52, 98, 103, 110, 137, 244
Emerson, Ralph Waldo, 35, 137, 200, 221–222

Empson, William, 241
Encyclopedia of the Documentary Film (Ian Aitken book, 2006), 179
Erwartung (Arnold Schoenberg opera, 1924), 50
Ether, God, and Devil (Wilhelm Reich book, 1949), 67
Eumenides, 24
Euripides, 98, 102, 249n5
Every Man for Himself (1980), 50
Exterminating Angel, The (1962), 57

Faerie Queene, The (Edmund Spenser poem, 1590), 52, 139
Family Plot (1976), 28
Faulkner, William, 243
Fauré, Gabriel, 40
Fear and Trembling (Søren Kierkegaard book, 1843), 152
Fellini, Federico, 205
Ferzetti, Gabriele, 205
Film as Art (Rudolf Arnheim book, 1933), 245
Film as Film: Understanding and Judging Movies (V.F. Perkins book, 1972), 241–245, 247n1
Films of Josef von Sternberg, The (Andrew Sarris book, 1966), 250n9, 251n16
Fitzgerald, F. Scott, 9, 211
Flaherty, Robert, 171, 182, 198, 251n2
Fontaine, Joan, 95, 221
Ford, John, 1, 114, 136
Forest of Bliss (1986), 191
Four Nights of a Dreamer (1972), 177
Frechette, Mark, 211
Freud, Sigmund, 34, 56, 59, 72, 76, 237
From Reverence to Rape: The Treatment of Women in the Movies (Molly Haskell book, 1974), 3
From the Other Side (*De l'autre côté*, 2002), 184–191

Function of the Orgasm, The (Wilhelm Reich book, 1927), 67
Funny Games (1997), 218–219
Funny Games (2007), 218

Gable, Clark, 94
Garbo, Greta, 95, 152, 221
Gardner, Robert, 191, 200, 251n2
Garfield, Allen, 22, 24
Gaslight (1944), 27, 95, 100, 110, 221
Gibson, Henry, 10, 31
Girardot, Annie, 222–223
Godard, Jean-Luc, 2, 34–54, 58, 129, 138, 173, 179, 180–181, 197, 216, 247n1
Gold Rush, The (1925), 14
Goldblum, Jeff, 19
Gospel according to Matthew (1964), 211
Gould, Elliott, 21
Grant, Cary, 83, 94, 100, 127, 130–132, 150, 156, 247n2
Griffith, D.W., 2, 16, 106, 114, 124

Hail Mary (*Je vous salue, Marie*, 1984), 4, 34–54, 58, 118, 180–181, 216, 247n1, 248n7
Halprin, Daria, 211
Hamlet (William Shakespeare play, c. 1601), 194
Haneke, Michael, 4, 207, 215–226
Happy Mother's Day (1963), 196
Hardy, Thomas, 140
Harris, Barbara, 17
Harris, Richard, 207
Haskell, Molly, 3
Hawks, Howard, 247n2
Hearne, Vicki, 22
Heart Is a Lonely Hunter, The (Carson McCullers novel, 1940), 1
Heath, Stephen, 67
Heidegger, Martin, 5, 20, 72, 79–81, 85, 96, 114, 143, 171, 174, 191, 242

Heine, Heinrich, 96
Hélas pour moi (*Oh, Woe is Me*, 1993), 36
Helen (Euripides play, 412BC), 98, 102
"*Helen in Egypt*" (Hilda Doolittle poem, 1961), 98
Hepburn, Katharine, 94, 247n2
Herbert, George, 155
His Girl Friday (1940), 94, 131
Histoire(s) du cinema (1989), 54, 181
Hitchcock, Alfred, 1, 2, 28, 154, 200, 213, 218–221, 242, 245
Hitchcock's Films (Robin Wood book, 1965), 250n9
Hitchcock: The Murderous Gaze (William Rothman book, 1982), 67, 251n15
Hitler, Adolf, 55, 86–87
Hölderlin, Friedrich, 210
Homer, 98, 249n5
Hopkins, Tom, 24–25, 28
Howe, Susan, 4, 242, 245
Hud (1963), 2
Huillet, Danièle, 210
Huppert, Isabelle, 207, 219, 222, 224

I Confess (1953), 242–243, 245
I'm No Angel (1933), 126
Ibsen, Henrik, 55
Ideology and the Image (Bill Nichols book, 1981), 250n7
Idiot, The (Fyodor Dostoyevsky novel, 1869), 141
Imaginary Signifier, The (Christian Metz book, 1977), 248n6, 250n11
Immanent Frames: Postsecular Cinema Between Malick and von Trier (Caruana and Cauchi book, 2004), 248n6
In Vanda's Room (2000), 184
Innocence Unprotected (1968), 56
Intervals of Cinema, The (Jacques Rancière book, 2014), 251n4

It Happened One Night (1934), 94

Jacobs, Lea, 249n3
Jannings, Emil, 109
Je tu il elle (1974), 180–184
Jeanne Dielman, 23 quai du commerce, 1080 Bruxelles (1975), 4, 181–184
Jelinek, Elfriede, 222, 224–225
Johnson, Samuel, 180
Jourdan, Louis, 221
Just Watch! Sternberg, Paramount, and America (Peter Baxter book, 1993), 249n3, 250n8

Kant, Immanuel, 174, 182
Kaplan, E. Ann, 249n2, 250n7
Karina, Anna, 173, 194
Keane, Marian, 248n1
Keaton, Buster, 2, 106
Keats, John, 211
Kerman, Joseph, 242
Kiarostami, Abbas, 217
Kierkegaard, Søren, 12, 140, 152
King Lear (William Shakespeare play, 1606), 151
Kino-Pravda (1922), 172
Kipling, Rudyard, 158
Klevan, Andrew, 251n1
Kupferberg, Tuli, 60–61, 76–77, 84, 87

L'Argent (*Money*, 1983), 178, 243
L'Avventura (1960), 4, 205–214, 220
Lacoste, Philippe, 34
Lady Eve, The (1941), 94, 110
Lang, Fritz, 106, 114, 148
Larkin, Philip, 200
LaRoy, Rita, 127
Last Tycoon, The (F. Scott Fitzgerald novel, 1941), 9
Last Year at Marienbad (1961), 1, 173, 181
Late Spring (*Banshun*, 1949), 244
Laugier, Sandra, 247n2

Lawrence, D.H., 4, 10, 12, 27, 57–58, 74–75, 88, 140, 197, 244
L'Eclisse (1962), 211
Le joli mai (1963), 4, 167, 172–175, 197
Leacock, Richard, 196
Leavis, F.R., 2, 4, 12, 50, 200, 241, 244, 251n14
Leavis, Q.D., 4, 241, 242
Lenin, Vladimir Ilyich, 78
Les parents terribles (1948), 1
Les rendez-vous d'Anna (*The Meetings of Anna*, 1978), 190, 206–207, 219–220
Lesage, Julia, 250n10
Letter from an Unknown Woman (1948), 27, 95, 110, 151, 221–222
Letters Upon the Aesthetic Education of Man (Friedrich Schiller book, 1794), 212, 244
Lhomme, Pierre, 172
Locke, Maryel, 247n4
Lopate, Phillip, 248n2
Loren, Sophia, 206
Lorre, Peter, 147
Love Affair, or the Case of the Missing Switchboard Operator (1967), 56
Lovers, The (1958), 225
Lowell, Robert, 9, 27
Lubitsch, Ernst, 14, 106
Lumière brothers, 153, 171
Luther, Martin, 194
Lynch, David, 212

M (1931), 147, 154
Maazel, Lorin, 55
Macbeth (William Shakespeare play, 1606), 23, 112, 148
MacDonald, Flora, 1
Magic Mountain, The (Thomas Mann novel, 1927), 224
Mahler, Gustav, 55
Makavejev, Dušan, 4, 56–90, 248n1

Making Meaning: Inference and Rhetoric in the Interpretation of Cinema (David Bordwell book, 1989), 245
Mallarmé, Stéphane, 48
Malle, Louis, 206, 225
Man Who Shot Liberty Valance, The (1962), 1
Mating Urge, The (1959), 82
Mann, Thomas, 128, 159, 219, 224, 226
Marker, Chris, 4, 167, 172, 174, 197, 245
Marshall, Herbert, 96, 109–110, 117–118
Massari, Lea, 205–207, 220
Mayne, Judith, 250n10
McCullers, Carson, 1
McDaniel, Hattie, 123, 128, 148
McElwee, Ross, 4, 193–203, 248n7
McLaglen, Victor, 109
Melville, Herman, 50, 250n6
Meshes of the Afternoon (1943), 140
Metz, Christian, 248n6, 250n11
Mirror (*Zerkalo*, 1975), 217
Mizoguchi, Kenji, 180, 221
Modern Times (1936), 14
Monsieur Verdoux (1947), 14
Montenegro (1981), 57
Monteverdi, Claudio, 229–230
Moore, Dickie, 97
Morin, Edgar, 4, 167–175
Morocco (1930), 93, 133, 154
Mouchette (1967), 227–228, 251n2
Mozart, Wolfgang Amadeus, 40, 55
Murder of Christ, The (Wilhelm Reich book, 1953), 67
Muriel, or the Time of Return (*Muriel ou le temps d'un retour*, 1963), 215–216
Murmur of the Heart (*Le Souffle au coeur*, 1971), 206
Murnau, F.W., 16, 106, 154
Murphy, Michael, 12, 23, 24

Must We Mean What We Say? (Stanley Cavell book, 1969), 245
My American Uncle (*Mon oncle d'Amérique*, 1980), 216

Nanook of the North (1922), 79, 251n2
Nashville (1975), 4, 11–30, 33, 42, 54, 58, 111, 114, 136, 206, 218, 221
New Criticism, The (John Crowe Ransom book, 1941), 243, 245
News from Home (1977), 183–184
Nichols, Bill, 250n7
Nietzsche, Friedrich, 12, 139, 162, 171, 174, 221
Night and Fog (*Nuit et brouillard*, 1956), 1, 209
Nortier, Nadine, 228, 230
Nosferatu (1922), 16
Notorious (1946), 131
Notre Musique (*Our Music*, 2004), 54, 199
Now, Voyager (1942), 27, 50, 95, 100–101, 221, 223
Nowell-Smith, Geoffrey, 252n1

October (1927), 212
Odyssey, The (Homer epic poem), 99, 249n5
Oliver Twist (Charles Dickens novel, 1838), 227
Ollendorf, Dr. Robert, 76
Olson, Charles, 4
On Beauty and Being Just (Elaine Scarry book, 1999), 174
Only Angels Have Wings (1939), 57
Opening Night (1977), 221
Opera as Drama (Joseph Kerman book, 1988), 242
Ophuls, Max, 95, 221
Orpheus (*Orphée*, 1949), 138
Ozu, Yasujiro, 55, 244

Index   265

Pasolini, Pier Paolo, 41, 55, 179, 196, 211, 251n1
Passenger, The (*Professione: Reporter,* 1975), 211
Passion (1982), 50
Pasternak, Boris, 247n3
Pather Panchali (1955), 212
Perkins, Victor, 5, 83, 241–245, 247n1
Persona (1966), 206, 209
Petrarch (Francesco Petrarca), 130
Philadelphia Story, The (1940), 94, 97, 131
Phoenix: The Posthumous Papers of D.H. Lawrence (D.H. Lawrence book, 1972), 12
Piano Teacher, The (*La pianiste,* 2001), 207, 215–226
Picasso, Pablo, 131
Pickpocket (1959), 177, 178, 251n2
Pierrot le Fou (1965), 216
Pindar, 92, 110–115, 119, 132, 138
Plato, 156, 174, 197
Playmates (1941), 82
Pound, Ezra, 4
Poussin, Nicholas, 242
Prénom Carmen (1998), 54
Promise, The (1996), 228
Proust, Marcel, 129
Psycho (1960), 67, 154, 218, 251n15
Psychoanalysis of the Unconscious and Fantasia of the Unconscious (D.H. Lawrence book, 2004), 12
Pursuits of Happiness: The Hollywood Comedy of Remarriage (Stanley Cavell book, 1981), 28, 94, 247n2, 251n1

Rabelais, François, 119
Raines, Cristina, 22
Rancière, Jacques, 184–187, 251n4
Ransom, John Crowe, 3, 9, 241, 243–245
Ray, Satyajit, 212

Rear Window (1954), 218
Rebecca (1940), 221
Red Desert (*Il deserto rosso,* 1964), 207, 211, 217
Reflections in a Golden Eye (Carson McCullers novel, 1941), 1
Reich, Eva Moise, 66, 68–70
Reich, Wilhelm, 55–56, 58–90
Renoir, Jean, 15, 17
Resnais, Alain, 173, 181, 209, 215–218
Richards, I.A., 244
Rilke, Rainer Maria, 57, 131, 175, 185, 192
Ritual in Transfigured Time (1946), 140
Rivette, Jacques, 173
Rocco and His Brothers (*Rocco e i suoi fratelli,* 1960), 220
Rode, Thierry, 34
Rosetta (1999), 4, 227–239
Rossellini, Roberto, 211, 221
Rothman, William, 67, 172, 198, 230, 248n1, 249n4, 251n15
Rouch, Jean, 4, 167–175, 249n4
Roussel, Myriem, 34
Rule, Janice, 206
Rules of the Game (*La règle du jeu,* 1939), 17–18, 79

Sans soleil (1983), 197
Sansho the Bailiff (*Sanshô dayû,* 1954), 180
Sappho, 98, 119
Sarris, Andrew, 2, 250n9, 251n16
Scarry, Elaine, 174
Schiller, Friedrich, 185, 187, 212, 244
Schönberg, Arnold, 50
Schopenhauer, Arthur, 34
Schubert, Franz, 220, 223, 225–226
Scorpio Rising (1963), 2
Screening the Sexes (Parker Tyler book, 1972), 250n11
Searchers, The (1956), 136

Sebond, Raymond, 194
Second Shepherd's Play (Anonymous c. 1500), 36
Senses of Walden, The (Stanley Cavell book, 1981), 251n3
Seventh Continent, The (*Der siebente Kontinent*, 1989), 215–217
Seventh Seal, The (*Det sjunde inseglet*, 1957), 2, 198, 211
71 Fragments of a Chronology of Chance (*71 fragmente einer Chronologie des Zufalls*, 1994), 218
Seyrig, Delphine, 181, 215
Shakespeare, William, 50, 55, 102, 133, 194
Shanghai Express (1932), 93, 109, 153
Sharaf, Myron, 64–65, 73–74
Shelley, Percy Bysshe, 111, 132
Shepard, Sam, 55
Sherman's March (1985), 200
Shoah (1985), 67
Short Cuts (1993), 218
Sight of Death, The (T.J. Clark book, 2006), 242
Signoret, Simone, 197
Silence, The (*Tystnaden*, 1963), 206, 219
Spenser, Edmund, 2, 52, 139
Stalin, Joseph, 55, 84–87
Stanwyck, Barbara, 94, 95, 221
Stella Dallas (1937), 27, 95, 221, 251n3
Sterritt, David, 247n1
Stesichorus, 99, 114
Stevens, Wallace, 131, 210
Stewart, Alexandra, 197
Stewart, James, 218
Straub, Jean-Marie, 210
Stravinsky, Igor, 110
Strike (1925), 212
Stromboli (1950), 211
Suspicion (1941), 221
Sweet Movie (1974), 56

Swift, Jonathan, 12–13, 54
Symposium, The (Plato book), 156

Tanaka, Kinuyo, 180
Tarkovsky, Andrei, 38, 205, 217, 245, 247n3
Taste of Cherry (*Ta'm e guilass*, 1997), 217
Tate, Allen, 3, 9, 178, 241, 244
Taylor, Charles, 248n6
Tender is the Night (F. Scott Fitzgerald novel, 1934), 211
Theory of Literature (Wellek and Warren book, 1942), 243
Thoreau, Henry David, 2, 102, 167, 172, 200, 251n3
Three Women (1977), 206
Thulin, Ingrid, 219
Time Indefinite (1993), 4, 193–203
Time of the Wolf (*Le temps du loup*, 2003), 217
Tokyo monogatari (*Tokyo Story*, 1953), 55
Toles, George, 251n14
Tolstoy, Leo, 50, 152
Tomlin, Lily, 16, 17
Touch of Evil (1958), 148
Toute une nuit (1982), 177
Train Arriving at a Station (1895), 153
Truffaut, François, 2
Two or Three Things I Know About Her (*2 ou 3 choses que je sais d'elle*, 1967), 216
Two Women (*La ciocara*, 1960), 206, 213
Tyler, Parker, 250n11

Ullmann, Liv, 209
Ulysses (James Joyce novel, 1920), 77, 79
Un chien andalou (1929), 135
Une femme douce (1971), 154

Vagabond (1985), 227–228, 231
Valéry, Paul, 50

Van Gogh, Vincent, 24, 96
Varda, Agnes, 179, 227, 232–233, 252n2
Verdi, Giuseppe, 40
Vertigo (1958), 200
Vertov, Dziga, 171–172, 245, 249n4
Viaggio in Italia (*Voyage to Italy*, 1954), 211
Visconti, Luchino, 219–220
Vitti, Monica, 205, 207, 212, 220
Vivra Sa Vie (1962), 197, 216
Von Goethe, Johann Wolfgang, 159
Von Sternberg, Josef, 4, 91–163, 221–222, 224, 249n3, 250n7
Von Stroheim, Erich, 106
Vow, The (1946), 248n9

Wagner, Richard, 46
Walk in the Spring Rain, A (1970), 82
Warhol, Andy, 82
Warren, Austin, 243
Warren, Robert Penn, 3, 241
Wayne, John, 136
Weil, Simone, 34
Weiss, Andrea, 250n10
Well Wrought Urn, The (Cleanth Brooks book, 1947), 243
Wellek, René, 243
Welles, Gwen, 18
Welles, Orson, 114, 147
West, Mae, 126
Whitman, Walt, 245
William Faulkner: Toward Yoknapatawpha and Beyond (Cleanth Brooks book, 1963), 243

Williams, Hank, 11
Wilson Knight, George, 4, 23, 241
Winckelmann, Johann, 185
Window Shopping (1986), 177
Winter's Tale, The (William Shakespeare play, 1623), 102, 167
Winters, Yvor, 4, 244, 250n6
Without a Stitch (1968), 198
Wittgenstein, Ludwig, 191
Woman Under the Influence, A (1974), 160, 221
Women and Film: Both Sides of the Camera (E. Ann Kaplan book, 1972), 249n2
Women in Love (D.H. Lawrence novel, 1920), 88
Wood, Natalie, 136
Wood, Robin, 2, 83, 216, 224, 250n7
Woolf, Virginia, 99
World Viewed, The (Stanley Cavell book, 1971), 2, 12, 192, 195, 241, 248n5
WR, Mysteries of the Organism (1971), 4, 54, 55–90, 130, 158, 212, 248n4
Wuthering Heights (Emily Brontë novel, 1847), 104
Wynette, Tammy, 11
Wynn, Keenan, 18

Yeats, W.B., 244

Zabriskie Point (1970), 211
Zavatsky, Bill, 248n2
Zavattini, Cesare, 180
Zulu (1964), 2

Also in the series

William Rothman, editor, *Cavell on Film*

J. David Slocum, editor, *Rebel Without a Cause*

Joe McElhaney, *The Death of Classical Cinema*

Kirsten Moana Thompson, *Apocalyptic Dread*

Frances Gateward, editor, *Seoul Searching*

Michael Atkinson, editor, *Exile Cinema*

Paul S. Moore, *Now Playing*

Robin L. Murray and Joseph K. Heumann, *Ecology and Popular Film*

William Rothman, editor, *Three Documentary Filmmakers*

Sean Griffin, editor, *Hetero*

Jean-Michel Frodon, editor, *Cinema and the Shoah*

Carolyn Jess-Cooke and Constantine Verevis, editors, *Second Takes*

Matthew Solomon, editor, *Fantastic Voyages of the Cinematic Imagination*

R. Barton Palmer and David Boyd, editors, *Hitchcock at the Source*

William Rothman, *Hitchcock: The Murderous Gaze, Second Edition*

Joanna Hearne, *Native Recognition*

Marc Raymond, *Hollywood's New Yorker*

Steven Rybin and Will Scheibel, editors, *Lonely Places, Dangerous Ground*

Claire Perkins and Constantine Verevis, editors, *B Is for Bad Cinema*

Dominic Lennard, *Bad Seeds and Holy Terrors*

Rosie Thomas, *Bombay before Bollywood*

Scott M. MacDonald, *Binghamton Babylon*

Sudhir Mahadevan, *A Very Old Machine*

David Greven, *Ghost Faces*

James S. Williams, *Encounters with Godard*

William H. Epstein and R. Barton Palmer, editors, *Invented Lives, Imagined Communities*

Lee Carruthers, *Doing Time*

Rebecca Meyers, William Rothman, and Charles Warren, editors, *Looking with Robert Gardner*

Belinda Smaill, *Regarding Life*

Douglas McFarland and Wesley King, editors, *John Huston as Adaptor*

R. Barton Palmer, Homer B. Pettey, and Steven M. Sanders, editors, *Hitchcock's Moral Gaze*

Nenad Jovanovic, *Brechtian Cinemas*
Will Scheibel, *American Stranger*
Amy Rust, *Passionate Detachments*
Steven Rybin, *Gestures of Love*
Seth Friedman, *Are You Watching Closely?*
Roger Rawlings, *Ripping England!*
Michael DeAngelis, *Rx Hollywood*
Ricardo E. Zulueta, *Queer Art Camp Superstar*
John Caruana and Mark Cauchi, editors, *Immanent Frames*
Nathan Holmes, *Welcome to Fear City*
Homer B. Pettey and R. Barton Palmer, editors, *Rule, Britannia!*
Milo Sweedler, *Rumble and Crash*
Ken Windrum, *From El Dorado to Lost Horizons*
Matthew Lau, *Sounds Like Helicopters*
Dominic Lennard, *Brute Force*
William Rothman, *Tuitions and Intuitions*
Michael Hammond, *The Great War in Hollywood Memory, 1918–1939*
Burke Hilsabeck, *The Slapstick Camera*
Niels Niessen, *Miraculous Realism*
Alex Clayton, *Funny How?*
Bill Krohn, *Letters from Hollywood*
Alexia Kannas, *Giallo!*
Homer B. Pettey, editor, *Mind Reeling*
Matthew Leggatt, editor, *Was It Yesterday?*
Merrill Schleier, editor, *Race and the Suburbs in American Film*
Neil Badmington, *Perpetual Movement*
George Toles, *Curtains of Light*
Erica Stein, *Seeing Symphonically*
Alexander Sergeant, *Encountering the Impossible*
Brendan Hennessey, *Luchino Visconti and the Alchemy of Adaptation*
William Rothman, *The Holiday in His Eye*
Jason Sperb, *The Hard Sell of Paradise*

www.ingramcontent.com/pod-product-compliance
Lightning Source LLC
Chambersburg PA
CBHW070756230426
43665CB00017B/2385